D1396676

# A PRIMER FOR
# EASTERN RACING

## OPENING PANDORA'S BOX

A BOX LOADED WITH DISAPPOINTMENT AND SPIRITED FUN, AND ALWAYS CHUCK FULL OF TREASURE FOR LUCKY GUYS AND DOLLS.

# A PRIMER FOR
# EASTERN RACING

**NORMAN D. KISAMORE**

**DODD, MEAD & COMPANY**
**New York**

COPYRIGHT © 1963 BY NORMAN D. KISAMORE

ALL RIGHTS RESERVED

NO PART OF THIS BOOK MAY BE REPRODUCED IN ANY FORM
WITHOUT PERMISSION IN WRITING FROM THE PUBLISHER

LIBRARY OF CONGRESS CATALOG CARD NUMBER: 63-14373

PRINTED IN THE UNITED STATES OF AMERICA

# CONTENTS

# ACKNOWLEDGMENTS

The following publishers have kindly granted us permission to reprint their copyrighted material.

A. S. Barnes & Company, Inc.—from *Down the Stretch,* The Story of Colonel Matt J. Winn as told to Frank G. Menke. Copyright, 1945, by Smith and Durrell. Reprinted by permission of A. S. Barnes & Company, Inc.

A. S. Barnes & Company, Inc.—from *This Was Racing* by Joe Palmer. Copyright, 1953, by A. S. Barnes & Company, Inc.

The Citadel Press—from *Across the Board* by Toney Betts. Copyright © 1956 by Anthony Zito. Reprinted by permission of The Citadel Press.

Coward-McCann, Inc.—from *Thoroughbred Racing and Breeding* by Tom R. Underwood. Copyright, 1945, 1948, by Coward-McCann, Inc.

Doubleday & Company, Inc.—from *War Has Seven Faces* by Frank Gervasi. Copyright, 1952, by Frank Gervasi. Reprinted by permission of Doubleday & Company, Inc.

Houghton Mifflin Company—from *The Autobiography of Will Rogers,* selected and edited by Donald Day. Reprinted by permission of Houghton Mifflin Company.

*Sports Illustrated*—the photograph of Eddie Arcaro. Herb Scharfman for *Sports Illustrated.*

Triangle Publications, Inc.—charts and past performances printed in this book are copyrighted by Triangle Publications, Inc. and reproduced by special permission of *The Morning Telegraph.* Reproduction prohibited.

*Turf and Sport Digest*—the frontispiece cartoon by Jim Lavery reprinted by permission of *Turf and Sport Digest.*

Vanguard Press, Inc.—from *John D., A Portrait in Oils* by John K. Winkler. Copyright, June, 1929, by John W. Winkler. Reprinted by permission of Vanguard Press, Inc.

# INTRODUCTION

THE word "Primer" in the title of this treatise is defined as an "elementary textbook," and, dear friends, if there ever was an elementary textbook, this is it. The term "Eastern Racing" refers to thoroughbred running races in the following states:

| | |
|---|---|
| Maine | Delaware |
| New Hampshire | Maryland |
| Massachusetts | West Virginia |
| Rhode Island | Ohio |
| Michigan | Arkansas |
| New York | Louisiana |
| New Jersey | Florida |
| Kentucky | |

This book was written with the novice and the "know-nothing" racing fan in mind, along with the uninitiated and the resolute godly souls who do not approve of roulette wheels with horseshoes, for no other reason than that they know nothing about them. "Ignorance breeds contempt," or some such palpable rot.

The fact that this work is intended for the novice does not set it apart from the bulk of other racing literature. The reason for such an alienation of intentions is because any racing fan who has been to a race track as many as three times already knows all there is to know about racing, and if you don't think he does, just ask him and he'll tell you.

There is another, bigger reason for aiming didactic writing at the beginner. During World War II, many people were surprised at how quickly the Armed Forces could teach reluctant, uninterested men all the various military technical skills in a relatively short time. As an alumnus of a couple of those service schools, I can pinpoint one outstanding reason for their success: The service schools operated on the premise that all members of the student body knew nothing save three things: 1. Name 2. Rank 3. Serial number.

They assumed further that all members of the student body experienced great difficulty in remembering that damnable serial number and thus did not stress that point too strongly. Hence the list of assumptions regarding readily available knowledge was shortened to two. Since virtually none of the student body had any appreciable rank, the list shrank even shorter. The point of it all being that the instructor who begins his task by assuming the student is already familiar with the subject matter is off on the wrong foot. *Exhibit A:* The college professor who assumes the tall one there in the first row already knows how to read, although the gangling goon is present only because he can throw (or is it drop?) a round ball through a hoop with amazing efficiency.

Now just who is this bigmouth know-it-all who feels qualified to enlighten the masses concerning the whys and wherefores of Eastern Racing? I'll begin to answer that by stating first what I am not. I am not a freeloading newspaper writer of long-standing dormancy who perennially picks up his free clubhouse pass and then mechanically watches the proceedings without giving a particular damn about which horse finishes where. I am not an "improver of the breed" who goes to the races to be seen. I am not a sports writer who fell into a racing assignment as the result of someone else's afterthought. I am not a deviser of new and foolproof systems. I am not a race track owner soliciting more attendance; hence, more wagering; hence, more profits; hence, more race tracks. I am not . . . but then the list of what I am not would get quite lengthy. It might fill the whole damn book.

I am, stated in the simplest terms, a racing fan—one of the $2 punters over in the grandstand who is trying to root home some tired and wobbling 10-1 shot. I've been to Charles Town in the snow and to Monmouth in the mud. I've watched cheap races at Timonium and stakes races at Belmont Park. I've been to Atlantic City many times and have never seen its beach. I've been to Lincoln Downs in the daytime and to Shenandoah Downs at night. I've seen 'em run at Aqueduct, Hagerstown, Narragansett, Bowie, Jamaica, Bel Air, and on and on. As I said, I'm a racing fan.

Then there's the paper work—the research—to give it a high-sounding name. Reading this turf article and then that one, and then this book and then that one . . . and all the while trying not to sink in the morass of extraneous minutiae which tends to envelop the reader—authors so far back among the trees and so busily engaged in expounding the virtues of fetlock, furlong, and track variant, that they can't see the forest . . . much less point it out to me.

All right, so I'm a racing fan who can read. Now just

what kind of people go to race tracks? Let's get the answer from racing's grand ol' man, the late Col. Matt J. Winn. He gave the most concise yet most comprehensive answer possible in his autobiography *Down the Stretch,* a book most assuredly required reading for turf fans of every dimension:

Race track people live in a world of their own, which is something other folks, chiefly the "reformers," never can understand. They are not, in other things of life, any different than all the other people. But when the subject is horse racing, or they are within a race course, they are a distinct species.

They do not interfere, or try to interfere, with anyone else's sport. They do not try to bring discredit on any other sport, or the peoples of any other sport. All they ask is to be left alone to enjoy their own sport in their own way. They want to choose their own horse in their own particular way; they want to back him with their own cash; and they want to see what their choice can do.

They are quaint people, too, in the fact that they resent criticism of their sport, and the slurs upon its honesty by outsiders—yet some cry out louder, in their losing moments, and make wilder charges than all the enemies of racing put together. A race or two later, when they've won a bet, they grow enthusiastic again, and happy, because horse racing exists, and they call it the grandest and most thrilling sport in the world.

One final thought—if you're wondering what the "Dr." in front of the name stands for, it's Doctor of Dental Surgery; or, to be blunt: Dentist. Now don't hold that against me; just remember the sentiment as expressed by, I believe, W. C. Fields when he said, "Any man who hates dogs and little children just can't be all bad."

## 1st. OF CABBAGES AND RINGS

ALONG about 1937 or thereabouts (memory's a little fuzzy) I, along with three or four boyhood friends, was on the Fair Grounds of our local Cumberland Fair and Running Races. Having no money and no prospects of any, we were listening to the specious spiel of a side show barker and soaking up any loose fragments of free entertainment which may have been oozing forth. Presently, amidst some shouting in the background, one of our group yelled, "Hey, the horses are running! Let's go watch 'em."

Since the spectacle of horses pounding around a half mile strip also came under the heading of free entertainment, we all sped toward the race track to take a look. While we were hurrying to a vantage point along the outside rail, another member of the group suggested, "Let's all pick a horse and see who wins. I'll take number two!"

"I'll take number seven!" another shouted.

My lucky number was six, and naturally I joined in with the swing of things, "I'll take number six!" (I guess it was luck, or fate, or something that my lucky number wasn't nine, or ten, or anything beyond eight . . . else I wouldn't even have had a participant in the race.) With a lusty "Come on, number six!" I got ready to watch my first horse race. (And no, I very definitely was not standing in my father's wagon—for two reasons: First, my father had no wagon; he had a Whippet. Second, my father would not have gone to a race track if they were giving 20-1 on Citation in a walkover.)

We reached the head of the stretch about the same time the horses did, and as the field swung around the turn, there was ol' number six out front and winging—and so on across the finish line.

A couple of disgruntled losers began to make excuses about how their horses could have won, or should have won, but one die-hard—there's always at least one die-hard—stayed right with it. He kept watching the horses go across the finish line and then informed us, "Hey, they're going around again!"

I looked back and he was right. Number six was still out there, but he didn't look like a horse who had just won a race; he looked like a horse who was very much in a race. He still had about a half mile to go.

"Come on, number six!"

A lot of my lung power kept number six striding smoothly, but I could have saved my breath. The way he was running he could have made ten revolutions around that bull ring and the field never would have caught him. Number six, whoever he was, win big. Thus, on a hot afternoon back in the thirties my percentage of winning selections stood at 1.000. Since then it has dropped some.

All right, so a few years ago a hillbilly lucked onto a winner. So who cares? Who shows any interest in dirty ol' horse racing?

Well now, friends, some of the fruits of all that research are about to pour forth; it's time to list some figures. Figures are treacherous, though, in that you can prove about anything you want with them—depending upon how you add them up; however, these won't be added up; they'll simply be listed. In 1941, some thirteen and a half million people went to the races and bet over 500 million dollars. In 1952, 26,434,903 people went to the races and bet $1,915,220,517. In 1961, 35,056,244 people bet $2,577,-093,615. I want you to take another peek at that last figure: $2,577,093,615. That's in the billions . . . and that means that someone, somewhere, is showing an awful lot of interest in dirty ol' horse racing.

Billions—that's a good series of figures, friends. Why, when you're discussing anything in terms of billions of dollars, you're hobnobbing in the same league as the monumental farm surplus lunacy. We may all die of gluttony of the grain elevators, but we'll all go with the ark of the dole held high, and we'll all know that whenever whatever happens—we'll always be well fed—or bled—depending upon which side of the dole you happen to be standing.

Billions. Another example—that's the same series of figures used to discuss foreign aid. Foreign aid—that's when we send a few billion dollars to some have-not nation to "develop" it; albeit, some people say to "exploit" it. Again it depends upon how you look at it. Anyhow, the billions flow and we give aid and comfort to the downtrodden; yea and verily, we make them literate, and their first literary work is always the same—whatever the country. The most learned one in the group always gets a paintbrush and a bucket of red paint and writes on the nearest wall, "Yankee, go home!" There's our reward, friends, the little savage can now read and write. His blood-colored scrawl on the wall cost us a few odd billion—and it was all money well spent, I say. Of course at about the same time an ancient, antiquated school burns down in one of our major cities and kills a hundred or so kids—but I really think they probably would have just grown up into delinquents anyhow. But I digress.

And so, 35,056,244 people went to the races and bet over 2½ billion dollars. (Actually, friends, I have a feeling that that total attendance figure is misleading. I don't really think it was 35,056,244 separate souls. I believe that total paid attendance figure contains some of the same people who went to the races more than once. See, I told you figures were treacherous.) But you vehemently sit there, cocksure and smug, and hold tenaciously to the dogma that you will never go to the races; or, at best, will only tolerate racing or coexist with it because you have heard those immortal words, "You can't win." And by "win," I assume that you in your vile and smutty little mind mean to win money, or loot, or the root of all evil, or bread, or whatever you choose to call it.

So now let's talk about winning—that is, winning money. Your chances of winning money at a race track are small, just as are the chances of your forsaking week-end golf and successfully hitting the tournament trail. In the meantime you wonder about the golfers who do play golf successfully on the circuit. The fact that they make a living playing golf and you can't break a hundred does not mean that you should hastily jettison your golfing gear into the depths of the nearest water hole. No, it means nothing of the sort. You play because you like to play and you know that the day is going to come when you will not only break a hundred, but will break ninety as well; albeit, a few strategic flicks of the toe may be needed to improve a few unfortunate bad lies.

In the meantime—how much are you winning? And, remember now, by winning, we are discussing money. And also in the meantime—you will be buying golf balls, a set of irons (Can't play decent golf with half the clubs missing.), golf balls, a putter, golf balls, a set of woods (Can't reach those long par 3's with an iron, and besides, might as well complete the set now that all the irons are there.), golf balls, a golf bag (Where else to put all those clubs?), golf balls, a cart (How else to get all those clubs around over the course?), golf balls, golf shoes (Side-hill lies are made easy when you don't slip.), golf balls, a glove (Can't play golf with a handful of blisters.), golf balls, a hat (That shanked shot there on the 9th hole was a direct result of the sun being in your eyes.), golf balls, tees, golf balls, possibly a lesson or two (Not that any was needed—that slice would have straightened itself out with a little practice.), golf balls, hood covers (Lot of money tied up in that set of woods—can't have them getting wet.), golf balls, shag bag, golf balls, another putter since the old one never *quite* put the ball in the hole, golf balls, sand wedge (Would have saved 6 strokes on that last round.), golf balls, pitching wedge, (Don't know what this one is for, but all the pros use one.), golf balls, whiffle balls for practicing in the back yard, golf balls, and finally—some practice balls to put in that shag bag . . . almost forgot—golf balls.

And then there's the expense of all those hours out at the driving range, bashing out bucket after bucket of balls —at 60c per bucket—to tend to the little matter of straightening out that slice. You later decided the easy way out was to simply turn around and then let the damn thing go ahead and bend. Of course, later on, out on the links, when you played a hole with a jungle paralleling the left side of the fairway, you always had the hideous suspicion right at the top of the backswing that this may be the time the drive straightens out. Then there you'll be, the unmitigated ass who hit a beautiful 200-yard-plus drive—straight out into the wilderness.

And then there's the matter of green fees (unless you happen to own a golf course) and transportation to and from the golf course (unless you happen to live on one). Naturally, you can economize some here by joining, say for instance, the Dale Acres Golf and Country Club. The outlay of such a gambit is considerable and then there's all those charity drives and the "Let's Make Dale Acres A Better Place To Play Golf Fund." And then there was that unfortunate lawsuit that cropped up after the Spring Festival and Pageant went amiss.

And let's not forget the 19th hole, the bar of justice

where you always get your comeuppance for overestimating your prowess out on the course.

And now, friend, there's one thing that's beginning to worry me, and that's this: "How are your winnings holding out?" What's that? You say you haven't won a dime? You say for some inexplicable reason the whole damn mess is costing *you* money? Amazing. Baffling. A real puzzlement. How about last year? The year before? The year before that? Next year? If the slice straightens out . . . Hope springs eternal.

Such inverted logic could be extended to tennis, hunting, fishing, and all other participation sports—right on down to croquet and tiddlywinks, but we won't belabor the point. We'll move on to turnstile sports and "win" some more money.

From 1947 to 1950 here in the Monumental City we had an aggregation of beefy young men called the Baltimore Colts. The Baltimore Colts were a professional football team, complete with band, and played football, well, maybe not exactly football, but it was close. During this period of woe and tribulation the Colts, and thus the Colt fans, weren't winning much. The fact is they ran up a consecutive losing streak of eighteen games. And the band played on.

Losing is always bad, but the one-sidedness of the scores made it all the more distressing. A sampling: 56-0, 48-0, 70-27, 55-13, 45-2. Such a display of awesome inadequacy left the fans with very little to shout about. The only demonstration of sentiment they could show effectively was to stay home, and this they did in great numbers.

In January of 1951 the team was mercifully abandoned, and so it came to pass that the Baltimore Colts were deflated, defeated, dispersed, and defunct. Very little winning here. In 1951 and 1952 there were no Baltimore Colts. Yet the band played on.

In 1952 there was another professional football team going through the same perilous throes as had done the Colts in. This was a New York team called the Yanks. The Yanks were ready to get out of New York and seek greener pastures. There was an idea or a rumor, or the hopes of one, of transplanting the Yanks to Baltimore. But since one team had just gone down the drain here, it didn't seem like such a good idea at the time. No, heavens, no. Not when the big money boys and the free spenders in the Lone Star State started making rumbles about what a bonanza professional football would find in Texas. And so the ex-Yanks did not come to Baltimore; they went to Dallas and became known as the Dallas Texans. And right about there more troubles began.

There was one factor about the attendance of the Texans' home games which stymied the eagerly awaited windfall of cash. And that, very briefly, was this: nobody showed up. After four games in the Cotton Bowl, the powers that be were ready to leave Dallas to the cotton pickers. The small sum of $50,000 would have kept the team in Dallas for the balance of the season, and from tales of Texans I've heard that figure of $50,000 would appear to be in the neighborhood of one oil baron's cigar money. But throughout the length and breadth of Texas, the $50,000 proved

to be an insurmountable sum. Hard to believe. The owners were ready to cry "Uncle," or "Oil well," or whatever
it is they cry down there. The Texans then became known
as the "Orphans" or the "Vagabonds" since they had no
home and were forced to hit the road. They played one of
their remaining home games in Akron, Ohio, and the other
one in Detroit. I mention that just to show that they were
moving around. I also had to mention that Akron game
because it was the important one—that's *the* game they
won.

In the winter of 1952, then, the Commissioner of professional football was confronted with two problems which
were paradoxically related. On the one hand he had a
city with no team—Baltimore, which was proceeding with
a court action as a result of its disenfranchisement; and on
the other hand, he had a team with no city—the New York-
Yank-Dallas-Texan-Orphaned "Vagabonds." The solution
to both problems could be realized by one audacious stroke:
move the Vagabonds on to Baltimore. And the band
played on . . . and now it did so with more gusto, since
it had prospects of being reunited with a team.

Of course the transfer of the Vagabonds to Baltimore
wasn't made bing-bang-bing, just like that. Hardly. Seems
there was some fine print down there at the bottom of the
page. The fine print brought out a technicality about some
money, $300,000 worth of money, to be exact. The Com-
missioner stipulated that before Baltimore was given the
Dallas team it would have to sell 15,000 season ticket books
and deposit the thusly acquired cash—$300,000 cash. No
"Buy Now, Pay Later" schemes, no I O U's, no pledges or

promises—just money. The Commissioner made his offer December 3, 1952, and gave Baltimore six weeks to sell the 15,000 season books.

Sell 15,000 books of tickets in six weeks, with the Christmas shopping period right smack in the middle. Sell 15,000 books of tickets which allow the purchasers to sit through six afternoons of frustration watching a nebulous team of mediocre capacities going nowhere in particular. Sell 15,-000 books of tickets to a football team which in its last year of competition logged a win-1, lose-11 record and finished at the bottom of the pile. Find 15,000 fanatics who are willing to amass $300,000 to obtain a team which while playing last year in Texas, the cash register of the continent, couldn't muster $50,000 worth of interest. In short, raise $300,000 and resurrect the Colts, whatever their capabilities; that was the proposition.

Well, sir, to make a short story shorter, the nonparsimonious, pitifully piqued parlay pickers pulled it off. (Which gives the impression they must have picked some good ones.)

I'd like to mention that Baltimore Colt band one more time. The band stuck together through thin and thinner, team or no team, and I believe their two-year effort through 1951 and 1952 may very well qualify as the longest halftime ceremony in the history of organized football.

So now, via a turnstile sport, I'm ready to win something. Well, in the first year of the resurrection, 1953, I didn't win a hell of a lot. I cheered lustily but to no avail. The "new" Colts staggered through a win 3, lose 9 season. Just to show that was no fluke, they repeated the performance in

1954. Again I won nothing.

In 1955 the Colts improved, almost reached a .500 percentage with a 5-6-1 record. The team looked like a comer and I thought I was on to something. In 1956 they got rid of that one tie, but put it in the wrong column when they finished 5-7. I was disappointed. In 1957 heretofore unused muscles began to flex and except for the customary *rigor mortis* out in the Golden State the Colts might have done it. Win 7, lose 5. I had kind of a feeling that next year would be the year and got ready for a jackpot.

Well, sir, in 1958 the much-maligned Colts rose up out of their valley of sin and smote the whole damn league. In New York City, which had kind of a familiar ring to the New York-Dallas-Baltimore Colts, they defeated the Giants in the "Greatest Football Game Ever Played" for the NFL championship. O joy of joys. My cup runneth over.

And then came the sad news, the most unkindest cut of all; nobody came around and gave me a damn thing. Nothing. Not a dime; yea, verily and forsooth—not a farthing. I didn't mind losing when they were losing. I could see there were no available profits when the team was cast to the winds. I could even be patient with the new and incompetent version of the Colts. But now here I stood at the summit, nobody left to defeat, and the only payment I got was the news that if I wanted a season book of tickets, I had better shag off to the ticket office and get in line because the management now had a real, live, breathing champion to exhibit.

And then there's the Baltimore Orioles. The Orioles are a baseball team, of sorts, which was transferred here from

St. Louis after the spectacle of a midget being used as a pinch hitter served only to antagonize a lot of baseball's brass. . . . They said something about how such shenanigans made a travesty of the game.

Each year the Oriole fans are told, "If the good Lord's willin', and the creek don't rise, the Orioles *might* finish fifth." Now just how much exhilaration we're supposed to feel over a probable fifth-place finish, I don't know. We're also told that the Orioles play "interesting" baseball. By "interesting" I assume they mean that everyone knows they're going to lose—the question is, "How?"

As a for instance: The opposition has just rallied to tie the score. No outs. Runners on second and third. An Oriole relief pitcher is called in from the bullpen, a relief pitcher who must have been listening to another game on the radio while out there in the bullpen; the one being played here apparently bored him.

On the first pitch the batter hits a hard grounder right back to the pitcher's mound and the base runners take off. The relief pitcher spears the ball and throws it to first base with great dispatch . . . while the winning run scores from third. I'll say this about his fielding play: he threw that batter out by 10 feet.

Now there you have an interesting game, friends. It was interesting in that the Orioles didn't have to lose it, but they did. But I'll say this about the Orioles: they try. And each year they draw 800,000 to 1,000,000 paying customers. As I say, it's interesting. So far I haven't won anything from the Orioles either, and really don't expect much anywhere in the foreseeable future.

All of which brings us back to the proposition and to the idiotic notion that if you can't win money at a sport, you can't enjoy it. And to that notion I say "Balderdash!"

And now after exploring some other sports and finding the pecuniary possibilities nil, we have swung full circle and are back to horse racing, where profit is possible, if not likely. We're back to America's No. 1 spectator sport; back to where over 2½ billion dollars are involved annually in the racing fans' battle with the iron men; back to the sport which relies upon audience participation for its very existence; back to the blare of the bugle and that familiar daily challenge, "Ladies and gentlemen, these are the horses for the first race"; back to the color and the spectacle of racing silks flashing in the sun; back to that period of self-inflicted anxiety as we wonder just how this damn race is going to turn out; back to the sound and the fury of thoroughbreds battlin' it out to the wire; back to . . . But let's call in Colonel Winn again and let him explain it:

Life has moved swiftly since the time of my birth in Louisville. Miracles have been wrought. Men fly over the earth almost in swarms like the locust; men sail far beneath the surface of the oceans. The automobile has come to move the human race across the land at incredible speed; men talk into rubber mouthpieces and, in a flash, their voice carries along wires to the far ends of the earth; men talk into small instruments, and their voices, without wires to carry them, go to all the places in the world.

Moving pictures have come—and talking pictures. Astounding inventions have revolutionized chemistry and industry. Refrigerators are here—and dehydrators; electricity has been harnessed as to revolutionize the habits of life itself.

All this within my 83 years.

Once a friend, commenting on what has happened since 1861, offered, in reflection, the question:

"And what were those thousands of millions of people doing who inhabited this earth up to 83 years ago?"

I didn't know but a good many of them, I told him, were having their fun just as they are today—playing the horses.

We have now finished speaking of cabbages and rings and are ready to sally forth into the subject of Eastern Racing; however, the discussion must first be prefaced by acknowledging the following truism, to wit: Horse racing is a matter of opinion. Virtually every statement or idea concerning racing is subject to debate. An example: One might say, "You should always bet on the horse that comes in first, that is, wins." And then all the learned gentry will majestically nod their heads in agreement, as all great men do when they ponder and accept a new and beneficial morsel of wisdom. But then there's always that one die-hard yard-bird who rises up and retorts, "Sometimes the horse that comes in first is disqualified and placed last. How about that?" Yeah, how about that? And so it goes. You just have to remember Will Rogers' classic comment, "A difference of opinion is what makes horse racing and Missionaries."

With that formality justly stated, I will add that the opinions expressed herein are mine and that I don't expect everyone to agree with them. I even suspect there will be much weeping and wailing and gnashing of teeth, mixed with an abundance of adamant disagreement. And that's as it should be. However, to return to the original purpose of this treatise, the novice and/or the uninitiated racing fan should glean a sufficient amount of racing information to enable him to attend a race meeting and to participate in its excitement with more than an aimless, thoughtless series of blind stabs. He will recognize and understand the problems that beset him when he undertakes the task of selecting a winner. How well he succeeds will depend upon him.

## 2nd. THE HORSE

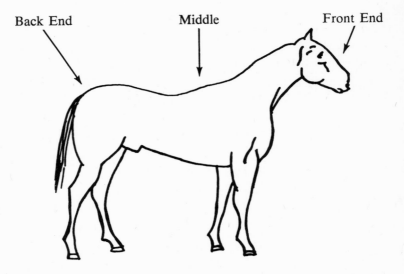

Back End             Middle             Front End

THIS is a horse. The front end, back end, and middle have all been clearly labeled. Thus ends our discussion of equine anatomy. (Now don't laugh, friends; we have to start some place.)

16

More specifically, this is a race horse, also known as a Thoroughbred, Bangtail, Gee Gee, Beetle, Plug, Oat-burner, Hayburner, Hoss, Steed, Nag, and on those occa-sions when he happens to blow a four length lead in the stretch and winds up a staggering fourth, he then takes on a whole new series of names . . . which won't be listed here since this work may fall into the hands of innocents.

Even with the discreet omission of the base epithets shouted by the momentarily upset losers, the pictured sub-ject has still more names. We'll start at the beginning and follow his multi-monikered progress. As we proceed with this piece (later chapters), we'll learn that he has even more names.

In the first place, when the little rascal is born, whether male or female, he is called a foal. And there he stands, all wiggly and unsteady; doesn't even realize that he is a member of the aristocracy regarding things equine, no milk route for him. Unless, of course, it develops that he can't run very fast; then it's a case of every hoss for himself. Foals do not race. Too little. After being weaned away from his mammy, he is called, of all things, a weanling. Weanlings do not race either. Too little.

On January 1st of the following year, regardless of the actual date of his birth, he becomes one year old and is called a yearling. In other words—all horses have the same birthday—January 1st—no matter when they were born.

And now sex, or the lack of it, enters onto the scene. If the yearling is a male, he is called a colt. If the yearling is a female, she is called a filly. If the yearling is an unsexed male, that is, a castrated colt (gelded colt), then he (it?) is called a gelding. If you are wondering why anyone would deprive a horse of his divine right, it's because some male thoroughbreds are too cantankerous and too mean to be useful. Castration mellows them early in life and makes them manageable. That's true. But somewhere there must be those who believe such action isn't really playing the game. Next, there's Mr. In-between. This is a thing called a ridgling, which is defined as: a male thoroughbred of any age with one or both organs of reproduction absent from the sac. Now I don't know exactly what that means either, friends, but you'll have to admit it sounds like a wonderful conversation piece.

Yearlings do not race. Too little. Yearlings are important in another respect, though, and I'll mention it in case you should feel inclined to gamble on horses in the grand fashion—by buying one or some. A yearling is the progeny sent by breeding farms to the auction sales. And there he stands, a nameless, totally unknown quantity of equally unknown potential. That colt standing there may be another Citation just waiting for the chance to get out on the track and show his stuff. . . . Then, on the other hand, he might be just another colt. Should you want to join in the bidding during an auction sale of yearlings but are hesitant because you don't know exactly which one to buy, a good rule of thumb to follow is by breeding, by guess, and by God.

On the following January 1st (second birthday) the yearling becomes a two-year-old. The terminology stays the same:

| Two-year-old male: | colt |
| Two-year-old female: | filly |
| Two-year-old gelded male: | gelding |
| That other one: | ridgling |

(With the facts of biology being what they are, the gelding and the ridgling do not figure in the thought we are trying to develop. A two-year-old gelded male is called a gelding, and so is a 3, 4, 5, 6, 7, 8, 9, etc.-year-old gelded male. However, the broad terms pertaining to their age group, listed subsequently, do apply.)

Two-year-olds do race. Big enough. Should the two-year-old come to the races immediately after his second birthday, he will begin his career via winter racing in one of the southern states. The races for these brand-new two-year-olds are very short and are spoken of as "baby races."

Should the two-year-old begin his racing efforts later on in the year in one of the middle Atlantic or northern states, the races in which he competes will be somewhat longer, but they will still be referred to as juvenile races, or, races for youngsters, or, more simply—races for two-year-olds. The first year of competition of the thoroughbred is called his freshman campaign and hence, two-year-olds are often called freshmen, to give the appropriate connotations that they are in their first year of racing.

On the following January 1st the thoroughbred becomes a three-year-old. Since this is his second season of racing, it is referred to as his sophomore campaign, and consequently the three-year-olds are called sophomores. Again the exact nomenclature stays the same:

Three-year-old male:    colt
Three-year-old female:   filly

This particular age group of thoroughbreds is very important, especially to the casual racing fan. If you have heard of any horse race at all, you have probably heard of the Kentucky Derby. To enlarge that supposition slightly, you may even have heard of the Triple Crown of racing: the Kentucky Derby, the Preakness Stakes, and the Belmont Stakes. These high-caliber races are strictly for three-year-olds—the sophomores. Thus you can readily see that a thoroughbred gets only one chance at these racing prizes; he is three years old only one season. When a good horse, say, for instance, Native Dancer, is defeated in the Kentucky Derby, there is to be no consolation in the phrase, "Wait till next year." There is no next year.

One more birthday and our thoroughbred has become four years old—and he's called just that, a four-year-old.

Four-year-old male:    colt
Four-year-old female:   filly

However, on the fifth birthday the terminology changes. The five-year-old male is called a *horse*. There it is, and we were a long time getting there. The five-year-old male may also be called a stallion—for no other reason than to generate some confusion. Actually the term "stallion" connotes a male horse which has been retired from racing for stud purposes. The five-year-old female is called a mare, and a mare retired from racing for breeding purposes is called a broodmare, which is about as homey a term as you can get. To complete the cycle, when the above horse

and mare produce a foal of their own, the father is called a sire and the mother is called a dam, not a damn anything, just a dam. To go on—as grandparents, they're called grandsire and granddam.

Five-year-old male:     horse
Five-year-old  female:   mare

Now then—with all of the preceding information carefully digested, we'll move on to the next point.

There's a trick question which periodically passes around among racing folk. There is always one wiseacre who loves to ask you, "How many *horses* have won the Kentucky Derby?" After you mentally subtract 1875 (date of the first Kentucky Derby) from the current year and announce your answer, he is delighted to tell you that you are wrong. He will then enlighten you that such and such number of *colts,* and one filly, have won the Kentucky Derby, but no horses. To his way of thinking, no horse has ever even participated in the Kentucky Derby, since it is a race exclusively for three-year-olds.

Well now, he's sort of right and yet he isn't. For the answer we'll go all the way back to the first sentence under the picture on page 16: "This is a horse." The term "horse" is a general one which applies to all the preceding types and age groups given. All of them. The colt, weanling, ridgling, mare, foal, all of them. All things equine. When out at your local track, or any track, the track announcer never says, "Ladies and gentlemen, these are the two-year-old colts and geldings for the first race." Or, "Ladies and gentlemen, these are the fillies and mares for the fifth race."

Nay. Nay. Nay. (Neigh?) It's always, "These are the *horses*."

It may also be pointed out that the roster of "Horse of the Year" award winners includes colts, example: Citation; fillies, example: Busher; and a gelding, Armed. To repeat a statement, "This is a horse."

An explanatory chart follows:

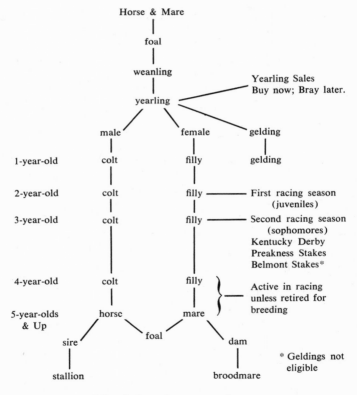

All of the above are horses.

## 3rd. THE JOCKEY

WE now have the first prerequisite for a horse race—the horse. The second necessity is someone to ride and steer this 1,100 pounds of nervous, high-strung, temperamental thoroughbred. This someone is a smallish man called a jockey, and although small in stature, he has an overly large portion of many admirable traits; the fact is, he is composed of rather stern stuff. A poll of sports writers was made a few years ago to select the most dangerous job in American sports. The result of the poll was not the 250-300-pound professional football players who knock heads on Sunday afternoons; it was not the boxer whose sole aim is to flatten or maim his opponent; nor was it the baseball player who stands up at home plate and lets a baseball (I almost said horsehide) whiz by his head at about 90 m.p.h. No, it was none of these. The dubious honor went to the plucky little man who time after time through the course of a single afternoon will charge with his mount into a tangle of hard-running race horses and try to steer his way through.

He's in the midst of a mild stampede—hell for leather aboard lunging, hard-headed horses. One unfortunate cuppy hole in the track, one misstep by one of the front runners, one shattered foreleg that couldn't stand the strain, and the jockey may find himself viewing that stampede from the worst possible angle. Yes, the jockey is gritty, rugged, courageous, and doggedly determined, but there is one thing he is not, and that is clairvoyant. You have undoubtedly heard somewhere that jockeys know just exactly which horse is going to win each race, possibly the 1st and 2nd horse, or even the 1-2-3 result, with the payoff on the winner thrown in for good measure. Some cynics have even been heard to remark that the races are rehearsed the night before just to insure interested parties against grievous errors.

Well, let's pause and contemplate the vistas awaiting a race rider who knows each and every time the horse he is riding is going to win. He will ride three to six mounts a day, six days a week, for as many weeks as he cares to. Each mount, each day, each week, each month, he knows when he is going to win and can bet accordingly. (Jockeys can bet on races—as long as they bet on the horses they're riding. For them to bet on a horse other than the one they're riding is decidedly frowned upon.) Now the question is, just how long will he have to continue risking life and limb out there on the track before he has more money than he can fold? Assuming he gets something resembling "his share" of winners, he shouldn't have to ride more than six months to a year—two years at the very most. Now how many jockeys can you name who made such a fat roll of money in two years of riding that they were ready to retire? I think you can tally the list on the fingers of one finger.

Or, to look at it another way, the reason Johnny Longden has been riding for over thirty years is because he has always known when he was going to win. Ted Atkinson rode for over twenty years for the same reason. But they say one picture is worth 10,000 words, so let's look at a picture:

If the picture simply showed just a jockey lying in the mud at Belmont Park, it might not mean much. But that is not just a jockey lying there in the mud. That's Eddie Arcaro, a jockey of some renown. Many people say he was the best—and by the all-American standard, dollars, he was. His mounts won over $30,000,000 during his thirty-one years of riding.

The picture shows Eddie's finish in the 1959 Belmont Stakes—face down in a quagmire, awaiting an ambulance and hospital care. Take another look at that picture; that's a picture of a man who, beginning in 1931, knew every time he was going to ride a winner.

And yet I'll say this. There have been times when I saw what I thought were some very peculiarly run horse races. Not very often, but now and again. And maybe they were; and maybe they were not. But I'll also say this. I can remember reading about a certain World Series played between Cincinnati and Chicago which wound up in some sort of a fiasco. Charges, countercharges, investigations, lawsuits—stuff like that. I also remember an investigation into some basketball games played in Madison Square Garden where such terms as "point shaving" were brought out. (You don't have to lose; just keep it close.) And then there's an occasional golf calcutta where Joe Snodgrass with a bogus handicap of 12 suddenly shoots a 66 and walks off with all the money.

That's the way it was. That's the way it is. And that's the way it's going to be. As long as there is a pot of money involved, there will always be the spasmodic appearance of a plot and a counterplot, always the specter of some sinister skulduggery afoot.

And then I'll say this. No sport does more to prevent the occurrence of such instances than does horse racing. And I'm not going into a long-winded diatribe about a film patrol, Pinkertons, etc., since I believe racing is above and beyond the era in which it must constantly walk around apologizing for itself. And the fact that racing can combat and cope with its myriad problems and subtle bits of chicanery over and in spite of a thing called a "State Racing Commission" makes its success all the more amazing. And what is a "State Racing Commission"? The answer can be found in the glossary of racing terms in Toney Betts' book, *Across the Board*:

*State Racing Commission:* An official board, generally composed of zombies; usually a triumvirate, appointed by a governor in payment for his cheapest political debts.

And finally I'll say this. If you feel racing is all dishonest and crooked, if you feel it is all for the advantage of some mysterious inner clique, then for the mutual benefit of everybody, don't go. No one will browbeat you into going out to the track; no one will coerce you into visiting the mutuel windows; and no one will inflict bodily harm upon you if you do not open up your wallet and buy some tickets. Just stay home.

But I was talking about jockeys. They have to learn their trade, just as everyone else does. And they start at the bottom of things, just as the productive majority do. A beginner does such menial tasks as walking "hots" (horses which have to be cooled out after a workout or after a race are called hots; they are walked around in a ring—around and around), cleaning out stalls (a nice way of saying shoveling dung), cleaning muck (another nice way of saying dung) out of the horses' feet, fetching water, and on and on—every thankless job that nobody else wants to do.

Then if all goes right, the beginner will be allowed to gallop some horses—the morning workouts. If he hasn't gotten too fat, or if he hasn't changed his mind somewhere along the line (tired of shoveling dung), he will finally get a mount in a real honest-to-goodness horse race. After complying with all the qualifying trivia about a license, contract, etc., of course.

And pretty soon he'll be a race rider, and then when he battles it out through the stretch with a couple of other horses and finishes third because he didn't have enough horse, there will always be that irate loser who shouts, "Did you see that crooked little gangster pull that horse up? He didn't even try to win!" Makes it seem like all that dung shoveling was for nothing. The owner or trainer could have picked any uninterested kid off the street to come in and ride a loser.

Or, to try the same thought from another angle, if you should ever be walking through the stable area of a race track and see a diminutive, determined, rawboned little man diligently shoveling horse dung, you can sagely surmise to yourself that he is shoveling away so that someday he can get out on the track, ride a shady string of consecutive losers, and then hurry back to his dung pile and his shovel—ideally without missing a stroke. Fascinating stuff, horse dung.

A jockey who is just starting his riding career is called an apprentice jockey, or an apprentice rider, or—simply—an apprentice. As an apprentice he is allowed to ride with a specified amount of weight subtracted from the original weight the horse was supposed to carry. The exact amount of weight he is allowed to deduct depends upon where he is doing his riding. The weight allowance, or apprentice allowance, as it's called, varies among the different states (states' rights, state Racing Commissions, political debts).

The rule as set forth in the New York Jockey Club's Rules of Racing will serve as an example. This rule states that an apprentice is allowed a weight allowance of five (5) pounds until he has ridden forty (40) winners. With that being the state of affairs, the new jockey may grow up, live, and die—all as an apprentice. Such a contingency could arise if he performed in such lackluster fashion that he simply couldn't boot home forty winners. Actually I'm very much afraid that if he didn't get those forty winners with something at least approaching competent proficiency he'd be right back at ye ol' dung pile. Such action would save embarrassment all the way around and would prevent his apprenticeship from reaching any such ridiculous proportions.

But then nobody likes to discuss losers. Let's talk about winners. What about the apprentice who rides his forty winners quickly? Just to veer off into fantasyland for an instant, let's assume some hotshot apprentice rode winners the first forty times he went to the post. Such a miraculous performance would render his apprenticeship period very short if there were not more to the Jockey Club rule given previously. However, the rule goes on to say that if an apprentice rides forty winners prior to the end of one year from the date of his first winner, the 5-pound apprentice allowance continues until the end of that year. He may even keep a 3-pound apprentice allowance the succeeding year, provided he is still riding for his original contract employer. Thus saith the Jockey Club.

At other tracks in other states the actual figures pertaining to the apprentice allowance will vary. You will see apprentice allowances of 10 pounds, 7 pounds, 5 pounds, and 3 pounds. The only thing that remains constant in spite of whoever dreamed up the rule is that the amount of weight allowed varies inversely to the number of winners the apprentice has ridden. I hope that's clear.

In summation, then, a beginning jockey is called an apprentice, and as an apprentice he is allowed to ride with less weight than a full-fledged jockey would have to ride. To illustrate with an example, we'll say that a horse named Old Reliable is slated to carry 121 pounds. By putting an apprentice on the horse, the apprentice allowance reduces the imposed weight to 116 pounds, unless—there are always exceptions—the conditions of the race specifically deny any apprentice allowance being claimed. Example: Kentucky Derby. All colts carry 126 pounds. All fillies carry 121 pounds. Apprentice or no. Which is one reason why apprentice riders don't figure too heavily in many big races; the salient reason for their use, less weight, has been nullified.

Now just how does the casual racing fan know when a horse is being ridden by an apprentice? He surely wouldn't be expected to know experienced riders from beginners simply by their names. Of course not. On his official track program the apprentice rider will be marked by an asterisk or "bug" (*). The "bug" appears immediately in front of the weight, thus:

Old Reliable     *116

The asterisk is a signpost informing all interested parties that the horse is being ridden by an apprentice.

Since the apprentice always rides with this "bug," both he and his apprentice allowance are referred to as "bugs" in the vernacular of the race track. He is a "bug," or a "bug boy," and rides with a "bug." When his apprentice-ship is terminated, he is said to have lost his "bug." Some people say apprentice riders are called bugs because they ride like they had one up their breeches, since they've never been thrown, or knocked down, or hung over the rail, or experienced any such mellowing eventuality. But that's just hearsay.

All right, so Old Reliable is going to race with an apprentice rider in the saddle. What does that mean? Is it good or bad? Well, just like about everything else under the sun, there are at least two schools of thought on the problem. The first theory is that since he is being ridden by an inexperienced apprentice he is actually competing under a handicap, less weight or no, and the outcome may very well be that he will finish away up the track when he didn't necessarily have to. A more experienced rider, even with the additional 5-pound impost, may have made fewer mistakes and got a better performance out of the horse.

In the main, I would say that such a line of reasoning is basically correct. Most beginning jockeys never do amount to much, just as most of all the wide-eyed rookies in the Major League tryout camps eventually wind up back on the farm, or back in college, or wherever they came from. Even the bulk of the moneybag bonus babies prove to be seriously deficient. (I'll be home shortly, Mom; they're starting to throw the curve ball.) Most of these bonus babies simply go back home, sit down, and count their money; or, they knock around in the bush leagues for a few frustrating years and then sink slowly into oblivion.

However—and it's a big however, just to keep two sides to everything and just to keep controversy stirred up— every once in a while *one* of these bonus babies proves to be a very good investment. He takes up on the Major League diamond right where he left off in high school, actually knows how to play baseball.

And, similarly, on the race track there is occasionally a red-hot apprentice, a boy who can actually ride a horse. The fact that he hasn't been riding very long is little or no detriment to his capabilities. And the fact that he always gets five pounds off the assigned weight makes his services all the more attractive.

To get back to the question, "Is having an apprentice rider good or bad?" we can only say that with all other factors being equal, things around a race track are no different than around anyplace else. In this respect: "The rich get richer and the poor play bingo."

The apprentice who starts off slowly by riding very few winners and a good many losers doesn't find his services sought feverishly by trainers who have their horses conditioned for a top effort. And so he goes right on riding "stiffs," "dogs," "chronic also-rans," in short—losers. At the end of the race meeting he will have ridden two winners: one paid $36.80 and the other one paid $87.60.

On the other hand, the hotshot who starts off with a flourish and boots home a few winners will soon be sought out by interested parties who have "live" mounts, "ready" horses, in short—the solid contenders. And then the thing snowballs. The boy rides more winners and gets more "live" mounts. Things may reach such a state of affairs that the "bug boy's" agent may be able to pick and choose just which horses to ride and which to pass up. This "bug" may wind up as the leading rider at the meeting.

*Note:* According to Jockey Club rules, the apprentice must be under contract to one specific owner or trainer for a period of at least three years. During these three years he must, of course, ride the horses entered by his contract employer. But since the owner or trainer holding his contract must have a minimum of only three horses in training, on many days there will be races in which the apprentice may pick and choose his mounts; or, if not pick and choose, he can at least be available.

If the manner in which a brand-new jockey gets started on his riding career is so all-fired important, then the smart play would be to start with a successful, first-class, high-caliber racing stable, a stable that gets more than its share of wins. That's true—very true. The only thing wrong with such a notion is that a few hundred other youngsters have already had the same thought. The would-be jockey trying to become a part of such an organization may never get off the dung pile. The awful truth is he may never even get *on* the dung pile.

It would be about like applying for a job as a pinch hitter on the heaviest-hitting team in baseball. No room. Or, if allowed to stay, the newcomer may die of a petrified *gluteus maximus*. He'd be better off going on down the scale to the weakest-hitting team and trying to make the grade there. If he had any talent at all, he would make this team and then he would at least be playing. Yes, sir, that's about the size of it; he'd be playing. His team would struggle through a win 62, lose 100 season, but he'd be playing.

Similarly, the boy aspiring to become a jockey could forsake the dung pile of Moneybag Stables, Inc., and move on down the scale a ways. He could find a patchwork stable of modest means which needed a rider. And that's the important thing—to ride. Yes, sir, that's about the size of it; he'd be riding. Of course the horses would be more or less a broken-down sort held together with chewing gum and string—but he'd be riding. You see, there just is no easy way. And it's all done so that one irritated loser can vent his spleen by shouting, "Did you see that crooked little bastard hold that horse back!!" And that's the loser's privilege, friends. He's paid his $2.

Well, is having an apprentice rider up on your horse good or bad? I'd say it depends. The first factor governing the answer would be: Which apprentice? Is it an out-and-out novice who has never ridden a winner? Is it a Johnny-come-lately who's been cutting a rather dismal swath through the turf world? Is it a good, hard-riding youngster who is about to graduate from the apprentice ranks? Is it the hottest rider at the meeting who has been getting more than his share of live mounts? The answers to these questions would have a direct bearing on whether or not the prospect of having an apprentice rider on your horse is good or bad.

For some kind of a line on the particular apprentice who is going to ride your horse, look at the jockey standings listed in your program or in your racing paper and see if he is listed, and where. This will be hard to do on the first day of the meeting, but then everything is hard to do on the first day of the meeting, with the possible exception of losing money. If no jockey standings are given, due to the fact that the meeting has just started, consult the final jockey standings for the meeting just concluded in your area. If there has been no meeting in your area recently, one final opportunity is available for getting a line on the apprentice rider in question. This last resort will be mentioned later, much later.

Or, to take the easy way out, confine your handicapping to selecting the right horse and let the trainer worry about selecting the right jockey. He knows more about such things than you do anyway. And it must always be remembered that no jockey, apprentice or otherwise, can win if he doesn't have enough horse under him. He can't get off and carry the damn thing.

There's only one more point I'd like to make about the apprentice rider. Ofttimes a hotshot "bug boy" enjoys a very meteoric career—only to burn out just as quickly as he initially appeared on the horizon. The first thing that happens when he leaves the apprentice ranks is that he loses his 5-pound "bug." He's lost one of his stellar characteristics right there, and at about the same time the owners and trainers begin to notice a new kid who sits well on a horse. He rides a few losers and then one thing leads to two and the next thing he knows his snowball is in reverse. He's gone from feast to famine, just as does the slump-ridden .344 hitter who suddenly can't buy a base hit and sees his team-leading average sink to an anemic .187.

The jump from "bug" to successful jockey is a big one. It is somewhat comparable to the all-conquering golf amateur who turns pro and then finds out much to his chagrin that he can't win a nickel on the play-for-money circuit. Similarly, the leading apprentice rider during the current meeting may be a complete has-been by next year.

# 4th. THE RACE TRACKS

WE now have the horse and the jockey. The next item needed is a specific site or locale for the horse and the jockey to compete. Such a locale is called a race track, or a race course, or a racing plant. The latter term is a broad one used mostly to refer to the racing establishment in its entirety—all the necessary buildings, the race track proper, auxiliary gear, everything out there. Since most race tracks are ovoid in shape, they are also called ovals, the one in your area, the local oval. At other times a race track may be referred to as a strip, the one in your area, the local strip. And of course that cynic is still with us and he refers to all of the above as separation centers.

All race tracks have a name. They are named to enable all the prospective turf patrons in the area to know just where it is they want to go. Continuing with generalities, many tracks are referred to as Parks. Examples: Beulah Park, Belmont Park, Delaware Park. Others are referred to as Downs. Examples: Wheeling Downs, Scarborough

Downs, Churchill Downs. Others want to leave absolutely no doubt in the minds of visitors as to just what kind of enterprising venture they are entering. They see to this by putting the phrase "Race Course" right in their names. Examples: Cranwood Race Course, Bowie Race Course, Detroit Race Course. Other tracks have simply a short, curt name. Examples: Timonium, Saratoga, Keeneland.

Race tracks in the East come in an assortment of sizes ranging from one and a half miles on down to half a mile. The size spoken of here means the distance around the track—the distance covered by one revolution—or one lap.

Here is a diagram of a race track which has the bare essentials, i.e., a fenced-in oval.

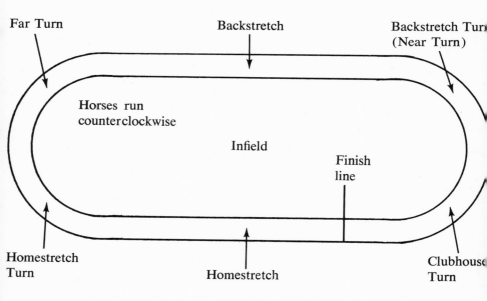

In addition to the minimum requirements as shown above, a race track may have one or more extensions called chutes. A chute, if present, allows for a fairer race by giving the horses a longer run on a straightaway course before encountering any turns. In other words, a long run on a straight course tends to separate the wheat from the chaff before the cumbersome field has to negotiate a turn. Crowding and bumping among the contenders may thus be minimized. Chutes also afford the horses positioned on the outside an opportunity to *get to the front* (in race track lingo—get to the top) and assume a better racing position along the inside rail. In the preceding sentence the phrase "get to the front" is very important. The jockey on the outside horse cannot simply charge diagonally across the track and hang all the other horses over the rail. Such a maneuver is called cheating and is frowned upon.

In addition to chutes, a race track may have a turf, or grass, course paralleling the main, or dirt, course. Such a race track, with two chutes, would look like this:

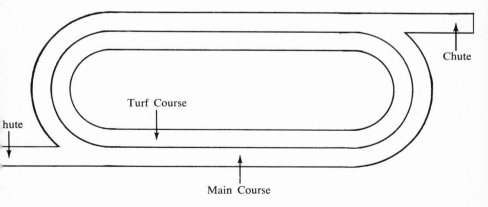

Chute

Turf Course

hute

Main Course

All other terminology the same as that given previously.
Enough of generalities, let's get down to cases and name
names. There follows an alphabetical listing of the race
tracks which comprise Eastern Racing. The state in which
the track is located and the size of the track in miles are
also given:

| Track | State | Size |
|---|---|---|
| Aqueduct | New York | 1⅛ |
| Ascot Park | Ohio | ¾ |
| Atlantic City | New Jersey | 1⅛ |
| Bel Air | Maryland | ¾ |
| Belmont Park | New York | 1½ |
| Berkshire Downs | Massachusetts | ½ |
| Beulah Park | Ohio | 1 |
| Bowie | Maryland | 1 |
| Brockton Fair | Massachusetts | ½ |
| Charles Town | West Virginia | ¾ |
| Churchill Downs | Kentucky | 1 |
| Cranwood | Ohio | ⅝ |
| Cumberland Fair | Maryland | ½ |
| Delaware Park | Delaware | 1 |
| Detroit Race Course | Michigan | 1 |
| Fair Grounds | Louisiana | 1 |
| Garden State | New Jersey | 1 |
| Great Barrington Fair | Massachusetts | ½ |
| Gulfstream Park | Florida | 1 |
| Hagerstown | Maryland | ½ |
| Hamilton | Ohio | ½ |
| Hazel Park | Michigan | ⅝ |
| Hialeah | Florida | 1⅛ |
| Jamaica | New York | 1 |
| James C. Ellis Park | Kentucky | ⅝ |
| Jefferson Downs | Louisiana | ⅝ |

| | | |
|---|---|---|
| Keeneland | Kentucky | $1\frac{1}{16}$ |
| Latonia | Kentucky | 1 |
| Laurel | Maryland | $1\frac{1}{8}$ |
| Lincoln Downs | Rhode Island | $1\frac{3}{16}$ |
| Marlboro | Maryland | $\frac{1}{2}$ |
| Marshfield Fair | Massachusetts | $\frac{1}{2}$ |
| Maumee Downs | Ohio | 1 |
| Miles Park | Kentucky | $\frac{5}{8}$ |
| Monmouth Park | New Jersey | 1 |
| Narragansett Park | Rhode Island | 1 |
| Northampton | Massachusetts | $\frac{1}{2}$ |
| Oaklawn Park | Arkansas | 1 |
| Pimlico | Maryland | 1 |
| Raceway Park | Ohio | $1\frac{1}{16}$ |
| Randall Park | Ohio | 1 |
| River Downs | Ohio | 1 |
| Rockingham Park | New Hampshire | 1 |
| Saratoga | New York | $1\frac{1}{8}$ |
| Scarborough Downs | Maine | 1 |
| Shenandoah Downs | West Virginia | $\frac{5}{8}$ |
| Suffolk Downs | Massachusetts | 1 |
| Sunshine Park | Florida | 1 |
| ThistleDown | Ohio | 1 |
| Timonium | Maryland | $\frac{1}{2}$ |
| Tropical Park | Florida | 1 |
| Waterford Park | West Virginia | 1 |
| Weymouth Fair | Massachusetts | $\frac{1}{2}$ |
| Wheeling Downs | West Virginia | $\frac{1}{2}$ |

That's fifty-four race tracks—more than there are cards in a deck—and just as shuffled. However, it must be pointed out that race tracks are like everything else constructed by man in that they come and go. The year 1959 marked the last racing season at Jamaica. Progress said the plant had to be torn down to make room for a housing development, and thus one chapter of New York racing is finished. On the brighter side of things, a "New Aqueduct" has opened and is taking up any slack which may have been brought about by the departure of New York's "Ugly Duckling." Down in Kentucky, a "New Latonia" has entered the racing scene. Shenandoah Downs in West Virginia held its inaugural meeting in 1959 (night racing). And in upstate New York, Finger Lakes race track held its inaugural meeting in 1962. Tracks come and go.

With the facts of progress being what they are, Jamaica Race Course will not be considered any further . . . and while speaking of things which will not be considered, I will add that there is a two-day meeting in New York called United Hunts which will not be discussed, since by the time you find out it's open, it's closed.

I trust you saw your local oval somewhere in the preceding list of race tracks. If you did, then you can follow its progression or its regression as we proceed with this piece. If you did not, then you can still tag along, since the over-all approach to racing as set forth in this work is applicable to racing anywhere.

Besides this roster of over half a hundred race tracks, I've heard it said that in certain strange places such as Pennsylvania and Virginia they actually race horses without the benefit of pari-mutuel betting. What a waste. For the purpose of discussing Eastern Racing in this work, such strange places will be referred to as limbo.

Now to attack this unwieldy list of race tracks and to establish some kind of order, to formulate some feasible approach to the problems and intricacies abounding in such a multiplex structure.

As a first stroke we will divide the list into two parts by separating all the tracks which conduct what is loosely referred to as winter racing. The term "winter racing" is getting to be a semi-passé or incipiently outmoded one. Charles Town is in operation right up until January, provided of course the starting gate hasn't gotten snowbound or the racing strip hasn't become a sheet of ice. On the other side of the Potomac, Bowie kicks off the Maryland season in early February amidst snowing and blowing, and even staid ol' New York has nudged its opening date up a few days from the traditional April Fool's Day inaugural (no connection). Perhaps "Southern Racing" would be a more accurate term. For the moment, however, we, in the interest of confusion, will assume the term "winter racing" is still a valid one.

And here are the tracks engaged in winter racing:

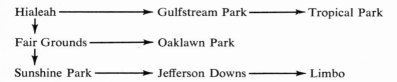

You will notice that the tracks are no longer listed alphabetically. In fact, they seem to have assumed some graduated, or echelon, formation. Now just what are the reasons for such strange markings?

Stated briefly, there are race tracks, and then there are race tracks: some big, some little, some great, some near-great, some indifferent. To draw upon other sports again for illustrative purposes, we could say that golf has an amateur and a professional classification; baseball has both Major and Minor leagues (1962); football has the professional game and a "built-in" Minor League system, college football. (Although at times the college player who turns professional may have to take a cut in salary and lose some of his fringe benefits.) Racing is no different in this "big" and "little" respect; it has both Major League and Minor League competition, although such a division is not publicized, since no race track entrepreneur wants to advertise the ignominious fact that his race course offers second-string or even third-string racing. It is better business to indulge in some imbecilic tub thumping by proclaiming that the horses campaigning at the local oval this year are *perhaps* the best which have ever raced over the track. Now that sounds good; may even represent the truth, since the horses present last year and all the years before weren't any good either; the speciousness of the gobbledygook hurts no one, and like the man said, "That's show biz."

And so the seven race tracks embracing winter racing have been evaluated and listed in order of their descending significance. You will note that there are various levels or plateaus present in the scheme of things. These are to denote twilight zones or transitional areas where any differences in the caliber of racing offered are slight. Also, in the first row:

Hialeah ⟶ Gulfstream Park ⟶ Tropical Park

the single row, or layer, is more or less mandatory since when one of these tracks closes, the next one opens and it is *virtually* a case of the same horses moving on to the next track. It has to be virtually, but not entirely, since the three tracks actually open and close in this order:

Tropical Park ⟶ Hialeah ⟶ Gulfstream Park

So you can see there has been some rearrangement.

To take a long view of winter racing—there is not much difference in the type and caliber of racing offered at Gulfstream Park and that offered at Tropical Park. In the same fashion, there is not much difference in the racing staged at the Fair Grounds when compared to that offered at Oaklawn Park. But there is a *lot* of difference between the racing at Hialeah and the racing at Sunshine Park.

One popular, though inaccurate, notion concerning a method of determining the quality of racing at any given track is to rely solely upon the actual size of the track. In this respect there are only two sizes: mile tracks and half-mile tracks. The "mile" signifies Major League racing while the term "half-mile" means Minor League racing. (Other descriptive phrases for the "half-milers" are "bull rings," "bush leagues," and the "Gyp circuit." "Gyp" as used here is an abbreviation of "Gypsy" and does not connote dishonesty—as a rule, the Minor League tracks conduct short meetings and the horsemen, or the "Gypsies," are constantly on the move.)

However, this overly simplified device to separate Major and Minor League racing is like most everything else that is too easy to do—it is filled with errors and is worthless, since race tracks vary in size from a half mile to a mile and a half, and—in addition—just to thoroughly confuse the issue—there are many instances in which it is possible to witness the spectacle of half-mile racing on a mile track. I would say that simply noting the size of the track you are visiting is not a foolproof index as to its quality of racing, but it certainly gives strong indications.

On just what basis was the preceding chart of Southern race tracks founded? What are the available criteria for "rating" race tracks? By what reasoning does it come about that an evaluation of all the tracks engaged in winter racing should place Hialeah at the top and Jefferson Downs at the bottom? Here I assume you will have anticipated me to the extent that the tabulation of the seven winter race tracks was a precursor of bigger things to come. We still have forty-six tracks to go.

Well now, friends, since I'm making all the evaluations and tabulations, I can use whatever to me seems to be logical and equitable. Therefore, the classification of the tracks engaged in winter racing and the subsequent classification of tracks engaged in "summer racing" were deftly formulated by the astute use of the following:

1. Personal experience and observation.
2. Personal prejudice.
3. Concentration.
4. Malice.
5. Austere comparison and devious manipulation.
6. Some pertinent figures concerning the various tracks. To wit:
   A. The record attendance for one day.
   B. The All-American standard and sacred deity—dollars —the one thing blessed among men, the badge of social grace, the all-holy, omnipotent, long green. This immaculate standard was used in the following ways:
      (1) The record amount of money bet at the track in one day.

(2) The average net purse distribution per race.*

(3) The minimum claiming price carded at the track.*

The two terms marked * will be explained in the following chapter. Right now I am aware that such terms as "purse distribution" and "claiming price" may mean nothing to you, but you can still differentiate large numbers from small ones. The quality of racing at any given race track is directly proportional to the size of these two numbers. In other words, the average net purse distribution per race and the minimum claiming price should be as large as possible.

And now that you have some inkling as to how the previous race track chart was derived, we'll examine it again:

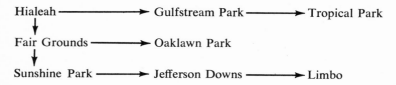

Now to look at these tracks with some relevant figures. The figures are from the *American Racing Manual, 1962* and have been rounded off in the interest of clarity.

| Track | Record Attendance For One Day |
|---|---|
| Hialeah | 42,000 |
| Gulfstream Park | 33,000 |
| Tropical Park | 21,000 |
| Fair Grounds | 21,000 |
| Oaklawn Park | 18,000 |
| Sunshine Park | 7,000 |
| Jefferson Downs | 7,000 |

| Track | Record Amount of Money Bet in One Day |
|---|---|
| Hialeah | $2,800,000 |
| Gulfstream Park | $2,400,000 |
| Tropical Park | $1,400,000 |
| Fair Grounds | $1,000,000 |
| Oaklawn Park | $1,000,000 |
| Sunshine Park | $284,000 |
| Jefferson Downs | $248,000 |

Now even the novice must be aware that there has to be some difference between the racing at Hialeah and the racing at Jefferson Downs. Compare $2,800,000 with $248,000.

| Track | Average Net Purse Distribution Per Race (1961) |
|---|---|
| Hialeah | $6,000 |
| Gulfstream Park | $4,400 |
| Tropical Park | $3,300 |
| Fair Grounds | $2,200 |
| Oaklawn Park | $2,800 |
| Sunshine Park | $1,000 |
| Jefferson Downs | $1,000 |

| Track | Minimum Claiming Price |
|---|---|
| Hialeah | $3,500 |
| Gulfstream Park | $3,000 |
| Tropical Park | $2,500 |
| Fair Grounds | $2,000 |
| Oaklawn Park | $2,000 |
| Sunshine Park | $1,500 |
| Jefferson Downs | $1,500 |

And now to attack the remaining forty-six tracks. The first step will be to divide them into two groups, Major

League tracks and Minor League tracks. And these, in descending order, are the Major League tracks:

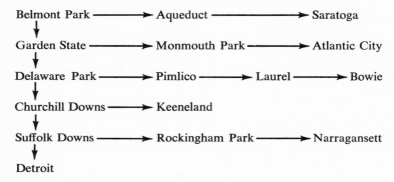

Belmont Park ⟶ Aqueduct ⟶ Saratoga
↓
Garden State ⟶ Monmouth Park ⟶ Atlantic City
↓
Delaware Park ⟶ Pimlico ⟶ Laurel ⟶ Bowie
↓
Churchill Downs ⟶ Keeneland
↓
Suffolk Downs ⟶ Rockingham Park ⟶ Narragansett
↓
Detroit

And these, again in descending order, are the Minor League tracks:

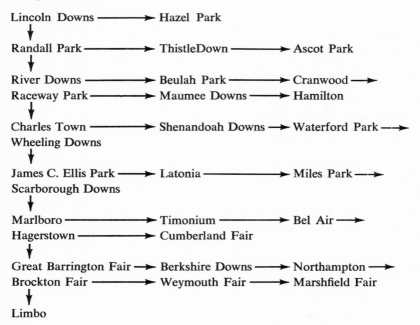

Lincoln Downs ⟶ Hazel Park
↓
Randall Park ⟶ ThistleDown ⟶ Ascot Park
↓
River Downs ⟶ Beulah Park ⟶ Cranwood ⟶
Raceway Park ⟶ Maumee Downs ⟶ Hamilton
↓
Charles Town ⟶ Shenandoah Downs ⟶ Waterford Park ⟶
Wheeling Downs
↓
James C. Ellis Park ⟶ Latonia ⟶ Miles Park ⟶
Scarborough Downs
↓
Marlboro ⟶ Timonium ⟶ Bel Air ⟶
Hagerstown ⟶ Cumberland Fair
↓
Great Barrington Fair ⟶ Berkshire Downs ⟶ Northampton ⟶
Brockton Fair ⟶ Weymouth Fair ⟶ Marshfield Fair
↓
Limbo

It may help if I enlarge the charts to show how the tracks have been grouped by states, or by circuits. This grouping accounts for the fact that Wheeling Downs has been grossly misplaced; it should be a way down the scale, but in the interest of keeping it with the balance of the West Virginia tracks, I gave it the benefit of a very large doubt. Other than that miscarriage of values, I hope you are not too upset by the graduated placement of tracks. If your local oval didn't fare too well, don't take it too badly, since my hometown track, Cumberland Fair, didn't exactly emerge as any world beater either.

And in case you are wondering about what may seem to be some peculiar groupings, such as Kentucky & Maine and Rhode Island & Michigan, I'll admit that the geography is not too good, but money-wise they approach the same brackets. The charts again to show their groupings:

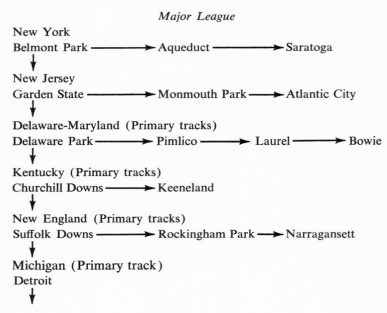

*Major League*

New York
Belmont Park ⟶ Aqueduct ⟶ Saratoga

New Jersey
Garden State ⟶ Monmouth Park ⟶ Atlantic City

Delaware-Maryland (Primary tracks)
Delaware Park ⟶ Pimlico ⟶ Laurel ⟶ Bowie

Kentucky (Primary tracks)
Churchill Downs ⟶ Keeneland

New England (Primary tracks)
Suffolk Downs ⟶ Rockingham Park ⟶ Narragansett

Michigan (Primary track)
Detroit

*Minor League*

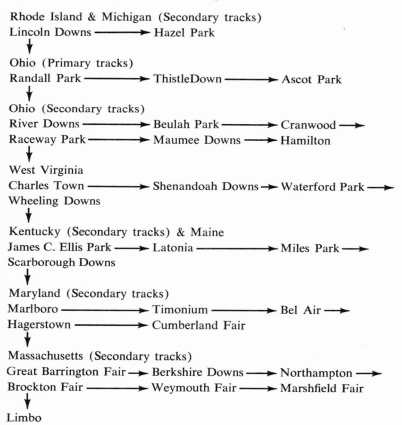

Rhode Island & Michigan (Secondary tracks)
Lincoln Downs ⟶ Hazel Park

Ohio (Primary tracks)
Randall Park ⟶ ThistleDown ⟶ Ascot Park

Ohio (Secondary tracks)
River Downs ⟶ Beulah Park ⟶ Cranwood ⟶
Raceway Park ⟶ Maumee Downs ⟶ Hamilton

West Virginia
Charles Town ⟶ Shenandoah Downs ⟶ Waterford Park ⟶
Wheeling Downs

Kentucky (Secondary tracks) & Maine
James C. Ellis Park ⟶ Latonia ⟶ Miles Park ⟶
Scarborough Downs

Maryland (Secondary tracks)
Marlboro ⟶ Timonium ⟶ Bel Air ⟶
Hagerstown ⟶ Cumberland Fair

Massachusetts (Secondary tracks)
Great Barrington Fair ⟶ Berkshire Downs ⟶ Northampton ⟶
Brockton Fair ⟶ Weymouth Fair ⟶ Marshfield Fair

Limbo

This time you will notice a continuity between the two charts and, in fact, there is. If you live in, say for instance, Rhode Island, you may be inclined to be uninterested in the relative merits of race tracks in other parts of the country since you never have visited them and never will. However, even if you don't move around, the *horses* do. And for that reason, if you live in Rhode Island, or in any other state in the East, and want to go out to the local oval and have some idea of what is going on, you're going to have to have a significant interest in the racing plants scattered about over the other sections of the country. If you will recall, the first thing you read in this treatise was that it was an elementary textbook, and, dear friends, with this being a textbook, and with textbooks being what they are, I will have to state here and now that you are going to have to have more than a nodding acquaintance with the preceding chart of race tracks. All of it. From Belmont right on down to and including Limbo. There's no rule that says a horse running on Major League tracks and losing must stay there and continue to lose. Likewise, there is no rule which states that a hard-hitting horse campaigning in the Minor Leagues for small purses must stay there. The losers can move down the scale; the winners can move up. Aye, and there's the rub; those little rascals are always shifting around.

To backtrack a trifle to pick up the "winter racing" tracks with respect to Major and Minor Leagues:

*Major League*

Hialeah ⟶ Gulfstream Park ⟶ Tropical Park

Fair Grounds ⟶ Oaklawn Park

*Minor League*

Sunshine Park ⟶ Jefferson Downs ⟶ Limbo

And since the horses engaged in "winter racing" and those engaged in "summer racing" are not actually two

distinct sets of horses, but rather the same ones moving back and forth between North and South, we will correlate the two groups with a series of reference points. Hialeah is the New York of the South, and Gulfstream Park is the New Jersey of the South. The horses at Tropical Park, the Fair Grounds, and Oaklawn Park are of about the same racing caliber as those racing in the Delaware-Maryland (Primary tracks), Kentucky (Primary tracks), and the New England Major League circuits. On the Minor League side, Sunshine Park may be considered the Charles Town of the South.

As a parting shot, I'll make the somber observation that things are going to get a lot worse, regarding the mastery of that race track chart, before they get any better. In this respect: you not only have to know the Major League tracks from the Minor League tracks, and the high Major League tracks from the low Majors, and the high Minors from the low Minors, and all the gradients in between— but you have to be able to do it using not the name of the track, but by using its racing paper abbreviation. Now "Pim" for Pimlico and "Beu" for Beulah Park may be easy; but, on the other hand, "Elp" for James C. Ellis Park and "Mth" for Monmouth Park may not be so easy. You are not going to "write any equations" until you know the symbols. And then to make the task completely humbling, keep in mind that since this is a Primer, only Eastern tracks are being considered. A horse in a Western state is not necessarily exiled out there; he may move in to Eastern tracks. And then what strange markings from distant places will he bring with him? And then there are Canadian tracks, and Mexican, and Cuban (?). And then there are imports from Ireland, France, England, Argentina, Australia, Chile, etc. Now put that trusty hatpin back down. Don't give up. If you can handle the tracks listed here, you will have the necessary background material to enable you to competently assimilate new and unfamiliar race courses and their relative merits—or demerits.

A complete rundown of the Eastern tracks and their abbreviations will be given later when the racing papers are discussed.

# 5th. THE RACES

NOW, friends, if you put one jockey on one horse and put said horse and rider out on a race track, you have the makings of a horse race. Of course it won't be much of a race with just the one racing interest out there; forsooth, the horse could walk over the required distance and come in a winner. And that's just what such a horse race is called— a walkover. And just to show you how lily-livered race track owners are, they don't allow any betting on a walkover. Damnation. Just when we had a good thing going. But then that's neither here nor there.

To start at the start, we'll say first that all race tracks in the East have a contrivance called a starting gate. This is a large steel beamed affair containing separate, padded stalls to hold the horses in position in preparation for a fair start. All the entries in the race will be together at least once during the course of the race—in the starting gate. When all of the horses are lined up and in an alert position, the official starter pushes a button, the gates open, and the horses are running. But that is *not* the official start of the race. The official starting line is twenty to thirty yards up in front of the starting gate. While the horses are in position in the starting gate, or nearly so, look up the track a few yards and you will see a man standing in the infield holding a red flag. This man is standing on the official starting line. As the horses come out of the gate, he holds the flag up over his head, and as they go by him, he swooshes it down, à la Indianapolis 500, to signify the race has officially started. In other words—although the starting gate is used to line the horses up, the horses actually get a running start for each race. For purposes of officially timing the races, both this man and his red flag may in many instances be looked upon as examples of featherbedding, since automation has moved in and the actual timing at many race courses is done by an electronic gizmo called a Teletimer.

Now just how far are these horses going to run before the race is over? Such a question naturally brings up the category of distance; and, friends, around a race track distance is discussed for the most part in terms of furlongs. How long is a furlong? A furlong is ⅛ of a mile. A furlong is ⅛ of a mile. A furlong is ⅛ of a mile. Therefore, we can chart thusly:

| | | | |
|---|---|---|---|
| 2 furlongs | ¼ mile | 6 furlongs | ¾ mile |
| 3 furlongs | ⅜ mile | 7 furlongs | ⅞ mile |
| 4 furlongs | ½ mile | 8 furlongs | 1 mile |
| 5 furlongs | ⅝ mile | 9 furlongs | 1⅛ miles |

In some quarters a furlong may at times be referred to as a panel. If you should read that a horse raced 5 panels, you would know that he raced 5 furlongs, or ⅝ of a mile.

Now to return to those horses that just came out of the starting gate. How far are they going to run?

All the horses campaigning in the East, or campaigning anywhere, for that matter, can be divided into four groups. The first group consists of horses which come out of the starting gate quickly and show a high turn of speed (early foot)—and then the farther they go, the slower they get. Or in other words—the finish line hadn't better be too far away, else they'll never make it. This group has a lot of speed but can't carry it very far. Such horses are called *sprinters,* and the short races in which they compete are called *sprints.* If this group of horses sounds fainthearted, I'll add that being a sprinter is certainly no disgrace; most of the races run are sprints, anyhow.

The second group consists of horses which come out of the starting gate without any great burst of initial speed— and then the farther they go, the faster they run—up to a point, of course. Such a horse would have little or no chance in a sprint; the race would be over before he hit his best stride; or, in other words, this horse needs more room. Such a horse is called a *router,* and the long races in which he competes are called *routes.* Since this horse runs so slowly in the early stages of his races, he may also be referred to as a plodder.

And then there's the versatility group. These horses can be rated to run a race depending upon the existing conditions. They can break out of the gate and sprint; or they can plod slowly and turn on the speed in the latter stages of the race. When in top form and when favorably placed, members of this group may simply sprint their way to victory in a route race. While the others are plodding and biding their time, these speed horses with staying power may go right to the top and open up such a long lead that the plodders can't catch them. Five furlongs or a mile and a half, it makes no difference to the members of this group; they'll give it a good effort, and at the end of the race they'll be there or thereabouts.

And lastly, to round out the different types and to lend symmetry to the classification, it must be confessed that there are those horses which can't win at any distance. Five furlongs or a mile and a half, it makes no difference to the members of this group; they don't care where the finish line is because they're not going to win anything anyhow. Such horses are said to suffer from the "slows."

How long is a long race? A route? How short is a short race? A sprint? The dividing line is 7 furlongs. All races up to and including 7 furlongs are sprints. All races 1 mile and over are routes.

At this juncture we are going to have to backtrack momentarily to gather up one loose end which has been dangling. In the preceding chapter you were told a race track may have one or more extensions called chutes. Then you were shown via a diagram the positioning of these chutes. Since up until that time no mention had been made concerning the different lengths of races, no mention was made concerning the size of the chutes.

When speaking of the "size" of a chute, what is meant is the length of the *races* run from that chute. Using a one-mile track as an example, the chute at the head of the backstretch is a 6-furlong chute (or a 7-furlong chute, of course, if it's ⅛ of a mile longer). The chute at the head of the homestretch is a 1¼-mile chute. To repeat: The 1¼ miles means that the races run from the end of that chute are 1¼ miles long. It does not mean that the chute is 1¼ miles long, else you would have the paradox of the chute being longer than the entire track. And do try to remember the positioning of the 6-furlong chute, at the head of the backstretch, because most races run on the Major League tracks are just that—6 furlongs. Notice that when these races start at the top of the backstretch, the horses will be almost completely out of view. The horses come out of the gate, sprint for position out of the chute, speed down the backstretch, swing around the turn, and go for the wire. And that's it. That's the whole race. By the time you have positively located your horse visually, either by the color of the racing silks or by the number on his saddlecloth, you don't know whether you should urge, "Hold him out there!" or, "Get him up there!" The track announcer will have been giving a running description of the race, but then when you are out there frantically clutching your pari-mutuel tickets, who wants secondhand information?

And now for a statement of some importance, probably the most important statement made up to this point: *At every race track and for virtually every race there has been some attempt or some effort made to give all the competing horses an equal chance to win.*

The horses for each day's races are not simply drawn out of a hat and numbered. Down deep in the bowels of every race track there dwells an evil, suspect man called a racing secretary. This diabolical soul works all day and into the night formulating (carding) races in which he tries, in his ruthless way, to get all the horses entered in each race to finish at once—a grand and glorious tie, or "dead heat" as it's called around the track. What a twisted mind.

Now you can see that you, or I, or anybody who tries to pick a winner, and this despicable man are at complete and total loggerheads. He works all night trying to bring all the horses in at once and we work all night (with modifications) trying to pick the *one* outstanding horse. We have to select a winner now and again to prevent the day's activities from becoming a complete financial disaster. He has to provide "interesting" races since the turf public does not want to come out and witness eight or nine consecutive runaways—unless of course the public happened to have its money on the horses which won in a breeze. By "interesting" here we mean that there will be many diverse opinions among the throng attending the races as to which horse will win—opinions worthy of being backed by cash. Ideally, from the racing secretary's point of view, all the races should be close and hard-fought; give the crowd something to shout about; get the money going into the machines.

And now strictly in the interest of understanding, I want you for the moment to put yourself in the racing secretary's place and endeavor to draw up some imaginary races in which all the horses have an equal chance to win. Yes, you. You with your knowledge of racing limited to what you have learned thus far in this book.

As a starter, you could card a race for 2-year-olds. That's a step in the right direction; it sorted out all the juveniles as being eligible and eliminated all the sophomores and all the older horses. To limit the number of eligible horses further, you could take in the sex factor. Since even among horses females are supposedly the weaker sex, you could place further restrictions by making the race: For 2-year-olds. Colts & Geldings. Or: For 2-year-olds. Fillies.

To consider older horses, you could start your conditions for a race: For 3-year-olds. Colts & Geldings. There you have eliminated all the females, all the 2-year-olds, and all those horses 4 years of age or older. But how about distance? Is this race for the speed merchants or is it to be a route? (Distance wasn't mentioned in the sample race for 2-year-olds since almost all the races for 2-year-olds are sprints.) Bringing the distance factor into consideration, you could specify: For 3-year-olds. Colts & Geldings. 6 Furlongs. Now we know that it is to be a sprint and the routers, for all practical purposes, have been eliminated.

And by now you should be able to card an assortment of races—still based solely on the three factors: age, sex, and distance. Examples:

> 3-year-olds & Up. Fillies & Mares. 5 Furlongs.
> 4-year-olds & Up. 7 Furlongs.
> 3-year-olds. 1 Mile.

In the last two examples you will notice there was no mention made as regards sex; the fillies and mares do quite often compete against the menfolk, and with some success, I might add.

Up to this point in an attempt to produce races in which all the contending horses have a chance to win, one great factor has been omitted. If races were carded on the basis of age, sex, and distance alone, they would of necessity prove to be grossly unfair; and, from the racing secretary's point of view, overwhelmingly boring . . . which equals no interest . . . which equals no money . . . which is bad.

To elaborate—if you designated a race as being for 2-year-olds only, you would eliminate the possibility of men competing against boys. To improve the situation somewhat, you could stipulate further: Fillies; and then the eventuality of girls competing against boys would be avoided. Lastly, you could bring in the distance factor and separate sprinters from routers. And in all of this sorting out—you have completely ignored perhaps the greatest single factor of all, the factor of *quality*.

You are proceeding on the shaky premise that a race for 2-year-olds, Fillies, 5 Furlongs, will tend to give some kind of favorable result since all of the entrants are female, all of them are 2 years old, and all will be asked to run 5 furlongs. Such an assumption is comparable to saying that all golfers in the United States who are male and who are 21 years of age, would compete fairly and with much excitement in, say, for instance, a 36-hole tournament— just to bring the "distance" factor into play. Since all the participants would be male, all would be the same age, and all would be asked to play the same number of holes—they should all play the game equally well. Now you can see that we are in big trouble here. A golf tournament based on such an erroneous assumption would make for grossly inequitable competition. And why? Because there was no mention made of *quality*. Some of those golfers would be professionals, some would be competent players who fracture par now and then, and then there would be some so-so players, and lastly, there would be many sod-smashing duffers.

To get back to the horses—you can now see that the racing secretary must have more tools, more ways and means to ply his trade. He must have available a method or methods of further classifying and grouping the horses according to *quality* to produce close and interesting races. And, fortunately, or unfortunately, depending upon your sentiments, he does. And how he does.

The magnitude in the variance of capabilities amongst thoroughbreds may be shown by the following figures. In 1961 over 13,000 foals were registered in the United States. That's 13,000 anxious and eager would-be thoroughbred champions who are going to vie on American race tracks for top honors. The sad truth is that out of all this horde of horseflesh, perhaps only 30 will ever be really good. Others will be fair. And all the rest are simply left over. Joe Palmer in his *This Was Racing* painted an honest and accurate picture. Let me preface his quote by first saying that his figure of total foals is a little old, and then let me add—don't be unduly upset or too concerned about the unfamiliar terms he uses. It is just such terms which we are leading up to:

About half of racing, or maybe a little more, isn't worth happening or seeing. A $3,000 claiming race, for instance, can be bet on if you feel that way, but that's the beginning and the end of it. The horses are no good, they are inconsistent, they are usually more or less unsound. The jockeys are about a routine task and their effort is just to ride as fast as the horse can run.

But unfortunately this half of racing is necessary to produce the other half, which consists of anything from matching fairly competent horses against each other to the real thrillers, the big races which involve the crack horses and produce the epic struggles.

Breeders try to produce top horses. Now, there are about 8,000 foals a year and there are going to be maybe 20 or 30 which are really good, and several hundred others which are fair. Inevitably most of the attempts are failures. But the failures can't be tossed out—they cost too much. So you have the claiming races, the races for maiden 4-year-olds and up, the sprints for non-winners of $2,500 at any time, to keep breeding and racing from being too expensive for even the wealthy owners.

We will now investigate further the ways and means at the racing secretary's disposal to card races in which horses of fundamentally equal talents and capabilities can compete. Or, briefly, there are different types of races and we must examine and understand these types.

The instruction booklet published by "America's Turf Authority," the *Daily Racing Form,* lists about twenty different types of races. I say "about twenty" because it's complicated. It initially lists sixteen types, and then in the explanatory summary it picks up three or four more. Whatever the number, it's too big and too cumbersome and I'm relatively certain that a person who knew nothing about racing or races would know even less after he read that list. In about two pages of type and explanation it made only one brief allusion to the fact that there is such a thing as a "Claiming Race"—by referring the reader to another section of the booklet. So I'll take the time right here and now, dear friends, to tell you quite emphatically that there is such a thing as a "Claiming Race"—to the point that Claiming Races make up about 60-80% of all the races run. To refresh your memory with some sections of the *This Was Racing* quote:

About half of racing, or maybe a little more, isn't worth happening or seeing. . . .

But unfortunately this half of racing is necessary to produce the other half. . . .

Breeders try to produce top horses. . . . Inevitably most of the attempts are failures. But the failures can't be tossed out —they cost too much. So you have the claiming races . . . to keep breeding and racing from being too expensive for even the wealthy owners.

Nineteen or twenty types of races are too many for the novice who is just trying to learn fundamentals. This treatise will discuss four types and will make only the briefest mention of a few other types.

The four types of races:

       1. Claiming
       2. Allowance
       3. Handicap-Stakes
       4. Races for non-winners

I'm going to start with the Claiming Race since, as I've said before, Claiming Races comprise over half of all the

races run. And what is a Claiming Race? Now get all the
crap out of your ears and sit up and pay attention; you are
about to hear a definition of a Claiming Race that has
never been given before, and may never be given again.
To wit: Claiming Races are races carded for the cheapest
horses on the grounds. That sounded so good I think I'll
say it again. Claiming Races are races carded for the
cheapest horses on the grounds.

And now I have to digress again. It just galls me to
have to harangue about the next subject. It is one of those
things which is perhaps better left unsaid, but duty calls—
and I have to answer.

There are certain yardsticks in various fields of endeavor
which stamp or label the participant as a proficient, re-
spected performer, (or writer), of promise. The absence
of these yardsticks just as assuredly labels the participant
as an ignorant, nondescript, dumb ass clod. For instance,
if you are ever going to play contract bridge, you *must*
finesse. Makes no matter whether the finesse is indicated
or contraindicated, if you are going to be any kind of
bridge player worth his salt, you must finesse. If you make
a game contract and thereby win the rubber and finish
plus 38, you are still a total loss as a bridge player if you
didn't finesse something somewhere along the line. For
shame, you callous, uncouth maker of contracts. You will
never amass any master points. On the other hand—if you
should be in a grand-slam contract, finesse successfully,
and then go down 12, the whole wretched mess is still an
unqualified success. Why? Because you finessed and finessed successfully. Aye, that's the hallmark of the elite.

Perhaps if you hadn't finessed you would have made the slam—but then where would be the "stamp" of the polished player? Don't try to wiggle off the hook; there's no denying it; you're an ass.

In the same vein, when discussing golf and golfing, you must never mention a slice. A slice is an affliction of the masses. Only proles slice. You must always discuss your hook. Only decent, self-respecting golfers hook. So always discuss your hook, and always talk about how you have a tendency to smother the ball, even though in reality the only thing you have a tendency to smother is your score card at the end of the round.

By the same token, if you are going to discuss horse racing anytime, anywhere, among any group, you *must* somewhere along the line mention, and this hurts, the Selling Race. So now I've mentioned it. I have now met the paramount qualification toward being an oracle on horse racing. I said it: Selling Race. What is it? Nothing. There's no such thing. It is simply a throwback to a by-gone era. What it used to mean was that when a Selling Race was over, they sold (via auction) the winning horse —to anybody—even to the original owner.

Now, friends, let's have a funeral and bury this damned empty carcass. There is no such thing as a Selling Race; it went out about the time wireless came in. With your permission, I will give the appropriate eulogy:

Dearly Beloved, we are gathered here to inter a leftover relic from the yesteryear of racing. We would like to rid ourselves of this hanger-on once and for all. The Lord giveth and the Lord taketh away. He gave us the Selling

Race and he took it away, but it's like a good purulent dose; it just keeps coming back. We want to shove this antique into a good airtight tomb and hastily bar the door. We want to hear no voices from the grave; we want no apparitions haunting the here and the now of racing. Let not sentimentality transcend sanity. Let there be logic. What the good Lord has put asunder let no man try to ressurect. Ashes to ashes and dust to dust, ye old Selling Race, the good Lord doesn't want you . . . the devil must. Afurlong.

The next time you are in a group of race track authorities and one of them regally drops the term "Selling Race" into the conversation, I want you to smile at him knowingly, pat him on the shoulder, and then pick up a goodly sized piece of lumber and bash his goddamned head in. As he lies there in his pool of useless blood and inquires rather gurglingly over a hoped-for death rattle just what in the hell got into you, tell him you had a hot horse going at Jerome Park and simply got all carried away by the very spirit of the thing. That answer won't make a bit of sense, but then neither did his asinine reference to the golden years of racing. Chances are the senile, crotchety old coot will give you some money to get a bet down for him. Thus ends our discussion of the Selling Race.

But I was talking about Claiming Races and about how they are races for the cheapest horses on the grounds. Claiming Races are an attempt, or an approach, toward evaluating horses, using the almighty dollar as the indicator of worth. In this manner: any time a horse is entered in a Claiming Race, he is subject to being "claimed," i.e., "bought" by any other bona fide owner, or his agent, who has raced horses at the track. There are diverse and sundry ramifications into the claiming laws of the various states (States' rights . . . State Racing Commissions . . . political debts). The technicalities and the actual mechanics of the claiming procedure do not interest us here. (The only technicality we'll mention is that an owner cannot claim his own horse.) But whatever the whys and the wherefores of the actual manipulation of the law, the basic concept is always the same; just remember that whenever an owner puts his horse in a Claiming Race, he is hanging a "For Sale" sign on his horse, since the animal can then be "claimed" (bought).

And here is how such a bizarre arrangement tends to classify and equalize the horses entered in a race. You must first be aware that there are Claiming Races and then there are Claiming Races—big ones and little ones. Claiming prices, the amounts for which horses can be claimed, vary from $50,000 on down to $800. (There may be Claiming prices higher than $50,000, but the point would merely be an academic one.) All those thousands of horses which can't be tossed out as factory rejects because they cost too much fall somewhere in this spectrum of $50,000 on down to $800. Any horse which does not fit into this scheme of things sinks slowly into limbo.

Horses definitely are not machines, but they can and do perform with a great deal of consistency, and by using dollars as the designator, they can practically be catalogued as to where they fit in this monetary scale.

To clarify by citing a few examples—some horses will be $5,000 Claimers, others will be $10,000 Claimers, and others will be $1,000 Claimers. When a horse is said to be a $2,000 Claimer, it does *not* mean that every time he is entered in a $2,000 Claiming Race he canters home an easy winner. No, it means nothing of the sort. It means that when he is *in form,* when he is going the correct distance, sprint or route, when he isn't being asked to carry too much weight, when he has a jockey up who knows how to ride a horse, when the track condition is favorable, and when all the other factors relative to a horse race are in his favor—then he will be properly placed and will give a *good* effort—not necessarily a winning effort.

All the other Claimers seek their level in the same fashion. And incidently, with all of this talk about "Claimers," I'll mention that the terms "Claimer" and "Plater" are the same thing. In the early days of racing when fields of mediocre horses competed, the winning owner received a silver plate and from this practice the mediocre, or cheap, horses came to be known as "Platers."

To illustrate the claiming principle further, let's assume that you owned a $5,000 Claimer. Again all the data about the horse having to be in form and all the other factors being considered—your horse could be counted upon to give a good account of himself when entered in a Claiming Race for $5,000. A good account of himself—again, *not* necessarily a win. Well, if all those factors have to be just right and then your horse still might lose, you may be tempted to reason, "Damn those $5,000 races; I'll run my horse in a Claiming Race for $2,000. Those cheapies I know he can beat." There's only one hitch to your "win 'em easy" plot. This time you won't lose the race; you'll lose the *horse.*

In fact, if your $5,000 plater runs a couple of smashers in the $5,000 bracket and garners a couple of purses (wins), you're going to have to elevate him up the scale and try to beat some of the better horses—the $6,000 or $7,500 company, or else someone will claim him for $5,000 and still have a bargain. And then when your horse battles his way to the wire against a couple of $7,500 horses and tires in the homestretch only to finish clear out of the money —it's all for the benefit of that raucous loser who will shout, "Did you see them hold that horse back!! The *owner* didn't even want to win!" The owner didn't want to win. He just got his charge into fine enough fettle to win two straight races, paid a jockey fee, paid a trainer, paid all the other bills, and then sent his horse out there to get beaten on purpose. If he wanted to lose, he could have sent out one of the stable ponies. The fact that the horse gave an honest effort, as witnessed by his being with the leaders into the stretch, and gave way only grudgingly to superior horses, never enters the loser's mind. There still is just no easy way. And yet the loser can and will yell, and that's his privilege, friends; he's paid his $2.

And now you are equipped to card some more "homemade" races of your own which will more nearly match equally talented horses. Examples:

6 Furlongs (Chute). 3-year-olds & Up. Claiming. Claiming Price: $4,000.

5 Furlongs. 2-year-olds. Claiming. Claiming Price: $6,000.

7 Furlongs (Chute). 4-year-olds & Up. Fillies & Mares. Claiming. Claiming Price: $25,000.

1 Mile. 4-year-olds & Up. Claiming. Claiming Price: $1,250.

And on and on. Now we could card races like that all day long; however, the question must be brewing in your mind—what about the owners who have horses of more than average merit and who do not want to place their horses in Claiming Races? We said all horses in Claiming Races were "For Sale." What about the owner who does not want to run the risk of having his horse claimed? Suppose a man owned a horse, which we will call Royal Whizbang for descriptive purposes, and thought his racer could beat about any horse on the grounds. Surely there must be some race or group of races in which he can enter his horse and be certain of maintaining ownership. And there is. Of course there is.

This reasoning brings us to the second type of race—the Allowance Race. And here is a genuine, authentic definition of an Allowance Race, regardless of whatever hogwash you may have read or heard before: Allowance Races are those races carded for all the horses which are too good to run in Claiming Races. That sounded so good I think I'll say it again. Allowance Races are those races carded for all the horses which are too good to run in Claiming Races. These are the horses Mr. Palmer referred to when he said, "and several hundred others which are fair."

Here is an example of an Allowance Race:

6 Furlongs (Chute).  3-year-olds.  Allowances.

With those being the conditions, *all* the Claimers can stay right back in the barn. No owner of a $1,250 Plater would consider placing his horse in such a race. Other examples of Allowance Races:

1¹⁄₁₆ Miles (Turf Course). 4-year-olds & Up. Allowances.

1 Mile. 3-year-olds. Allowances.

1 Mile & 70 yards. 3-year-olds & Up. Allowances.

5 Furlongs. 2-year-olds. Colts & Geldings. Allowances.

1¼ Miles (Out of Chute). Purse $4,500. 4-year-olds & Up. Allowances.

In the last example you will notice a new figure: Purse $4,500. This is the sum of money that the owners of the competing horses are trying to win. It has nothing to do with a claiming price. Do not get "Purse" and "Claiming Price" confused. To go back a step—the Claiming Race will also state a purse. The purse figure wasn't given previously because I did not want to confuse you with two sets of figures. Thusly:

6 Furlongs (Out of Chute), Purse $2,500, 4-year olds & Up, Claiming. Claiming Price: $3,000.

You will also notice that the purse (prize money for the winning owners) is considerably higher in the Allowance Race than in the Claiming Race. Since the Claiming Races are for the cheap horses—then they will also have cheap purses; the Allowance horses run for the richer purses, each getting his just deserts. And that's as it should be.

And now for another statement of some importance—a gem of wisdom to cut out and paste in your hat: *At any race track and in any type of race, the higher the relative figure of merit in which a horse is competing, the richer the purse for which he is competing.*

To illustrate—if you have a horse running at Timonium in low Claiming Races, then you are going to compete for low purses. If you have a horse of sufficient merit to run in the higher Claiming Races at Timonium, or good enough to campaign in the Allowance Races there—then you will likewise compete for higher purses. However, at whatever level your horse campaigns at Timonium, he is still at Timonium. You would be better off moneywise if you could get him out of Timonium (a Minor League track) and bring him to the Majors. There the purses would be considerably higher—and just to maintain the equine system of "checks and balances," the horses running there in the Majors would be correspondingly superior. In other words —if your horse is going to get close enough to win as much as five cents in the Major Leagues, then he had better have a lot of get-up-and-go, else you had better keep him right there in the bush leagues and keep going after those small purses. I repeat, friends, there still is just no easy way, and it is still all for the benefit of the disgruntled loser who wants to shout, "That crooked bastard didn't even try to win! !"

While on the subject of purses, we will mention "Purse Distribution." The figure stating the purse in the conditions of each race is the amount of money put up by the race track to be won by the owners of the horses which fare well in the race. The winning horse does not take home the entire purse; the purse is distributed. It is distributed, as a rule, among the first, second, third, and fourth place horses. The usual purse distribution is: first, 65%, second, 20%; third, 10%; and fourth, 5%. Thus in a race with a purse of $4,000 (an average Allowance Race purse at a Major League track) the distribution would be: first, $2,600; second, $800; third, $400; and fourth, $200.

We promised to explain the meaning of "Minimum

Claiming Price" and "Average net purse distribution per race" in reference to the chart of race tracks. You now know what a claiming price is, and putting "minimum" in front of the claiming price simply means the cheapest of the cheap. In 1961 the minimum claiming price at Belmont Park was $3,500. The corresponding figure at Marshfield Fair was $800.

Average net purse distribution per race simply means the average amount of money put up by the track to be won by the horse owners. In 1961 the average net purse distribution per race at Belmont Park was $6,557 and the corresponding figure at Marshfield Fair was $512. And therein lies one of the biggest differences between Major and Minor League racing.

To get another insight into the difference between Major and Minor League racing, look at the following figures. As stated previously, the average net purse distribution per race at Marshfield Fair was $512. The preceding figures which showed the distribution of a $4,000 purse at a Major League track indicated that the *second*-place horse received $800—or nearly $300 more than the whole damn purse at a Minor League track!

You now know what a Claiming Race is and what an Allowance Race is. To make mention of another type of race, there is a thing called an Optional Claiming Race. In this type of race the owner has the option of entering his horse to be claimed or entering his horse *not* to be claimed. This race is still a Claiming Race. It is not a slow Claiming Race. It is not a fast Claiming Race. Instead, it is a half-fast Claiming Race which serves three purposes:

1. It serves as a tranquilizing outlet for mixed-up owners who can't make up their minds as to just what kind of horse they do own.

2. It throws another factor into the pot to harass and perplex the already beleaguered handicapper.

3. It sells a lot of eyeglasses and keeps the optometrists busy, since people have a tendency to go cross-eyed from looking at all those little "ᵒ's" in the racing papers. To explain that last statement: when you see Clm. 5,000 in the racing paper, that means a Claiming Race for $5,000. But when you see (and now keep your eye on the bouncing ball) Clm. ᵒ5,000 it means an Optional Claiming Race for $5,000 and the horse was *not* entered to be claimed. Conversely, when you see Clm. 5,000ᵒ, it means an Optional Claiming Race for $5,000 and the horse *was* entered to be claimed. Or maybe it was the other way around.

Another type of race I'd better mention is what I call the "Chinese Allowance Race," although its official name is a Starter Allowance Race. When you read the conditions for an Allowance Race, make sure it is just that—an Allowance Race, and not one of the Chinese variety. Here is an example of such a race:

1 Mile. Purse $3,000. For 4-year-olds & Up. Starter Allowances. For horses which have started for a Claiming Price of $4,000 or less this year.

The underscored conditions just shot the race full of holes as far as its being a bona fide Allowance Race. This is simply a Claiming Race in which the horses entered cannot be claimed—a "Chinese Allowance Race." This is not a slow Allowance Race; it is not a fast Allowance Race. What this race really amounts to is that all the Claimers in a specific price range are brought together for some sort of a "championship" contest.

The cheap horses run in the cheap races, the Claiming Races. Horses too good for the Claiming ranks race in Allowance Races. Now what about the horse who wins the Allowance Races with commendable regularity? Are there no more lucrative contests for him to enter? Can't he continue on up the scale? Where are those $100,000 races I've heard about?

Such questions bring us to the third type of race—the Handicap-Stakes. These are the big money affairs and here is where the successful Allowance horse meets his big test. The horses that can win in this category are the "20 or 30 which are really good" to which Mr. Palmer referred. Here is where the champions are made, where the pretty good are separated from the great.

Things are still never easy, friends. If your horse fares better than average here in the Handicap ranks, then that evil man, the racing secretary, steps in and starts to make things uncomfortable for you and for your horse. He does this with weight—strips of lead are put aboard your horse to slow him down. Should your horse win carrying 115 pounds, the next time he will have to carry about 120 pounds. If he wins again, 125 pounds. Win again, 130 pounds. Again, 135 pounds. While your horse is lugging 135 pounds around the track, another horse which hasn't been doing too well lately and who is consequently in the race with a "feather" of only 105 pounds, will be trying to defeat you. So, you see, your horse not only has to be better than all the rest; he has to be about 30 pounds of lead better. Not many horses are in this class—maybe 2, maybe 1, maybe none—out of the original 13,000 who were ready and anxious to try it. Need I repeat? There still is just no easy way, friends. And when your handicap star wobbles in the stretch and weakens from carrying 135 pounds around over the track and finishes clear out of the money, it's still all for the benefit of that irate loser who will shout, "Did you see them hold that horse back! They didn't even want to win!" A win means the lion's share of a $100,000 purse, and yet the owner, trainer, and jockey simply were not trying. Fascinating people, those race-trackers.

Quite often here we have made reference to a man called a racing secretary. This man may also be called the "track handicapper," and for purposes of discussion the two terms are interchangeable since frequently it is the same man with both jobs. Here are some anecdotes from the literature to show you just how the minds of these men work. The first two are from *This Was Racing* and the third is from Underwood's *Thoroughbred Racing and Breeding*:

To preface the quotes we will say that one of the most famous (infamous?) handicappers of all time was the late, great John B. Campbell. It was Mr. Campbell, for those of you who may not know, who assigned the weights for the Carter Handicap at Aqueduct in 1944. Among the entries were these three horses which Mr. Campbell weighted thus:

|  |  |
|---|---|
| Brownie | 115 |
| Bossuet | 127 |
| Wait A Bit | 118 |

The result of the race? A *triple* dead heat. All *three* of the above horses won! And that, friends, is a pretty fair piece of handicapping.

Mr. Campbell is generally accounted the leading racing secretary and handicapper of his time. He is a robust man, and strong.

In 1949 he was able to lift 138 pounds and put it on Coaltown for the Suburban Handicap, when no other handicapper was able to handle much more than 130. This resulted in a stand-off. Narragansett Park got the gate attraction and Coaltown got a hollow victory. Mr. Campbell got a keenly contested Suburban without Coaltown and was able to look at himself calmly while shaving.

As an "aside": If you will look at the chart of race tracks and note the relative positions of Belmont Park and Narragansett Park, you will see why Coaltown's exodus from the Suburban Handicap and his subsequent triumph in the Roger Williams Handicap was regarded by Mr. Palmer as a hollow victory—this in addition to the $50,000 to $15,000 drop in purse money, of course.

Another great handicapper was Walter S. Vosburgh. Mr. Vosburgh happened to be the racing secretary when a certain colt was running roughshod over all the opposition. If you have ever heard of any one race horse in the United States, chances are that one horse is Man o' War. So now let's see how the fabulous Man o' War made out with the racing secretary, Mr. Vosburgh:

It was Mr. Vosburgh, for instance, whom the late Samuel D. Riddle asked what weight he would put on Man o' War at four. You understand that Man o' War would have been, with his towering reputation, the greatest gate attraction racing could have had in the present century. But Mr. Vosburgh was not in the admissions department.

"If he wins his first race," he said, "I'll put the heaviest weight on him that any horse has carried in my lifetime."

After Man o' War was in stud, Mr. Riddle accepted this as the greatest praise his horse had ever had, and he would tell the story proudly. In 1920, however, he considered it unfair and unjust and an infringement on the rights of all horsemen named Samuel Doyle Riddle.

And so, you see, the great Man o' War raced only as a juvenile and as a sophomore. Two racing seasons. Then the racing secretary retired him.

And as long as Man o' War is the only horse you've ever heard of, it might be fitting to add a couple of other tidbits about him. He ran a total of 21 races during those two racing seasons and won every race except one. After six straight wins as a 2-year-old, he lost the Sanford Memorial Stakes at Saratoga by half a length. The horse which defeated him was named, appropriately enough, Upset.

And if that wiseacre sidles up to you and wants to know in what year Man o' War won the Kentucky Derby, the correct answer is that Man o' War never won the Kentucky Derby, and for a very good reason—he was never entered in it. He did win the Preakness Stakes and the Belmont Stakes. So don't be taken back when you read over the list of Triple Crown winners and see that the great Man o' War isn't in there.

The third quote is self-explanatory:

A weight-for-age scale originated by Admiral the Honorable John Henry Rous, English racing expert, is the basis of racing in this country today.

Admiral Rous is recognized as the "first handicapper." He is credited with the first use of a classic reply for owners dissatisfied with weights. A horseman is said to have wound up a vigorous protest to the Admiral by asking if Rous thought his racer had a chance under the weights imposed.

"None whatever," answered the Admiral.

"None whatever." You see, friends, even in the early days of racing there just was no easy way.

Before we leave the Handicap-Stakes division, I want to make sure you are aware that such a term, as used here, is a "lumping together" of various types of "big money" races. Some big races are known strictly as Handicaps. Example: The John B. Campbell Memorial Handicap at Bowie. (Now there's a name that should sound familiar.) Other big races are known as Stakes. Example: The Flamingo Stakes at Hialeah. And then there are various names, titles, and subdivisions. Examples: Special Weight Stakes, Scale Weight Stakes, Weight-for-Age-Stakes, etc.—all big races. And let me add that a race does not have to have a monetary value of $100,000 to qualify as a Handicap-Stakes. Handicap-Stakes purses will range from $300,000 on down to $5,000.

However, we must also remark that the "Chinese Allowance Race" has a few homologues here in the Handicap-Stakes classification. When you are evaluating a horse as to his Handicap-Stakes ability, be certain he has raced in just that—Handicap-Stakes—and not one of the following:

An Overnight Handicap: This is a "Handicap" in which the racing secretary has let it be known that it might be morning before the horses finish.

Starter Handicap: This is analogous to the Starter Allowance and has the advantage of sounding even more impressive.

Handicap Claiming Race: This is a race run under Handicap conditions—but with a *Claiming* clause. Now there's an anomaly.

And here is perhaps the pinnacle of fame or the *pièce de résistance* as far as oddball races are concerned: The Optional Claiming Handicap. Now there, friends, is a race which has almost everything; too bad they couldn't have worked "Allowance" in there somewhere. This is not a slow Handicap. It is not a fast Handicap.

We started with the cheapest of the cheap horses, worked up through the Claiming ranks, discussed the better Allowance horses, and then moved right on up to the top—Handicap-Stakes horses. It would appear that we have covered about everything. But no, there is still one very large group of races we haven't touched upon—the races for non-winners.

What are races for non-winners? Friends, the term itself, non-winners, means just exactly what it says: horses which have not won a race. To give a textbook definition of a non-winner: A horse which has not won a race on the flat in any country. Notice the two phrases: "on the flat" and "in any country." Even though a horse has won a steeplechase or a hurdle race (which I've been told are not the same thing) and then forsakes the hedges and/or fences for flat racing, he is still a non-winner. And if a horse wins a race in Chile, or England, or France, or anywhere, and then comes to this country, he is not a non-winner. One more technicality: if a horse finishes first and then is disqualified, then he is still a non-winner.

The first point I want to make about non-winners is that the term non-winners is too long. Around a race track non-winners have another, shorter name: Maidens. A horse which has never won a race is called a Maiden, and let me add quickly that the term "maiden" as used here has no reference whatsoever to sex. It very definitely does not mean a coy, chaste little filly; it could just as well denote a grumpy, impure ten-year-old horse.

Here is an example of a Maiden Race, and I want you to examine it closely:

3 Furlongs. 2-year-olds. Maidens.

What's wrong with that race? The distance is there. The age group has been given, and the race is labeled as being exclusively for Maidens; yet, there's something wrong with that race. Here are a few more examples which may serve to jog your memory:

5 Furlongs. 3-year-olds. Maidens.
6 Furlongs (Chute). 3-year-olds. Fillies. Maidens.

And lastly,

1¼ Miles (Out of Chute). 4-year-olds & Up. Maidens.

What's wrong with those races? I'll give you a few final clues. In the first example: 3 Furlongs, 2-year-olds, Maidens, since the race is for 2-year-olds and since horses begin their racing careers at that age, it is highly conceivable that the horses in this race are making their first start, especially when the distance given, 3 Furlongs, smacks of being one of those "baby races" in one of the southern states. Naturally any horse which hasn't raced is a non-winner. Citation, Native Dancer, and Round Table were all Maidens before they made their first start.

In the next two illustrations the horses are 3-year-olds and one or two of them still could possibly be making their first start, but I doubt it.

The last example shows a race for Maidens, 4-year-olds & *Up*. These horses have raced before, a season or two at least, and are still Maidens.

The four examples given have one important factor missing. It is the same factor which went unheeded when you began carding races thusly:

1 Mile.    4-year-olds & Up.
1¾₁₆ Miles.    3-year-olds.
5½ Furlongs.    3-year-olds & Up.    Fillies & Mares.

What's the missing factor? If you don't know by now, then as a student reading a textbook you have flunked rather spectacularly up to this point and had better flip back to page 16 where it says "This is a horse," and start all over.

In the previously given examples of Maiden Races there was no reference made to *quality*. Yes, even among the Maidens, the non-winners, there are still good ones and bad ones, significant races and insignificant races.

When discussing Maidens, it is possible that we are also discussing first-time starters. As pointed out before, every horse is a Maiden until he has had a chance to race. Theoretically, all the 2-year-olds which are coming to the races for their first season can be looked upon as being equal. None of them can have a black mark against him if he has never raced. How then can you sort them all out as to Claimers, Allowance horses, and Handicap-Stakes candidates?

To understand the answer to that seeming stumper, you must first understand that horse owners are one of the most optimistic species on the face of the earth. And necessarily so, after all, for how much sense would it make for a horse owner to say, "I just went to the yearling sales at Saratoga and paid $37,000 for a colt. Next year when he's ready for racing I'm going to take him out to Rockingham Park and enter him in a *Claiming* Race"? Such a pessimistic owner would be admitting his horse was a flop without ever giving the colt a chance to demonstrate his value. The colt was ruled "guilty" without benefit of a trial. Why go down to the bottom of things and start a new colt in a Claiming Race? Why not start him at the top? Where is the top for non-winners? It is time to get the crap out of your ears again. Time to sit up and pay attention.

The top of the scale for non-winners, or the "Handicap-Stakes" classification for Maidens, is a race called Maidens Special Weights. That sounded so good I think I'll say it again: The top of the scale for non-winners, or the "Handicap-Stakes" classification for Maidens, is a race called Maidens Special Weights. Here is where all the optimistic, big-thinking owners start their horses. Here is where Man o' War, Citation, Count Fleet, Nashua, and Swaps all started. (Count Fleet needed three tries before he could win one of these races—then he went on to win the Triple Crown.)

All the starry-eyed owners bring their untried 2-year-

olds to the races and enter them in the Maidens Special
Weights races. There is just one winner in each of these
races—these are the juveniles who got off on the right foot.
They are now ready to enter the Allowance ranks. Some
horse owners who are overly optimistic or who are just plain
bare-faced snobs start their youngsters right off in the Allowance Races—skip the Maiden races altogether. At least
they skip the Maiden ranks until their horses run last in
the Allowance contests; then they may be inclined to re-
consider. And then there is the occasional out-and-out
aristocrat who enters his unraced colt right at the very top
—in the Handicap-Stakes division. Why fool around with
all that riffraff? The answer to that question is generally
given by the colt himself when he drags in a sorry last,
beaten fifty lengths or so, or else gets "distanced" to the
embarrassing extent that the jockey pulls him up to save
face—everybody's face.

But such practices are the exception and not the rule.
Almost all of the "big" horses start in races for Maidens
Special Weights. If you don't learn anything else from this
book, I want you to learn that races for Maidens Special
Weights are very hard to win. Have a lot of respect for the
horses campaigning in these races. For instance—when
Citation won his first race, some unfortunate, overmatched
horse ran eleventh (last). Now when Citation goes on to
become one of racing's super horses, just how much of a
disgrace was it for that victim of circumstances who ran
eleventh? All it proved was that he had no business being
in a race with Citation. Another example: When Nashua
came down the Widener Course at Belmont Park and won

his first race, some poor, pitiful victim of a complete mismatch ran twenty-first (last). That's not good, you understand, but all it proved for the moment was that the horse could not keep up with Nashua.

And right about here I'm sure we have some few cynics among us who are snickering up their sleeves and mumbling something to the effect, "Couldn't keep up with Nashua? My God, if he ran twenty-first and last, he must not have been able to keep up with *anybody*."

Well, friends, such a blanket accusation is not necessarily valid, and the reason is a horse racing factor called *pace*. Pace will be discussed later in the chapter on handicapping and for the time being we will suffice it to say that with a Nashua tucked in there among the entries, the pace is going to be terrific and some colts of medium merit will be "killed off" to the point where they have no chance to demonstrate what they might have been able to do if only the competition hadn't been so tough.

To return to the different types of races for non-winners —we have to get in reverse here and work down the scale. We'll work backwards by starting at the top and coming down; that's what all the owners do. What do the horses do when they can't compete against the best non-winners on the grounds? They have to get in a cheaper or weaker race. The loser's first stop on the way down is the Maiden Allowance Race. This is a race for all the losers from the Maidens Special Weights ranks, but still the owner hasn't given up. (Heaven forbid.) He wants to keep the horse and not risk the chance of a claim by some other owner. This type of race is simply an Allowance Race for Maidens.

If the horse still can't win, and if he doesn't give any indications of being able to win in the future—he goes right on down the scale. The next stop is a Maiden Claiming Race. The owner will still try to save face by entering him in a high Maiden Claiming Race. Example:

Maidens.  Claiming.  Claiming Price: $25,000.

No improvement?

Maidens.  Claiming.  Claiming Price: $12,500.

Still no improvement?

Maidens.  Claiming.  Claiming Price: $6,000.

Still runs last?

Maidens.  Claiming.  Claiming Price: $4,500.

Nothing?

Maidens.  Claiming.  Claiming Price: $2,000.

Still no good?  Well, we've just hit bottom here in the Major Leagues.  Better put that horse in a truck and we'll go try Charles Town.

Maidens.  Claiming.  Claiming Price: $1,500.

Marked improvement.  One more notch ought to do it.

Maidens.  Claiming.  Claiming Price: $1,250.

A win.  The horse is a Minor Leaguer and not a very good one at that; he never will amount to much.  He wasn't the worst of the lot, though—look at your chart of race tracks and you will see he still had a way to drop before he hit Maidens, Claiming, Claiming Price: $800 at Marshfield Fair.

And now you can card some sensible races for Maidens:

5 Furlongs. 2-year-olds. Maidens. Special Weights.

6 Furlongs. 3-year-olds. Maidens. Special Weights.

6 Furlongs (Chute). 3-year-olds. Maidens. Allowances.

6 Furlongs. 3-year-olds. Maidens. Claiming. Claiming Price: $10,000.

1 Mile. 4-year-olds and Up. Maidens. Claiming. Claiming Price: $2,500.

A final note about Maidens. Maidens do not always have to run in races which are exclusively for Maidens. For example, if the specific conditions for an Allowance Race state: "5 Furlongs, 2-year-olds, Allowances, For non-winners of two races", the Maiden 2-year-old meets these requirements. He can run 5 furlongs (if he can run any distance, that is); he is 2 years old, and he most certainly is a non-winner of two races—matter of fact, he's a non-winner of *any* races.

Maidens find their way into all the different types of races: Claiming (and here I don't mean Maidens, Claiming; I mean a straightaway Claiming Race—the regular, common, everyday, run-of-the-mill Claiming Race), Allowance (as shown previously), and even in the Handicap-Stakes. Other than first-time starters being in the Handicap-Stakes as Maidens, there are other examples. The only condition for a horse to be eligible for the Kentucky Derby is that he must be a 3-year-old, along with the necessary nominating and starting fees—which are considerable. In 1949 a 3-year-old Maiden named Seneca's Coin was en-

tered and ran in the Kentucky Derby. He lost the race by
a half a mile or so, but to this day his owner can still say
he owned a horse which ran in the Kentucky Derby.

Before we leave this lengthy discussion of the different
types of races, let me point out that the racing secretary's
job of carding races is still a bit more exacting and complicated than what we have shown here. For example, if
you should feel inclined at this point to dash out to the
corner newsstand and buy a racing paper, all fit and ready
to dig in for a first-hand examination of some actual races,
your first reaction would undoubtedly be, "Hey! There's
a lot of fine print in here he never said anything about!"
And so to offset any such premature accusations, I will have
to mention one more factor relative to the carding of races
—the factor of weight. And in so doing I am aware that
there are still people who do not believe in weight as a
matter of consequence in the final outcome of a horse race,
just as surely as I am aware that there are still people who
do not believe in witch doctors. Nevertheless, since all of
our handicapping scheme of things is based on weight, then
we must at least tolerate such a notion.

The "fine print" given in the conditions of a race deals
largely with weight. The racing secretary is penalizing the
successful horses and trying to help the ones which haven't
been doing so well lately. He does this with weight; he puts
it *on* the recent winners and takes it *off* the recent also-rans.
In other words—simply having different types of races and
classifying the horses still is not enough; there has been no
allowance made for the time factor—how is the horse doing
right *now*? (The fourth dimension, by God!) To illustrate

by investigating one stratum of the racing picture, we'll pick the $4,000 Claiming ranks as an example. Even in this one specific category there are still variations in the capabilities of its members. Why? Because some of these $4,000 Claimers are in "top form" and are running fine races, and then there are those which have passed their period of peak form and are now "stale." And then there are all the gradients in between—horses "coming to form" and horses "tailing off."

The fine print discloses, among other things, the final, actual conditions as laid down by the racing secretary in his last attempt to equalize the horses competing in the race. In the following example of an actual race, you will soon see that the "final, actual conditions" deal largely with time and dates, and accordingly, just so this race will make some sense, I will add that it was carded for the month of May:

1ST RACE SUFFOLK DOWNS

1⅛ Miles. (Whirlaway, July 15, 1942, 1:48⅕, 4, 130). Purse $2,000. 4-year-olds and Up. Claiming. For non-winners of two races since April 18. Weight 120 lbs, Non-winners of three races since March 30 allowed 3 lbs., two races, 5 lbs., a race 7 lbs. Claiming Price: $2,000.

Now put that trusty hatpin back down; this is just a little ol' horse race with all of its fine print. You do not have to be too concerned over all that stuff about dates and pounds. That's the racing secretary's job—let him worry about it. All you have to know is just what part of all that rigmarole to read. If you will examine those conditions with something more than a passing glance, which most horse players do not, you will see the same specifications, the same bare essentials we have been discussing all the time. To transpose all of the foregoing into our familiar terminology:

1ST RACE SUFFOLK DOWNS

1⅛ Miles. Purse $2,000. 4-year-olds and Up. Claiming. Claiming Price: $2,000.

To explain the very first line of the race, which undoubtedly puzzled you, since we had never discussed such markings:

1⅛ Miles. (Whirlaway, July 15, 1942, 1:48⅕, 4, 130.)

This information is always given in the racing papers immediately after the distance for the race. It is telling you the name of the horse which holds the track record for that distance at that track. It qualifies rather convincingly as a piece of what we might call useless information. The only purpose I can think of for such a piece of trivia is that the name of a high-powered horse there in the parentheses lends dignity and prestige to the track. Now everyone knows the great Whirlaway once visited Suffolk Downs. Such a piece of status-seeking can always boomerang, though, when a horse of little or no consequence happens to run one good race and gets his name etched into the record book of the track. How would it look if the line read:

1⅛ Miles. (Ol' Glue-Pot, July 15, 1942, 1:48, 8, 110.)

To return to Whirlaway:

(Whirlaway, July 15, 1942, 1:48⅕, 4, 130.)

Translation: On July 15, 1942, a horse named Whirlaway set a track record for 1⅛ miles at Suffolk Downs by running the distance in 1 minute, 48⅕ seconds. As of May, 1962, this record still stands.

The last two figures: 4, 130. Translation: Whirlaway set this record as a 4-year-old and carried 130 pounds.

You should now be able to read the conditions for a horse race and know what you are reading. If you can, that's fine. If you cannot, then you had better flip back to page 16, where it says, "This is a horse," and start all over.

## 6th. CORRELATION OF MAJOR AND MINOR LEAGUE RACING

WE now know what a horse race is; how it is composed of two or more racing interests, and how it all comes about via horses, jockeys, and race tracks. We even know that there are horse races, and then there are horse races. We have graded the various types of races thus:

Handicap-Stakes
↓
Allowance Races
↓
Claiming Races

And, off to the side

⟶ Races for Non-winners.

To proceed with the résumé, we now know that there are race tracks, and then there are race tracks. We went out on a limb and decided that the toughest place for a horse to win a race was Belmont Park in New York. Many people will not agree with that statement—but then that's what makes horse racing . . . and Missionaries, as the man said.

Now to combine these two basic principles: Since the most difficult locale to win a horse race is Belmont Park, and since the highest-caliber race run anywhere, at any track, is a Handicap-Stakes Race, then we can draw the conclusion that the toughest-type race to win anywhere, at any time, is a Handicap-Stakes Race at Belmont Park. And with all the usual tongue-in-cheek certainty of things equine —we can say that such a supposition is "unequivocally" true. Horses that can win in this category are the two or three we hear about each season that are really great. This classification includes the Donors, the Nashuas, the Tom Fools, the Capots, the Round Tables, etc., etc.—the really big ones. Horses which have won a Handicap-Stakes Race at Belmont Park command attention *whenever* they step out on a race track—any race track, anywhere, at any time. They may not *always* win. (The practice of using the term "always" is most difficult when discussing any phase of horse racing. Racing is booby-trapped with many ifs, ands, buts, and a generalized potpourri of multiple exceptions.) Nevertheless, when the winner of a Handicap-Stakes Race at Belmont Park steps out on any race track, he can be expected to give a good account of himself, and any horse who beats him will know that he has been in one hell of a horse race.

Enough for the high and the mighty. Let's take a look at the other end of the spectrum. We found that the most modest form of racing took place at Marshfield Fair in Massachusetts. The weakest, cheapest race we encountered was a Maiden Claiming Race with a Claiming Price of

$800. Now what about the horse that runs in a Maiden Claiming Race for a Claiming Price of $800 at Marshfield Fair and staggers in a distant last? What's to become of him? This horse has attacked the racing wars at the bottom of the bottom and has come out on the bottom. To borrow an oft-used phrase from the soap operas, "This poor waif has nowhere to go, no one to whom he may turn." This horse is treading on the very brink of oblivion, hovering near the abyss of limbo. Assuming there is no marked improvement in his efforts, this horse will choose one of the following:

1. Try his luck in jump races (steeplechases and/or hurdles).
2. Campaign at county fairs (no betting—limbo).
3. Be used by a riding academy ("Horses for Hire").
4. Be hitched to a milk wagon.

If the horse cannot jump, if he cannot campaign favorably at a county fair, if he is too high-strung and too ill-mannered to be used by a riding academy (dislodges riders on low-hanging tree limbs, bites, etc.), and if automation has done him in as a dairy worker—then this horse is truly on dangerous ground; forsooth, he is only about half a jump ahead of the glue factory or the cat-and-dog-food people.

Thus we can safely plot the two extremes of the racing graph. At the pinnacle of fame, or the apogee, rests the lofty Handicap-Stakes Race at Belmont Park; and, at the other extreme, or the perigee, rests the Maidens Claiming, Claiming Price $800 at Marshfield Fair. Notice that in giving the high and the low points, simply stating the type of race is not enough; the precise locale, i.e., the specific race course, must also be given. The fact is, that practically the only points we can locate with certainty are the two opposite poles. It's evaluating all that stuff in between where we get mixed up.

Simply saying that Handicap-Stakes Races are the most difficult to win, Allowance Races the next most difficult, and Claiming Races the easiest, is not enough—for two reasons. First, we still have those dangling misfits—the races for non-winners. They generate their fair share of confusion. Secondly, we have the grossly cumbersome problem of how to deal with the fact that there is both Major League racing and Minor League racing.

To touch upon the non-winners problem first. Let's look at a representative or sample listing of the different types of races run at a Major League track:

| *Handicap-Stakes* | *Races for Non-Winners* |
|---|---|
| Allowances | Maidens Special Weights |
| Claiming $50,000 | Md. Allowances |
| Claiming $25,000 | Md. Claiming $25,000 |
| Claiming $15,000 | Md. Claiming $15,000 |
| Claiming $12,500 | Md. Claiming $12,500 |
| Claiming $10,000 | Md. Claiming $10,000 |
| Claiming $7,500 | Md. Claiming $7,500 |
| Claiming $5,000 | Md. Claiming $5,000 |
| Claiming $3,500 | Md. Claiming $3,500 |
| Claiming $2,500 | Md. Claiming $2,500 |
| Claiming $2,000 | Md. Claiming $2,000 |

Now for the problems: Let us say that a Maiden was entered in a Maiden Claiming Race for $2,500 and ran flat last in his last start. Today he is entered in a *Claiming* Race for $7,500. Does he have a chance to win? According to all that's holy, the answer is heavens no ! ! He raced against a sorry field of non-winners in his last start and couldn't beat anybody. Today he's entered in a field of competent Claimers and consequently is very much overmatched. So far so good.

How about a Maiden who raced in a Maiden Claiming Race, Claiming Price: $10,000, finished a strong 4th and is entered today in a *Claiming* Race for $7,500? Now we have to start to hedge a bit. Is this damn horse dropping down the scale or isn't he?

And again—suppose a 2-year-old first-time starter made his debut in a race for Maidens Special Weights, led all the way until the final stride, and then lost in a photo finish. Does he figure to win an Allowance Race today? A Claiming Race for $10,000? He does? Well then, suppose instead of such an auspicious debut he had finished 7th in the 12-horse field and is entered today in a Claiming Race for only $5,000? On and on. Problems, problems. The combinations are limited only by the imagination of the racing secretary and the horse owners' desire to win.

And lastly, suppose a horse *won* his last start in a Maiden Claiming Race for $5,000 and is entered today in a Claiming race for $5,000. Is he moving up the scale, down the scale, or staying in the same classification?

The second problem—that of the bugaboo of Major League racing and Minor League racing. Here is where the task of selecting winning horses wanders off into a

Never-Never Land of confusion.

The fact stated bluntly is that the chart on page 97 giving examples of the different types of races run at a Major League track is vastly inadequate to be of any use. Most race track patrons looking at such a chart and then looking at the Past Performances of the entries listed for the day at their local oval would rapidly become aware of its shortcomings.

Complications arise, pile up, and multiply due to this double standard of racing: Major League racing and Minor League racing. Here is a chart giving examples of the different types of races run at a minimal Minor League track:

| | |
|---|---|
| *Handicap-Stakes* | *Races for Non-Winners* |
| Allowances | Maidens Special Weights |
| Claiming $3,500 | Md. Allowances |
| Claiming $3,000 | Md. Claiming $3,000 |
| Claiming $2,500 | Md. Claiming $2,500 |
| Claiming $2,000 | Md. Claiming $2,000 |
| Claiming $1,750 | Md. Claiming $1,750 |
| Claiming $1,500 | Md. Claiming $1,500 |
| Clamiing $1,250 | Md. Claiming $1,250 |
| Claiming $1,000 | Md. Claiming $1,000 |
| Claiming $800 | Md. Claiming $800 |

And now all the problems inherent in the Major League classification are repeated, only more so, since these horses are cheaper and hence more erratic and undependable. Possibly the owner and the jockey of any one particular entrant do not know what the horse is going to do either— so don't you feel badly about it.

Does a horse who finishes a stout second in a Maiden Claiming Race for $1,750 figure to compete favorably in a *Claiming* Race for $3,000? No. A Claiming Race for $1,750? Unlikely. For $1,250? Perhaps.

How about the 2-year-old who makes a good showing in a race for Maidens Special Weights? Does he figure to have a chance in today's Allowance Race? Today's Claiming Race for $3,000?

And lastly, what about the horse coming off a win in a Maiden Claiming Race for $1,000? Does he figure in today's Claiming Race for $1,000?

With problems mounting the way they are, it still must be borne in mind that up to this point we have kept a strict separation of Major and Minor League racing. Unfortunately, losing horses eat just as much as do winning horses. Therefore, horse owners who find themselves saddled with a weak string of chronic also-rans (losers) at the Major League level begin to cast their eyes toward seeking greener pastures. Not by buying some new and better horses (can't afford the ones they have now), but by seeking a lower level of racing. Weaker racing—cheaper competition. Albeit, when they make this move they are admitting their horses are flops—but then a man can stand to lose only so long. Right now such a horse owner wants to win a purse—any purse—even a small one.

Thus things now get confused to the state where when we venture out to Scarborough Downs, as an example, we will see sprinkled among the entries some refugees from a higher level of racing—Rockingham Park, Narragansett Park,

Suffolk Downs. Bear in mind that when you encounter these refugees from the big time, their racing records will be pretty wretched; that's why they're there.

8th Race Scarborough Downs.   Claiming.   Claiming Price: $1,500.

Horse #1: Refugee. Past Performances: Has run last six times in a row. That's bad. All these last six races were run at Narragansett Park. That's not so bad. Refugee is dropping down the scale: Major League racing to Minor League racing. How far did he drop down? Far enough? Or will he persist in running last? Will he improve? Can he actually *win* the race? Who knows? That's one of the things the man meant when he said you could beat a race but you couldn't beat the races.

Enough of losers. How about winners? How about the hard-hitting, consistent performer on the Minor League circuit? Must he forever be forced to compete for small purses? Obviously the answer is no, heavens no. Thus we now witness the complete reversal of the down-in-the-mouth habitual loser on the Big Apple—now we have the speedy "half-miler," or the "speedy cheapie," who always seems to finish well up in his efforts.

Thus to go out to Hialeah, as another example, you will see sprinkled among the entries some few horses who are the possessors of very fine racing records—not solely because they happen to be some sort of super horses, but due largely to the fact that they are from a lower plane of racing. Bear in mind that as a rule these Minor Leaguers moving up the scale will have a fine win percentage and a fine in-the-money consistency rating; that's why they're there. (In-the-money consistency rating: Found by dividing the number of starts a horse has made during the current year into the sum of the times he has finished first, second, and third. Example: A horse has started ten times during the current year, won twice, finished second once, and third four times. His in-the-money consistency rating is 70%. $\frac{7}{10} = 70\%$, which is very high.)

2nd Race Hialeah.  Claiming.  Claiming Price: $4,500.

Horse #1: Hot Shot. Past Performances: Has won his last three races in a row. That's good. The race before that he lost by only a neck and the race before that he finished a creditable third. That's good. His in-the-money consistency rating is a remarkable 83%. That's very good. One last factor about Hot Shot: He compiled his racing record at Sunshine Park. That's bad.

Now just what kind of horse is Hot Shot? How did he manage to compile such a fine racing record? Did he do it by simply showing up a complete bunch of nobodies over at Sunshine Park? And now here at Hialeah will the big leaguers run off and hide from him? And is he simply another bonus baby biding his time until the bus goes back to North Dakota? Or—is he in reality a game, tough little customer who is going to make a fine showing wherever he campaigns? Who in the hell knows? That's what the racing fans are out there to see. And that's another thing the man had in mind when he said you could beat a race, but you couldn't beat the races.

And now to attempt to evaluate the relative merits of Major and Minor League racing, since as we have seen the two are more or less enmeshed—by despair and by joy— not by design. To invite chaos, let me make two observations—still keeping Major and Minor League racing separate as two distinct entities, and still holding steadfastly to the proposition that the value of races declines thus:

Handicap-Stakes        Allowance Races        Claiming Races

It is entirely possible to be confronted with the following situation: Observe the Past Performances of a horse we'll name Misfit:

| Type of Race | Finish |
|---|---|
| Allowance | $1^1$ (First by a length) |
| Allowance | $1^2$ (First by 2 lengths) |
| Allowance | $2^{nk}$ (Second by a neck) |
| Allowance | $1^{no}$ (First by a nose) |
| Allowance | $4^5$ (Fourth by 5 lengths) |

Misfit has been racing in Allowance company and doing very well, thank you. He's won his last two races by comfortable margins and has a nifty in-the-money percentage of 80%. So far so good. However, today Misfit is entered in a *Claiming Race*. Now that's odd. For a competent campaigner in the Allowance ranks he seems to be backtracking or dropping down the scale backwards, and unnecessarily so.

With such a backward state of affairs, the first impression regarding the betting activity would be that Misfit is the odds-on choice of the betting public; a real cinch to win as far as the people who are shoving the money into the machines are concerned. And so we'll check the odds on Misfit; and there they are, out in the infield all lit up like a Christmas tree, flashing shamelessly for the whole world to see. Misfit is an unbelievable 26-1 (pays $54 for $2). Something must be wrong; this must be the day the machine stops. But no, it's a fact; the prevailing odds on Misfit's chances are correct and rightly so, since Misfit doesn't figure to win today's race anymore than he figures to sprout wings and fly out over the grandstand.

Why? Now why? How can it be that a bona fide Allowance horse suddenly has no chance in a Claiming Race? Again it's due to a shift in location. Misfit is jumping from a Minor League track up to the big time. His Allowance racing record was compiled at Beulah Park, for example, and today he is entered in a Claiming Race for $12,000 at Garden State. Overmatched. Overmatched to say the least. Misfit is about to learn that ambition is a grievous fault and grievously is he about to pay for it.

The second situation. Here is a condensed version of the Past Performances of a horse we'll name Gone Slummin':

| Type of Race | Finish |
|---|---|
| Claiming | $4^4$ (Fourth by 4 lengths) |
| Claiming | $8^{10}$ (Eighth by 10 lengths) |
| Claiming | $6^5$ (Sixth by 5 lengths) |
| Claiming | $12^{20}$ (Twelfth by 20 lengths) |
| Claiming | $8^6$ (Eighth by 6 lengths) |

Gone Slummin's record demonstrates clearly that he

certainly isn't exactly what you might call a "ball of fire."
He doesn't show a winning race and his in-the-money consistency rating is a weak-kneed "zip"—zero—00%. The
best he can show is a fourth-place finish which in itself is
only fair. And that twelfth-place finish kind of startles me.
Since most races have only twelve starters, it appears that
for one shining hour he must have been the most valiant
horse on the track, since he obviously chased all the others
all the way around to the finish line.

However, today Gone Slummin' is entered in an *Allowance Race*. Now there's another anomaly. He made a
move, all right, but at first glance it would seem he moved
in the wrong direction. After finding out he couldn't get
in the money against Claimers, he now wants to take a
crack at the Allowance ranks. This horse is obviously confused. His chances of coming home on the front end today
are virtually nil, and as a consequence his betting odds
must be of the boxcar or telephone number variety.

Let's take a look at the going price on Gone Slummin'—
Ye Gods ! ! Gone Slummin' is 1-1 (even money; pays $4
for $2). Something's wrong; there must be a mistake of
some sort. But no, the money is down, and it's down in
the right place.

Why? Now how can that be? How can a flop in the
Claiming ranks suddenly square off against Allowance
competition and be the overwhelming choice of the betting
public? Again it's due to that double standard: Major
League racing and Minor League racing. Gone Slummin'
has been a failure against moderately high-priced Claimers

on the big time circuit ($5,000 to $8,000), but has now changed his field of operations. Today, after a long, lean summer, he has finally found a field of horses he can beat. Today he is going to crack down and crack down hard. He's going out there and win himself a horse race—and will even make it look easy in the process.

Right now I have a feeling that one of the thoughts going through your mind may be something like this: "Well, the only race track I ever attend is Delaware Park, and since Delaware Park is a Major League track, I don't have to be bothered with all that other garbage." To repeat an earlier statement: Even if *you* don't move around, the *horses* do. And thus, when you make your annual outing to Delaware Park, how can you intelligently know what's going on if you know nothing of the relative merits of other, distant race courses—or far-away places, if that sounds better?

Today's second race at Delaware Park is a Claiming race for $4,000 and among the entries you may see horses from Pimlico, Monmouth Park, Lincoln Downs, Ascot (Ohio, not England), Detroit, Aqueduct, Marlboro, and on and on. Now in looking over the Past Performances of these entries and checking their form, in spite of all the arithmetic you may conjure up, and in spite of the fact that you may use an adding machine, an IBM computer, an abacus, a slide rule, or your toes—the one single most important factor is *where* did today's entries compile their racing records?

Horse A has raced 5 times and has won 3 races. That's

very good, but in today's race it may or may not mean a thing. Horse B has raced 5 times and hasn't won anything. That's not so good, but in today's race it may or may not mean a thing. The primary factor is *where* have horses A and B won or lost those races? And that's why the graded chart of race tracks on page 49 is so important, and that's why you are going to have to know it if you expect to go out to your local oval, wherever it is, and know what's going on.

Just how do the Major League and Minor League factions of racing mesh together? I'll have to preface the next few thoughts with a timely rebuttal before the opinions are set down. I don't suppose any two race track authorities would agree with the correlation figures to be presented. And I suppose that's as it should be; however, beyond any such inference I have the inspiration, the logic, and the philosophy of one Mr. Jan Christiaan Smuts to rely upon.

Now who, pray tell, is Jan Christiaan Smuts? Mr. Smuts is deceased; albeit, some of his thinking lives on. He was, among other things, the Prime Minister of the Union of South Africa from 1939-1948, which means he was the Prime Minister during a period of some international crisis. What does he have to do with horse racing? I don't know if Mr. Smuts ever as much as saw a horse race or not, but whether he did or did not makes no matter. I like the man's thinking.

Being the Prime Minister during a period of international conflict, Mr. Smuts frequently had cause to address the country's lawmakers with the end in view of requesting that larger appropriations be made for the national defense. And here, from Gervasi's *War Has Seven Faces,* is an illustrative personal glimpse of Mr. Smuts to show how the mind of a great man works, and also to show how an ignorer of protocol and a potential, heckling roadblock can be muzzled.

Immediately after South Africa's entry into the war, a Boer member of the opposition rose in Parliament and asked Smuts to tell the country exactly what remilitarization had cost the Union. The opponent knew it was an almost impossible job, that it would take weeks of research to trace in the Union's complex bookkeeping system just what the war had cost up to then. Smuts said he'd give the assembly an answer the next morning.

Next day, Smuts rose, cleared his throat, and said, "The figure I was asked for yesterday is 80,169,000 pounds, ten shillings, and sixpence. . . ." The house was silent for a moment and then burst into cheers. The gentleman of the opposition had a very red face.

A friend asked Smuts after the session how he'd managed to obtain the figures. "Easy," Smuts replied, "I didn't know what the figure was and still don't. What I did know was that it would take the opposition two months and twenty clerks to compute the true amount and prove me wrong."

And, similarly, I can spout information and not jot down figures concerning horse racing and its labyrinthine classifications, knowing full well that any dissenting rogues would need two and twenty months, yea, two and twenty years perhaps, to prove that my figures were conceivably incorrect. And even if they did, or even if they tried, I could still exercise my God-given right to climb atop a soapbox and in the generally accepted flush of righteous indignation shout for all to hear, "Rape!"

I would also like to say that the Lincoln Downs–Hazel Park–Ohio (Primary tracks) area of the race track chart may not apply too stringently to the following thoughts and figures. This area of the chart represents some sort of a damnable transitional area between Major and Minor League racing and doesn't fit exactly anywhere. However, with its purse distribution being what it is, it was placed at the top of the Minor League grouping. Minor League as used in the following discussion refers to the down-in-the-mouth, garden-variety type of Minor League racing.

And since we're speaking in terms of dollars, I'll add that the value of money goes up and down. The figures used here relate to the "Soaring Sixties"—which is another way of saying that dollar bills are worth only 40c. The relative figures concerning the net worth of a horse will vary proportionately to inflation or deflation—whichever way we happen to be going. For example, I have a couple of condition books for the Maryland Joint Autumn Meeting, September-October, 1945. Bowie-Laurel-Pimlico-Havre de Grace (Where?), and in the books are races written with a Claiming Price of $1,200. Today the minimum Claiming Price on that circuit is $2,500. The horses didn't get twice as good—the dollar bills became worth only half as much—same caliber horses, different caliber dollars.

And so—with all that introduction out of the way—the *best* horse on the grounds at a Minor League track is at best a $7,000 Claimer. And perhaps that $7,000 figure is being a bit generous. Most Minor League tracks won't have a horse worth that much. $5,000 may be closer to it. Thus when you go out to a Minor League track and see its Allowance competition and its Handicap-Stakes Races, in spite of all it may say on the official race track program, what you are actually watching are a bunch of medium to mediocre Platers. Therefore, when the consistent winner on the Gyp Circuit ventures out to a real race track and meets some real horses, he hadn't better be too optimistic. If placed in a Claiming Race over $7,000, he is over-matched.

Or—to bring the thought home in another manner—don't go out to Charles Town, sit down, and wait to see a Claiming Race for $10,000. If you do, you are going to have one hell of a long wait—because there aren't any. For two reasons: first and foremost, they very likely don't have a horse there *worth* $10,000. And secondly, if they *did* happen to have a horse worth $10,000, he wouldn't be Claiming Race material; he would be in their Allowance Races, prepping for their Saturday Handicap-Stakes Races.

Now there are certainly exceptions—and in both directions. As for example, in 1959 a consistent Charles Town colt moved over to Bowie to compete in the Prince George's Stakes, an overly ambitious assignment for a $7,000 Claimer; however, the shift from Minor League Allowance Races to Major League Handicap-Stakes racing apparently made no impression on the colt, since he led all the way and bounced home the winner to the tune of over 5-1. I'm sure there are a few thousand other exceptions—also exceptions on the negative side. Many Allowance horses on the half-milers couldn't get in the money running for $3,500 at a Major League track.

A monstrous chart:

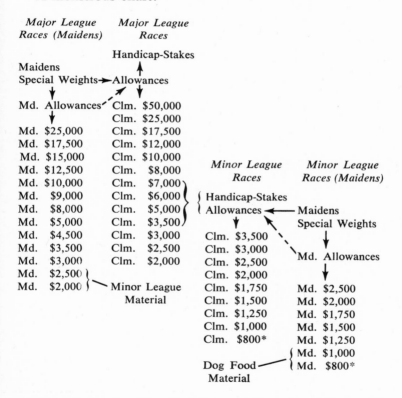

| *Major League Races (Maidens)* | *Major League Races* |
|---|---|
| | Handicap-Stakes |
| Maidens | ↑ |
| Special Weights→ | Allowances |
| ↓ | ↗ ↓ |
| Md. Allowances⟋ | Clm. $50,000 |
| ↓ | Clm. $25,000 |
| Md. $25,000 | Clm. $17,500 |
| Md. $17,500 | Clm. $12,000 |
| Md. $15,000 | Clm. $10,000 |
| Md. $12,500 | Clm. $8,000 |
| Md. $10,000 | Clm. $7,000 |
| Md. $9,000 | Clm. $6,000 |
| Md. $8,000 | Clm. $5,000 |
| Md. $5,000 | Clm. $3,500 |
| Md. $4,500 | Clm. $3,000 |
| Md. $3,500 | Clm. $2,500 |
| Md. $3,000 | Clm. $2,000 |
| Md. $2,500 | |
| Md. $2,000 | Minor League Material |

| *Minor League Races* | *Minor League Races (Maidens)* |
|---|---|
| Handicap-Stakes | |
| Allowances ← | Maidens |
| ↓ | Special Weights |
| Clm. $3,500 | ↓ |
| Clm. $3,000 | Md. Allowances |
| Clm. $2,500 | ↓ |
| Clm. $2,000 | |
| Clm. $1,750 | Md. $2,500 |
| Clm. $1,500 | Md. $2,000 |
| Clm. $1,250 | Md. $1,750 |
| Clm. $1,000 | Md. $1,500 |
| Clm. $800* | Md. $1,250 |
| | Md. $1,000 |
| Dog Food — | Md. $800* |
| Material | |

* The racing secretary at Marshfield Fair informs me that the $800 races have been discontinued.

Now I'll be the first to admit that the preceding chart closely resembles a Chinese laundry ticket or deciphering fodder for a Philadelphia lawyer. But a closer study will show that it isn't as complicated as it may have initially appeared. The figures and arrows are most assuredly *not* hard, set facts, but rather, they are indices or a series of what we might call "reference points." The chart illustrates what we have been discussing all the while and tends to simplify matters somewhat by putting all the reference points on one page. And lastly, and most important, it serves to further clear the muddied waters by showing the parallel between Major and Minor League racing and the continuity, or the unholy alliance between the two.

Using a few hundred or so frisky 2-year-olds as an explanatory medium, we can further clarify the theme of the chart. Some horses cost a lot of money when purchased as yearlings, and others don't cost so much. As a rule the high-priced ones can be looked upon as possible champions —or, at least, as above-average performers; the cheaper ones have a more modest outlook. Again there are exceptions in both directions. A horse called Pericles cost $66,-000 at auction and never won a nickel. And then there was a horse called Assault who went at the bargain basement price of $700 and went on to win over $600,000.

The promising 2-year-olds are brought to a Major League race track and entered for their first start—at the top: Maidens Special Weights. In each of the races there is one winner. This one winner can move right on to the Allowance ranks, and if things are still going well, he can move right on to the Handicap-Stakes division for 2-year-olds.

Other entries in these races for Maidens Special Weights do not win; however, their losing effort may have shown promise—maybe second, or third, or fourth—fifth—sixth—somewhere up in the bunch, and consequently they may merit another try, or a series of tries. And then there are all those others who, to be charitable, we may say simply that they made it safely around the track without mishap.

The chronic losers drop down a notch and try it again, this time in a race for Maidens Allowances. Again, each of these races will have one winner, and since these winners did win an Allowance Race of sorts, they are perfectly within their rights to take a token crack at the bona fide Allowance ranks—as shown by the broken arrow on the chart. Albeit, the horses and their owners soon learn that since they couldn't keep up with this particular group of horses last month, they can't keep up with them this month either, and the inevitable descent to the Claiming ranks begins. How far the plunge goes before the horse is again favorably placed is anybody's conjecture—as shown by the descending arrows.

The non-winners in the Maidens Allowance ranks likewise begin their descent into the Maidens Claiming Races. They drop down and continue to drop until they are advantageously placed. When they win one of these Maiden Claiming Races, they will assume their proper place in racing's over-all picture by becoming Claimers—the big "half" of racing which is necessary to support the other "half." As pointed out by the chart, the winner of a Maiden Claiming Race has to drop again when he moves over to the Claiming ranks of winners. A winner in a Maiden

Claiming Race for $10,000 is not a $10,000 Claimer, and likewise, a winner in a Maiden Claiming Race for $5,000 will have little or no success running against winners for $5,000. *Exactly* how far the recent graduate from the Maiden ranks must drop down is another one of those things the racing fans are out there to see, and that's another thing the man had in mind when he said you could beat a race, but you couldn't beat the races.

What about the *really* slow horses which just can't seem to hit it in any Maiden Claiming Race available—be it $25,000 or $2,000? Well, since they are in the Major Leagues, the future isn't necessarily all black—there is still much room for retrogression. These horses silently slink away in the still of the night and reappear at one of the Minor League tracks, where there is a ballyhoo specialist loudly proclaiming to the world that the horses campaigning at the local oval this year are perhaps the best horses the track has ever had. And the interesting thing is—he may be right; these may be the fastest slow horses ever to set foot on the local scene.

To maintain a certain quality of snob appeal, the habitual loser from the Major Leagues may start his half-mile career again at the top—Maidens Special Weights and/or at the very top—Handicap-Stakes. Here he will most likely come back a sorry loser, since the caliber of horses running against him represents in reality a bunch of moderately priced Claimers—and again, since he couldn't beat them last month (or last year), he won't beat them this time either.

What about the first-time starters in these races for

Maidens Special Weights here on the Minor League level? They can't very well be "washouts" from Major League racing; they've never raced before. Where did they come from? These are the racing hopes of the more modest stables—the yearlings whose breeding and whose capabilities were never too highly regarded in the first place. They too are seeking their proper level in racing.

And to round out the picture, we find that here on the Minor League level we have a complete parallel with Major League racing—with two notable exceptions. The first exception being that the consistent winners can move on to Major League racing and to bigger and better things— better pur$e$. The second exception being that the chronic losers have no place to go—other than limbo, of course.

Winners from the Maidens Special Weights ranks move on to the Handicap-Stakes and Allowance classification and note that the chart groups Handicap-Stakes and Allowances together in the Minor League level. This "lumping together" is done because many times it is actually the same field of horses running in the same races; albeit, the races have different names. On Monday a field of horses goes in a 6-furlong contest called an Allowance Race for 3-year-olds and up. On Saturday the same bunch of horses again races 6 furlongs, only this time we see via the official race track program that the contest is called the Potato Sack Purse.

Losers in the Maidens Special Weights ranks drop down into Maiden Allowance Races. The winners here take a token shot at the Handicap-Stakes and Allowance ranks, again as shown by the broken arrow. After a debacle or so in the upper stratum, they drop down into the "high" Claiming classification. And again, how far they must drop down is problematical.

The remaining non-winners drop down into the Maiden Claiming Races, and when they find a field of horses they can beat, they assume their proper place over in the low Claiming ranks.

And lastly, we must confess that the chart ends on a very sad note, for we see that even the *winners* in the lowest of the low Maiden Claiming Races have nowhere to go once they have won a race. As soon as they leave their den of mediocrity, they are overmatched against superior Claimers. We mentioned earlier how the persistent *losers* in the low Maiden Claiming Races had nowhere to go either. And thus, these slow-moving misfits are confronted by a most sticky wicket—the minimum-priced Maiden Claimer is faced with the dilemma of being damned if he does and damned if he doesn't. In either case he stands a very good chance of being canned or bottled—depending upon the going price of dog food or glue. Well, you can't win 'em all.

And so the chart, per se, is ended. It is ended only for academic reasons; as a source of discussion and controversy, it could be argued about ad infinitum. There are, however, a few more tidbits of information I would like to mention about the chart. First—let me say that with all things being considered, we ran the gauntlet of the biggest of the big to the smallest of the most insignificant in a most hurried fashion. Such a course was followed solely for reasons of expediency as we brashly cast this horse into this echelon and that horse into that one in order to demonstrate the *theory* of the racing process. In *practice,* however, as is most always the case in whatever field may be under discussion, the pieces do not fall into place by rote or in any such 1-2-3 fashion. As to exactly why the pieces do not fall into place with such a mechanical rapidity, we will have more to say later when a racing factor called "holt" is discussed.

Looking at the chart from various angles, we can see that a horse who can win a race for Maiden Allowances on the Gyp Circuit may also be able to win a race on the Big Apple. On the other hand—any horse in the Minors who is racing cheaper than Claiming $2,500 or Maiden Allowances had best stay put. From the other side of the fence we can see that a horse who can make a decent showing in a race for Maidens Claiming, Claiming Price: $9,000, could move over to a Minor League track and be one of the best horses on the grounds—if not *the* best. And lastly, we can see that there is not much difference in the relative merits of the high-priced Claimers in the Minors and the minimum-priced Claimers in the Majors.

However, there are a few thousand more intracacies and ramifications that have been omitted from the chart in the interest of maintaining brevity, clarity, and sanity. The different correlation reference points we have given refer only to racing's two major divisions: Major League racing and Minor League racing. Now with the different purse distribution figures being what they are, and with the best horses going where the best pur$e$ are—we have the completely humbling task of trying to reconcile the fact that there are variations and gradients within each of the two major divisions.

For instance, in looking at the graded chart of race tracks on page 49, you can readily see that there is quite a gap between Belmont and Detroit—both Major League courses. And, in the same fashion, there's a lot of room between Lincoln Downs and Marshfield Fair—both Minor League courses. And what all this amounts to is that a $7,000 Claimer at Bowie is not necessarily a $7,000 Claimer at Saratoga; forsooth, the $7,000 Claimer at Bowie may actually be a speedy half-miler up from Shenandoah Downs. And—on the other side of the coin—the $7,000 Claimer from Saratoga may prove to be very tough to handle for the $10,000 Claimers at Bowie.

On the Minor League side—a $3,000 Claimer at Thistle-Down may give a good account of himself in an Allowance Race at the Great Barrington Fair, while the Allowance racer from Great Barrington may find himself up against it in a $3,000 Claiming race at ThistleDown. And then there are multiple levels, merits, sub-merits, and demerits in between. And just how do all of these thousands of pieces fit together? Well, friends, that's what the racing fans are out there to see, and those myriad unsolved problems are what necessitate the expenditure of over 2½ billion dollars annually to kick around. As you can see, up to this point things have got complicated just getting the right horse to the right race track—let alone trying to get the right horse in the right race—with the right jockey, on the right day, under favorable track conditions, and with an advantageous weight distribution. It's a tough nut to crack, friends. Now put that trusty hatpin back down.

## 7th. THE RACING PAPERS
## AND HOW TO READ THEM

TO visit a race course and to participate intelligently in its challenges and its excitement, one must have access to authoritative sources of information which will give complete and accurate data concerning the competing horses. The sources of information available to interested parties are what we will call the "Racing Papers"—of which there are two. And that's an interesting commentary right there at the outset—the fact that there are two. It is interesting, since both are owned and published by the same company. With free enterprise being what it is as we know it in this country today, I would assume that there perhaps are two to give the appropriate illusion of competition generally demanded by the public. One racing paper is in competition with the other in much the same manner that your local telephone company is in competition with . . . with a . . . with a . . . Well, I can't think of anybody right off hand, but I'm sure there must be someone. The competition is comparable to that engaged in by your local gas and electric company, which is in vigorous competition with . . . with a  . . . the government? I'll try once more. The papers compete in the same manner as do the "Big 3" automobile manufacturers. The fact that all the new models rolling off the assembly lines happen to look a lot alike, and that all their price ranges miraculously coincide remarkably well, is sheer happenstance. But I digress.

To return to the racing papers—or to the Bibles of the turf world—one is the *Daily Racing Form* and the other one is the *Morning Telegraph*. Both contain the same information. There are slight variations and modifications between the two, and these differences will be noted and explained as we proceed.

To compare the *Form* and the *Telegraph*—the easiest way to draw a quick comparison between the two is to say that the *Telegraph* is a bit more grandiose than the *Form*. For instance—it's a bigger paper, literally—full newspaper size. The *Form,* on the other hand, is in the tabloid size and as a consequence it has the advantage, or the disadvantage, depending upon your individual preference, of being easier to carry around.

And now to the task of learning to read the Racing Papers. (As an aside, I'll mention that you can write to Triangle Publications, 525 West 52nd Street, New York 19, N. Y., and for the small fee of five cents to cover mailing, they will send you a booklet entitled: "How To Read Charts and Past Performances," which is interesting in itself since it shows that a nickel will still buy something.\*) However, I would strongly recommend that you put off reading this booklet and all its detail until after you have

---

\* This booklet now costs ten cents. Sorry.

read this piece. Note again the title of that booklet: "How To Read Charts and Past Performances"—I want to comment on that word Charts. Nowhere in this piece will we be concerned with reading charts. Charts are obituaries, perhaps a bit more than that; autopsies may be a better word. A chart gives a final summary of how a race was run. The race is over. You cannot bet on charts. If you can't pick the winner of a chart, then you had better give up on horse racing and apply yourself to something less taxing—like putting the round peg in the round hole and the square peg in the square hole, and not vice versa. To give the simplest procedure as to how to read a chart—the winning horse is placed at the top of the list, the second horse second, the third horse third, and similarly right on down the line. To pick the winner, read the name of the horse listed at the top, unless—there is always an unless— you should happen to notice a " Ⓓ " in front of the horse's name. That's the disqualification symbol and means that due to some irregularity on the part of the horse or his rider, he really didn't win after all. To repeat: forget about reading charts. There is an important reason for this aversion to charts—more so than a personal dislike on my part, and this reason will be noted later.

We are concerned here with how to read Past Performances. Past Performances are abbreviated summaries of the racing records of horses that are going to run *today*. There is a bit more of a problem in picking the winner than simply noting which horse is listed first. (Since the horses are listed in the racing papers according to their respective post positions, the fact that a horse is listed first means only that he will begin the race from No. 1 post position.) The winner is in there among the entries somewhere—the question is where?

The first thing to do in learning how to read Past Performances is to buy a racing paper—the *Form* or the *Telegraph*. If you buy the *Telegraph,* you are ready to read, since it sits there on the newsstand with all the dignity and grace of *The New York Times.* Not so with the *Form.* Should you buy a *Form,* the first thing you have to do is to tear it open. This isn't as difficult as it may sound, since it very conveniently has perforations to facilitate the tearing. There are still a few odd thousand things I don't know about horse racing, and why one must tear open his racing *Form* is one of them. The *Telegraph* costs fifty cents. In the East an Airplane Edition of the *Form* (from Chicago) costs seventy-five cents. I mention this to bring up the ogre of overhead; even horse players have operating expenses. A racing paper costs at least fifty cents, an official race track program costs twenty-five cents (and this is one instance where you really cannot tell one "player" from another without a program), track admission is about $2 (grandstand), and transportation to and from the track will be about $3 (train)—depending of course upon how far you have to travel. Should you drive instead of going via rail, then you will have car expenses and a fifty cent parking fee. Disregarding frivolous things, such as food and drink, it is apparent that the horse player is at least $6 in the hole the moment he sits down. No betting, no slow horses, no nothing—just getting there. But—he's there; probably the last of a breed of Americans still showing some initiative, still willing to hazard some of the life blood of his own personal economy against the uncertainties of some speed contests, still willing to pit his skill and luck against a soulless, bottomless machine. This bit of initiative and this attitude of uninhibited reckless abandon irks the zombies no end. They are appalled to note that here in this day and age our country is still plagued by a maverick group that does not understand and appreciate the blessings of a welfare state. And so the zombies must see to it that this restless, festering sore spot is liquidated. Their technique is simple and straightforward—they use their state-given powers to tax. And they tax, and they tax, and they tax. And one day, if all goes well, the mavericks and their race track follies will be stilled. Of course at about this time a big hole is going to appear in the state budget. But, have no fear, I have all the confidence in the world that the zombies will have the ability to spot and to exploit a new source of revenue. For example, since death and taxes are a certainty—they might toy with the idea of taxing deaths. However, I don't think this notion is too clever since the appointed zombies may only exacerbate the situation by creating a crop of bona fide zombies who would love to topple over and expire—only they can't afford it. No, I think the other end would be better: tax births. After all, the naked little con artist is an exemption and as such is going to gyp the state out of hundreds of dollars, so why shouldn't he pay a little tax—say $50, or $100 maybe. But I digress.

The racing paper has an index: *Telegraph*, page 1; the *Form*, page 3. Find the Past Performances for the track you intend to visit. And now we have to select a track for illustrative purposes, and we have a great number from which to choose. We'll make it Florida's Gulfstream Park. Here is the first information given as presented by the *Morning Telegraph:*

*LISTED ACCORDING*

# GULFSTREAM PARK,

zPreceding weight in today's race indicates 3 pounds

At Gulfstream Park the length of the stretch from

# 1st Race Gulfstream Park

As presented by the *Form:*

---

ENTRIES AND PAST PERFORMANCES

# GULFSTREAM PARK

## Hallandale, Florida

(Length of stretch from last turn to finish, 941 feet.)

---

Weather and track conditions appear on Page 3.
Percentage of winning favorites corresponding meeting 1960, .33; current percentage, .24. Percentage of favorites in the money, .68. United Starting Gate. Eye in the Sky Camera. Daily Double, first and second races. Field horses run as one; no entries in Daily Double races.

---

**1st G.P**    7 FURLONGS (chute). (Hornbeam, April 2, 1947, 1:22⅗, 7, 120.)
Purse $3,000. 3-year-olds. Claiming. Weight, 121 lbs. Non-winners of two races since Feb. 8 allowed 2 lbs.; two races in 1961, 4 lbs.; one race, 6 lbs. Claiming price, $4,000.

*Best time made at distance of race.*

| | | | | | |
|---|---|---|---|---|---|
| Major Chips | | Lois | | Yellow Moon | |
| Prom't'rs D'm Mar61 GP 1:26⅕ 116 | | Pan Out Nov60 CD 1:27⅗ 110 | | Surol Mar61 GP 1:26⅗ 112 | |
| Marble Carrier | | Miseracordia | | Intransit | |
| Pegs Lad Mar61 GP 1:26⅖ 114 | | Mt. Hood | | Belle Martin Oct60 Aqu 1:29⅗ 117 | |
| Repeat Question | | Early Song | | Classelayne | |
| My Chaperone | | | | | |

In looking over the size of Gulfstream Park's homestretch as given in the above headings, I see there is a difference of some 2 inches. Possibly somebody better get out there and

*TO POST POSITIONS*

# HALLANDALE, FLORIDA

**apprentice allowance claimed; \*5 pounds; \*\*7 pounds.**

**the last turn to the finish measures 941 feet, 2 inches.**

---

**7 FURLONGS. (Hornbeam, April 2, 1947, 1.22⅗, 7, 120.)**
**Out of chute. Purse $3,000. 3–year–olds. Claiming. Weight 121 lbs. Non–winners of two races since Feb. 8 allowed 2 lbs., in 1961, 4 lbs., a race 6 lbs. Claiming price $4,000.**

check that thing; it may be growing . . . or shrinking.

Note that the *Form* gives a bit of additional information —the best time each horse entered has run today's distance. The import of such data will be discussed in the next chapter on handicapping.

Also notice the *Telegraph* begins with a formal, long-hand: "1st Race Gulfstream Park" while the *Form* condenses the same information into "1st G.P," and that "G.P" exposes us to our first official racing paper abbreviation. Here is the complete list of race track abbreviations, again grouped as to Major and Minor League tracks. The abbreviations are the same for both the *Telegraph* and the *Form*; you do not have to master two lists:

Major League tracks and their abbreviations:

| | | | |
|---|---|---|---|
| Aqueduct | Aqu | Bowie | Bow |
| Atlantic City | Atl | Churchill Downs | CD |
| Belmont | Bel | Delaware | Del |

| | | | |
|---|---|---|---|
| Detroit | Det | Monmouth | Mth |
| Fair Grounds | FG | Narragansett | Nar |
| Garden State | GS | Oaklawn Park | OP |
| Gulfstream Park | GP | Pimlico | Pim |
| Hialeah | Hia | Rockingham | Rkm |
| Keeneland | Kee | Saratoga | Sar |
| Laurel | Lrl | Suffolk | Suf |
| | Tropical Park | TrP | |

Minor League tracks and their abbreviations:

| | | | |
|---|---|---|---|
| Ascot | Asc | Marlboro | Mar |
| Berkshire Downs | BD | Maumee Downs | MD |
| Beulah Park | Beu | Marshfield Fair | MF |
| Brockton Fair | BF | Miles Park | MP |
| Bel Air | Blr | Northampton | Nmp |
| Cumberland Fair | CF | Randall | Ran |
| Cranwood | Crn | Raceway Park | RaT |
| Charles Town | CT | River Downs | RD |
| Ellis Park | Elp | Scarborough Downs | ScD |
| Great Barrington Fair | GBF | Shenandoah Downs | ShD |
| Hagerstown | Hag | Sunshine Park | SP |
| Hamilton | HO | ThistleDown | Tdn |
| Hazel Park | HP | Timonium | Tim |
| Jefferson Downs | JnD | Waterford | Wat |
| Latonia | Lat | Weymouth | Wey |
| Lincoln Downs | LD | Wheeling | Whe |

This list of race tracks is still very important, since what any horse has done in the past, good or bad, is not nearly as important as *where* he did it.

Here is a one-line example of a horse's Past Performances as presented by the *Morning Telegraph*. This particular horse was chosen at random from our sample race, "1st

**Promoters Dream** $4,000   Ch g, 3, by Big Money—Exploitation, Arbywood Stable   M. A. Buxton
7Mar61–2GP   fst 7f .22⅖ .46   1.25⅗ Clm   5000   9   1   3² 3² 2² 54¼ JCulmone

Race Gulfstream Park," and is used to demonstrate the information given and the various symbols and abbreviations used in the presentation.

Explanation:

Promoters Dream: Name of horse. If the horse is a foreign-bred (Promoters Dream is not), then a small asterisk appears in front of the name, thus: *Promoters Dream.

A large asterisk after the horse's name, thus: Promoters Dream✱, denotes a horse which has been classified as a fair mud runner. An "×" in the same position, thus: Promoters Dream×, means a good mud runner, and the symbol "⊗" in the same position means a superior mud runner.

$4,000: Claiming Price. Promoters Dream is entered in a Claiming Race and can be claimed for $4,000. Hence, this figure appears only when the horse is entered in a Claiming Race.

Ch: Color of horse. In this instance—Chestnut. Other colors available: Bay (B), Brown (Br), Black (Blk), Gray (Gr), and Roan (Ro).

g: Sex. In this instance—the lack of it: gelding. Other possibilities: Colt (c), Filly (f), Horse (h), Mare (m), and Ridgling (rig).

3: Age. 3 years old.

by Big Money—Exploitation, by Sky Raider. Pedigree. Or, Promoters Dream was sired by Big Money. His dam is Exploitation. Exploitation was sired by Sky Raider.

Arbywood Stable: Owner of horse.

M. A. Buxton : Trainer of horse.

(H. G. Jones): Breeder of horse.

---

| y Sky Raider | | **115** | 1961 | 4 | M | 0 | 0 | $100 |
| | (H. G. Jones) | | 1960 | 0 | M | 0 | 0 | ——— |
| 116 14.05 82–12 Miss Standish 106²½ Colonel Hastie 116¹ Arctic Pilot 115¾ | | | | | | | Tired 12 | |

115: Weight to be carried in today's race. The *Telegraph* indicates an apprentice allowance by placing the amount of weight being claimed in a superscript position after the assigned weight. Examples: 113⁵, 111⁷.

1960 0 M 0 0 —— Last year's racing record. Promoters Dream did not race as a 2-year-old. Made no starts; had no wins, no seconds, no thirds; won no money. The fact that Promoters Dream was a non-winner last year is shown by the "M"—Maiden.

1961 4 M 0 0 $100: This year's racing record. Promoters Dream is still a Maiden, as shown by that "M." In 1961 the horse has started 4 times; won none, no seconds, no thirds. His in-the-money percentage is still 00%. He did get close enough in one of his races to earn $100.

7Mar61: Date of his last race.

2GP: He last competed in the 2nd race at Gulfstream Park.

fst: Track condition—fast. Other possibilities: sloppy (sly), good (gd), heavy (hy), slow (sl), muddy (my). And now another track condition has been added to cope with the current trend of affairs: frozen (fr). Turf Course (grass) track conditions: hard (hd), firm (fm), and soft (sf).

7f: His last race was a sprint of 7 furlongs.

.22⅘: The horse running *first* (*not* Promoters Dream) ran the first quarter mile in 22⅘ seconds.

.46: The horse running *first* (*not* Promoters Dream) ran the half mile in 46 seconds.

1.25⅖: The winner's final running time. The *winning* horse covered the 7 furlongs in 1 minute, 25⅖ seconds.

To repeat: These fractional times and the final running time *do not apply* to Promoters Dream. One more thing about times: In sprints, the time is given for the quarter, half, and finish. In routes, the time is given for the half, three-quarters, and finish.

Clm 5000: Type of race in which Promoters Dream last competed, a Claiming Race with a Claiming Price of $5,000.

9: Post position. Promoter's Dream ran from post position number 9.

1: Shortly after the field left the starting gate, Promoter's Dream found himself running first. Or—in race track lingo —Promoter's Dream "broke on top."

$3^2$: After the field of horses had raced one quarter mile, Promoter's Dream had dropped back to third place. AND HERE IS SOMETHING TO REMEMBER: Promoters Dream was 3rd by 2 lengths, *and that means he was running 3rd, 2 lengths behind the horse that was running first.* That "2 lengths" has nothing to do with the horse that was running 4th or with the horse that was running second. To repeat: $3^2$ means that the horse was running third, 2 lengths behind the horse that was running *first.* THIS STATEMENT DOES NOT APPLY WHEN YOU ARE READING CHARTS. So forget about reading charts; can't bet on charts anyhow.

$3^2$: After the field had raced one half mile, Promoters Dream maintained his position. Still third by 2 lengths. Still 2 lengths behind the first horse.

$2^2$: Coming into the homestretch, Promoters Dream moved up to second place. Second by two. Or did he really "move up"? After half a mile, he was losing the race by 2 lengths. Coming into the stretch, in spite of the fact that his position changed from 3rd to 2nd, he didn't move up a damn inch. He's still losing the race by 2 lengths. What has really happened is that one of the front runners has tired and has fallen back.

$5^{4-1/4}$: Final finish. Fifth by 4¼ lengths. Looks like somebody else got tired. Promoters Dream is still a Maiden. He finished 4¼ lengths behind the *first* horse.

JCulmone: Jockey.

b: Promoters Dream wore blinkers as part of his equipment. Also—all riders carry a whip as part of their equipment unless a special footnote denotes otherwise.

116: Weight carried.

14.05: Betting odds to the dollar. Must bet at least $2; therefore, a winning ticket on Promoters Dream would pay $30.10. Albeit, since he ran 5th, he didn't pay anything.

82-12: Speed rating and track variant. No comment.

Miss Standish $106^{2-1/2}$: The race was won by a filly named Miss Standish. She carried 106 pounds and finished 2½ lengths in front of the second horse.

Colonel Hastie $116^{1}$: The second horse, his weight carried, and his advantage over the third horse.

Arctic Pilot $115^{3/4}$: The third horse, his weight carried,

---

**Major Chips** $4,000 **B c, 3, by El Hawa II—Gallic Gal, by Daube**
**Dara-King J. E. King**

| | | | | | | | | | | | | | | |
|---|---|---|---|---|---|---|---|---|---|---|---|---|---|---|
| 11Mar61–3GP | fst 7f | .23 | .46⅖ | 1.24⅕ | Clm | 7500 | 4 | 8 | $7^{7\frac{1}{2}}$ | $8^{12}$ | $8^{17}$ | $8^{17}$ | FPannell |
| 8Feb61–2Hia | fst 1⅛ | .48 | 1.13⅕ | 1.53⅖ | Clm | 6000 | 5 | 10 | $10^{23}$ | $10^{21}$ | $8^{19}$ | $8^{22}$ | HGrant |
| 3Feb61–5Hia | fst 1⅛ | .47⅕ | 1.12⅘ | 1.54⅘ | Clm | 7000 | 10 | 6 | $6^{9}$ | $6^{8\frac{1}{2}}$ | $7^{10}$ | $6^{11}$ | JKurtz |
| 24Jan61–2Hia | fst 1⅛ | .47⅗ | 1.13⅖ | 1.53⅕ | Clm | 7000 | 12 | 12 | $12^{21}$ | $12^{25}$ | $10^{25}$ | $9^{28}$ | RYork |
| 10Jan61–3TrP | my 1 1/16 | .48 | 1.14⅘ | 1.50⅘ | Md Sp Wt | | 12 | 10 | $9^{15}$ | $9^{12}$ | $9^{9\frac{1}{2}}$ | $4^{7\frac{1}{4}}$ | JKurtz |
| 4Jan61–1TrP | fst 1 1/16 | .47⅕ | 1.12⅗ | 1.46⅖ | Md | 5500 | 10 | 8 | $8^{15}$ | $7^{12}$ | $5^{12}$ | $4^{9\frac{1}{4}}$ | JKurtz |
| 19Dec60–1TrP | fst 6f | .23 | .47⅖ | 1.13⅕ | Md | 4500 | 3 | 4 | $3^{2}$ | $2^{2}$ | $2^{1}$ | $2^{h}$ | JKurtz |
| 1Dec60–4TrP | fst 6f | .23 | .46⅘ | 1.13 | Clm | 5000 | 8 | 2 | $8^{5\frac{1}{2}}$ | $11^{14}$ | $12^{20}$ | $11^{17}$ | JKurtz |
| 8Apr60–3GP | fst 3f | | .22 | .33⅗ | Md | 10000 | 4 | 12 | | | $12^{15}$ | $12^{11}$ | WMorrisse |

**LATEST WORKOUTS Mar 10 TrP 3f fst .38 b Mar 4 TrP 3f fst .37**

and his advantage over the fourth horse.

Tired: *Telegraph's* comment on the horse's effort.

12: Number of horses in the race.

Below are the complete Past Performances of another horse entered in our sample race, 1st G.P. Again the horse was selected at random just to show the various symbols used by the *Telegraph*.

Other types of races are shown here besides Claiming Races. On 8Apr60 the "Md. 10,000" means a Claiming Race for Maidens with a claiming price of $10,000. Ran next to last. Odds were 43.10 to 1. The symbol "†" means that the horse was coupled in the betting as part of a mutuel "field"; note that in that particular race there were 13 horses. The betting machines at the track can handle only 12 separate racing interests so that in the event of races with more than 12 starters, certain designated horses will be coupled in the betting as a mutuel "field." In this particular race you could have bet two horses for $2 and if either one had won, you would have won. It is also possible to bet two horses for $2 in a field smaller than 13 in the event 2, or more, horses are coupled as an "entry." One racing interest may send out 2 horses to run in the same

| | | | **115** | 1961 | 6 | M | C | C | $200 |
|---|---|---|---|---|---|---|---|---|---|
| (L. Bushong) | | | | 1960 | 4 | M | 1 | C | $325 |
| b 115 | 186.30 | 75–14 | Joe's Man 114¹ Glass House 121¹¼ Level Streak 112⁴ | | | | Never close | | 9 |
| b 116 | 29.70 | 46–21 | DownCount 108¼ NightWreck114¹¾ Gray'sBlueMan113¹² | | | | No speed | | 10 |
| b 110 | 134.25 | 50–26 | d–Reel Thor 105¹½ Gypsy Ghost 109²¾ Bimenite 113²¼ | | | | No factor | | 12 |
| b 112 | 39.05 | 41–24 | Palestine Song 112⁵ Cadet's Miss 108⁴ Soups On 109⁸ | | | | Dwelt start | | 12 |
| b 119 | 46.90 | 41–32 | Blue Tattoo 119¹¼ Regards to Mabel 116² Aeroflint 119³½ | | | | Rallied | | 12 |
| b 118 | 6.45 | 61–22 | Be Welcome 113¹½ Night Wreck 113⁷ Lone Lady 108¾ | | | | Mild late bid | | 10 |
| b 114 | 13.40 | 76–20 | Belated News 112ʰ Major Chips 114⁴¼ Lois 114¾ | | | | Made sharp try | | 12 |
| 112 | 157.70 | 60–22 | Mighty Gone 115½ Bonova 107¹¼ Fly Dancer 110¹¼ | | | | Never a factor | | 12 |
| 121 † | 43.10 | 84– 5 | Sea Green 121² Kentucky Bid 116¹ Corlan D. 118½ | | | | Always far back | | 13 |
| **Feb 1 TrP 4f fst .53 b** | | | | **Jan 22 TrP 4f fst .49 b** | | | | | |

race. For instance, an owner may start 2 horses in the same race, and since these 2 horses will then be representing only one racing interest, the one owner, then they run as one. They would be numbered 1 and 1A, and you could bet both of them for $2 by asking for number 1. The fact that a horse raced as part of an entry is shown by the symbol "‡."

On 19Dec60 Major Chips raced in a Claiming Race for maidens with a Claiming Price of $4,500. Sharp try. Lost by only a head. Next effort: Maidens, Claiming; Claiming Price: $5,500. Mild late bid. Finished 4th.

In his next effort he tried Maidens Special Weights and did fairly well—again 4th. But note the jump in his odds. With Maidens Claiming $5,500 @6½ to 1. With Maidens Special Weights—almost 47-1.

His next effort was in a medium-priced Claiming Race—not Maidens Claiming—just Claiming; Claiming Price: $7,000. Like Mr. Coolidge, Major Chips did not choose to run. Dwelt at the start and finally got underway 21 lengths off the pace. Since then he has shown no speed against these medium-priced Platers, and that's one big reason why the Claiming Price today has been cut almost

---

**Noble Turn** **$15,000** **Dk br c, 3, by Noble Hero—Miss Linnett, by Alet**
**Elton Stable P. Roberts**

| | | | | | | | | | | | | |
|---|---|---|---|---|---|---|---|---|---|---|---|---|
| 11Mar61–2GP | fst 6f | .23 | .45⅗ | 1.11 | Allowance | 5 | 8 | $10^{8\frac{1}{4}}$ | $9^{11}$ | $7^{7\frac{1}{2}}$ | $7^{7\frac{3}{4}}$ | EMonacelli |
| 2Nov60–7GS | gd 6f | .22⅖ | .46 | 1.12⅘ | Clm 12000 | 2 | 7 | $7^{5\frac{3}{4}}$ | $4^{4\frac{1}{2}}$ | $3^{3}$ | $2^{no}$ | EMonacelli |
| 26Oct60–6GS | fst 6f | .22⅖ | .46 | 1.11⅗ | Allowance | 10 | 8 | $8^{6\frac{1}{4}}$ | $5^{6}$ | $5^{5\frac{1}{2}}$ | $5^{7\frac{1}{4}}$ | EMonacelli |
| 21Oct60–5GS | sl 6f | .22⅗ | .46⅘ | 1.12⅘ | Allowance | 11 | 1 | $8^{6}$ | $8^{3\frac{1}{2}}$ | $11^{5}$ | $12^{6\frac{1}{4}}$ | LGilligan |
| 4Oct60–4Atl | fst 7f | .22⅘ | .46 | 1.24⅗ | Allowance | 8 | 9 | $10^{2\frac{3}{4}}$ | $11^{13}$ | $10^{14}$ | $9^{17}$ | DBrumfield |
| 22Sep60–5Atl | fst 6f | .22⅘ | .46 | 1.11⅗ | Allowance | 6 | 8 | $8^{6\frac{1}{4}}$ | $8^{14}$ | $8^{13}$ | $9^{11}$ | DBrumfield |
| 18May60–7GS | sly 5f | .22⅘ | .47⅗ | .59⅘ | CherryHill | 5 | 13 | $14^{14}$ | $14^{16}$ | $14^{21}$ | $14^{28}$ | MNGonzalez |
| 22Apr60–3GP | gd 5f | .22⅘ | .46 | .59 | Md Sp Wt | 5 | 4 | $2^{2}$ | $2^{3}$ | $2^{1}$ | $1^{3}$ | RDever |
| 11Mar60–3GP | fst 3f | | .22⅕ | .33⅘ | Md Sp Wt | 2 | 7 | | | $4^{3}$ | $5^{4\frac{3}{4}}$ | MNGonzalez |
| 24Feb60–7Hia | gd 3f | | .22 | .33⅘ | Fla.Brdrs | 16 | 12 | | | $12^{5\frac{3}{4}}$ | $13^{6\frac{1}{4}}$ | SBoulmetis |
| 19Feb60–3Hia | fst 3f | | .21⅘ | .32⅗ | Md Sp Wt | 12 | 1 | | | $4^{3\frac{1}{2}}$ | $4^{3\frac{1}{2}}$ | SBoulmetis |

**LATEST WORKOUTS Mar 8 TrP 3f fst .37 bg Mar 2 TrP 5f fst 1.02⅗ b**

in half: Claiming Price: $4,000. Whether or not he can win this race is highly problematical—but the important thing is that that one race "$2^h$" at a Major League track lets the world know that he can win a horse race someday, somewhere, sometime. It may not be at Gulfstream Park; it may be Latonia, or Jefferson Downs or Sunshine Park—but someday, at some race track, he will be able to show his heels to a field of inferior horses. The future is not necessarily all black for Major Chips, unless—there is always an unless. Unless, he happens to blossom out into being a member of the "Ancient Maiden" set, a caste of untouchables we will discuss later when a list of "Horses To Avoid" is given. For the present we will mention only that today's race marks the eleventh (11th) attempt by Major Chips to win himself a horse race.

The complete Past Performances record also lists something at the bottom we haven't mentioned before: LATEST WORKOUTS. These workouts will be dealt with when the topic of "time" comes up in the next chapter.

One final example of Past Performances from the *Telegraph,* this time to show an Allowance horse. After all, all the races run aren't Claiming Races.

| | | | (C. G. Rose, Sr.) **109** | 1961 1 0 0 0 — |
|---|---|---|---|---|
| | | | | 1960 12 1 1 0 $3,100 |

| | | | | |
|---|---|---|---|---|
| 113 | 55.90 | 81–14 | Belair Road $118^{1}_{4}$ Jay Fox $118^h$ Swing Span $118^{1}_{4}$ | Had no mishap 12 |
| 115 | 7.40 | 80–24 | Lou Pelton $112^{no}$ Noble Turn $115^{2}_{2}$ Count Rose $115^1$ | Just nosed out 12 |
| 115 | 118.30 | 79–23 | Sailor Beware $117^4$ Relative $117^{1}_{4}$ Highland Lassie $114^2$ | Evenly 12 |
| 114 | 48.00 | 74–25 | Hellenic Hero $114^h$ Hasty Honey $115^{3}_{4}$ Copper Knight $114^{1}_{4}$ | No speed 12 |
| 117 | 44.70 | 63–20 | Wooden Nickel $117^{nk}$ Hellenic Hero $117^7$ Charlie Z. $117^2$ | No speed 12 |
| 117 | 34.70 | 76–16 | Great Scope $117^h$ Frankincense $117^2$ Wooden Nickel $117^{3}_{4}$ | No speed 12 |
| 113 | 31.70 | 63–23 | Iron Rail $113^{10}$ Song of Wine $113^{2}_{2}$ Relative $114^h$ | Far off pace 15 |
| 115 | 5.00 | 100–9 | Noble Turn $115^3$ Corvus $115^4$ Seminole Cadet $120^1$ | Scored handily 12 |
| b 119 ‡ | *1.05 | 89–6 | Dream On $116^{1}_{2}$ Foolish Youth $116^1$ Pepier $119^{1}_{4}$ | Made even effort 14 |
| b 120 ‡ | 10.80 | 87–7 | My Old Flame $117^{3}_{4}$ Carry Back $120^h$ Julitta $117^h$ | Had no speed 18 |
| b 113 † | 20.65 | 95–1 | Profit or Loss $118^{1}_{2}$ Wooden Nickel $118^1$ KingCroesus $118^1$ | Evenly 14 |

Feb 15 TrP 3f fst .38 b          Feb 6 TrP 5f fst $1.01^{2}_{5}$ h

Noble Turn is a bit more of a high-powered horse. Started in races for Maidens Special Weights. While still a Maiden he took a shot at the Handicap-Stakes end of things by running in the Florida Breeders Stakes. Finished 13th in an 18-horse field. Then as part of an entry he was bet down to just a little better than 1 to 1 and finished 5th. In this race he was the favorite, as shown by the little black star in front of his odds. (Being the favorite means that more money was bet on his chances of winning than was bet on any other horse in the race.) His next effort was a smasher when he bounced home in front by 3 lengths. The only sensible thing to do after such a convincing triumph was to take another shot at the "big boys" in the Handicap-Stakes ranks. So he hied off to Garden State and ran in the Cherry Hill Stakes. Much to his chagrin, he found out that since he couldn't keep up with that class of horses in February, he couldn't keep up with them in May either. He settled back to the Allowance ranks, and wasn't any world beater in that classification either. On the 2nd of November, 1960, he dropped down into the Claiming ranks—very high Claiming ranks too, $12,000. Just missed; or, as the *Telegraph* comment put it: "Just nosed out." Notice that when he came down out of the Allowance ranks and ran in a Claiming Race his odds also came down: from over 118 to 1, down to 7.40 to 1. His first start in 1961 was again in the Allowance ranks and again it didn't amount to much, and that's one big reason why today he is entered back in a high Claiming Race, Claiming Price: $15,000.

To compare the *Racing Form* with the *Telegraph,* we will

examine the same information as given by the *Form* for the same three horses: Promoters Dream, Major Chips, and Noble Turn.

**romoters Dream**     **115** Ch. g, 3, by Big Money—Exploitation, by Sky Raider.
Breeder, H. G. Jones.     1961   4   M   0   0     $100
wner, Arbywood Stable.   Trainer, M. A. Buxton.     **$4,000**
ar 7-61²G.P    7 f 1:25⅗ft   14   116   3²   3²   2²   54¼ CulmoneJ⁹   5000 82 M'sSt'd'h106   C'nelH'tie116 A'ticPilot 12

Promoters Dream:    Name of horse.

115:    Weight to be carried in today's race.

Ch:    Color—chestnut.

g:    Sex—gelding.

3:    Age—3 years old.

by Big Money—Exploitation, by Sky Raider:   Pedigree.

Breeder, H. G. Jones.

Owner, Arbywood Stable.

Trainer, M. A. Buxton.

$4,000:    Today's Claiming Price.

1961   4   M   0   0   $100:    This year's racing record. No mention is made of the fact that the horse did not race as a 2-year-old—other than by omission.

Mar 7-61:    Date of last race.

² G.P:    Second race, Gulfstream Park.

7f:    Distance—7 furlongs.

1:25⅗:    Winner's final time. No fractional times given.

ft:    Track condition—fast.

14:    Approximate odds to the dollar. Odds are "rounded off."

116:    Weight carried.

3²:    Position at the first call. Exact distance at which this first call is given varies with the length of the race. The fact that Promoters Dream broke on top is omitted.

$3^2$: Pre-stretch call. Varies with the length of the race, usually ¼ mile from the finish.

$2^2$: Stretch call. Usually 1 furlong from the finish.

$5^{4\text{-}1/4}$: Finish position. Promoters Dream finished 5th, 4¼ lengths behind the *first* horse.

CulmoneJ$^9$: Jockey and post position.

5000: Type of race—Claiming $5,000.

82: Speed rating—no comment.

Miss Standish 106: Winning horse and weight carried.

Colonel Hastie 116: Second horse and weight carried.

Arctic Pilot: Third horse.

12: Number of horses in the race.

The complete Past Performances of Major Chips as presented by the *Form:*

**Major Chips** **115** B. c, 3, by El Hawa II.—Gallic Gal, by Dauber.
Breeder, L. Bushong. 1961 6 M 0 0 $20
Owner, J. Dara & J. E. King. Trainer, J. E. King. **$4,000** 1960 4 M 1 0 $32

| | | | | | | | | | | | | | | | |
|---|---|---|---|---|---|---|---|---|---|---|---|---|---|---|---|
| Mar11-61$^3$G.P | 7 f | 1:24⅕ft | 186 | 115 | $7^{7\frac{1}{2}}$ | $8^{12}$ | $8^{17}$ | $8^{17}$ | PannellF$^4$ | 7500 | 75 | Joe'sMan114 | Gl'ssH'se121 | Lev'lStr'k | |
| Feb 8-61$^2$Hia | 1 1-8 | 1:53⅖ft | 30 | 116 | $10^{21}$ | $10^{21}$ | $8^{19}$ | $8^{22}$ | GrantH$^5$ | 6000 | 46 | D'nC't108 | N'tWr'k114 | Gr'y'sBlueM'n | 1 |
| Feb 3-61$^5$Hia | 1 1-8 | 1:54⅘ft | 134 | 110 | $6^{7\frac{1}{2}}$ | $6^{8\frac{1}{2}}$ | $7^{10}$ | $6^{11}$ | KurtzJ$^{10}$ | 7000 | 50 | ReelThor105 | GypsyGhost109 | Bimenite | 1 |
| Jan24-61$^2$Hia | 1 1-8 | 1:53⅕ft | 39 | 112 | $12^{21}$ | $12^{25}$ | $10^{25}$ | $9^{28}$ | YorkR$^{12}$ | 7000 | 41 | P'stimeS'g112 | C'det'sM's108 | SoupsOn | 1 |
| Jan10-61$^3$TrP | $1\frac{1}{16}$ | 1:50⅘sm | 47 | 119 | $10^{14}$ | $9^{12}$ | $8^{9\frac{1}{2}}$ | $4^{7\frac{1}{4}}$ | KurtzJ$^{12}$ | Mdn | 41 | BlueT'too119 | R'g'dstoM'b'l 116 | Aero't | 1 |
| Jan 4-61$^1$TrP | $1\frac{1}{16}$ | 1:46⅖ft | 6½ | 118 | $8^{15}$ | $7^{12}$ | $5^{12}$ | $4^{9\frac{1}{4}}$ | KurtzJ$^{10}$ | M5500 | 61 | BeWelcome113 | NightWr'k113 | L'neL'y | 1 |
| Dec19-60$^1$TrP | 6 f | 1:13⅕ft | 13 | 114 | $3^2$ | $2^2$ | $2^1$ | $2^h$ | KurtzJ$^3$ | M4500 | 76 | BelatedNews112 | MajorChips114 | Lois | 1 |
| Dec 1-60$^4$TrP | 6 f | 1:13 ft | 158 | 112 | $8^{5\frac{1}{2}}$ | $11^{14}$ | $12^{20}$ | $11^{17}$ | KurtzJ$^8$ | 5000 | 60 | MightyGone115 | Bonova107 | FlyDancer | 1 |
| Apr 8-60$^3$G.P | 3 f | :33⅗ft | 43f | 121 | 12 | | $12^{15}$ | $12^{11}$ | M'eyW$^4$ | M10000 | 84 | SeaGr'n121 | KentuckyBid116 | CorlanD. | 1 |
| Mar23-60$^3$G.P | 4½ f | :52⅕ft | 46f | 119 | 7 | $9^{14}$ | $10^{19}$ | $10^{17}$ | Mor'seyW$^8$ | Mdn | 81 | Bagpiper119 | GameJac114 | Pr'ceWil'm | 1 |

**March 10 TrP 3-8 ft :38b** **March 4 TrP 3-8 ft :37b** **Feb 1 TrP 1-2 ft :53b**

Notice now that his race for Maidens, Claiming $10,000, appears: M10000, and the fact that he was part of a mutuel field is shown in the odds: "43f." To denote an entry, the *Form* substitutes an "e" for the "f," thus: "43e."

Also take very careful note of the fact that a race for Maidens Special Weights appears in the *Form* as an innocent little "Mdn." Learn to have a lot of respect for such losing horses; they have been chasing the best non-winners on the grounds; or, they have been campaigning in the "Handicap-Stakes" division for Maidens.

Here are the Past Performances of Noble Turn as presented by the *Racing Form*:

**Noble Turn** **109** Dk. br. c, 3, by Noble Hero—Miss Linnett, by Aletern.
Breeder, C. G. Rose, Sr. 1961 1 0 0 0 (——)
Owner, Elton Stable. Trainer, P. Roberts. $15,000 1960 12 1 1 0 $3,100

| | | | | | | | | | | | | | | |
|---|---|---|---|---|---|---|---|---|---|---|---|---|---|---|
| Mar11-61 2G.P | 6 f | 1:11 ft | 56 | 113 | 10 8¼ | 9 11 | 7 7½ | 7 7¾ | Mon'celliE5 | Alw | 81 | BelairRoad118 JayFox118 SwingSpan | 12 |
| Nov 2-60 7G.S | 6 f | 1:12⅘gd | 7½ | 115 | 7 5¾ | 4 4½ | 3 3 | 2 no | Mon'lliE2 | 12000 | 80 | LouPelton112 NobleTurn115 C'ntRose | 12 |
| Oct26-60 6G.S | 6 f | 1:11⅗ft | 118 | 115 | 8 6¼ | 5 6 | 5 5½ | 5 7¼ | Mon'elliE10 | Alw | 79 | S'l'rB'w're117 R'l'tive117 Highl'dL'sie | 12 |
| Oct21-60 5G.S | 6 f | 1:12⅘sl | 48 | 114 | 8 6 | 8 3½ | 11 5 | 12 6¼ | GilliganL11 | Alw | 74 | H'l'nicH'ro114 H'styH'y115 Cop'rKn't | 12 |
| Oct 4-60 4Atl | 7 f | 1:24⅗ft | 45 | 117 | 10 2¾ | 11 13 | 10 14 | 9 17 | Brumf'ldD8 | Alw | 63 | W'denN'kel 117 H'nicHero117 Ch'lieZ. | 12 |
| Sep22-60 5Atl | 7 f | 1:11⅗ft | 35 | 117 | 8 6¼ | 8 14 | 8 13 | 9 11 | Brumf'ldD6 | Alw | 76 | Gr'tS'pe117 Fr'kinc'se117 W'd'nN'kel | 12 |
| May18-60 7G.S | 5 f | :59⅘sy | 32 | 113 | 14 14 | 14 16 | 14 21 | 14 28 | Gon'zMN5 | AlwS | 63 | IronRail 113 Song ofWine113 Relative | 15 |
| Apr22-60 3G.P | 5 f | :59 gd | 5 | 115 | 2 2 | 2 3 | 2 1 | 1 3 | DeverR5 | Mdn | 100 | N'bleTurn115 Corvus115 Semin'leC'd't | 12 |
| Mar11-60 3G.P | 3 f | :33⅘ft | 1e▲ | 119 | 7 | | 4 3 | 5 4¾ | Gon'zMN2 | Mdn | 89 | DreamOn116 FoolishYouth116 Pepier | 14 |
| Feb24-60 7Hia | 3 f | :33⅘gd | 11e | 120 | 12 | | 12 5¾ | 13 6¼ | Boul'sS16 | SpwS | 87 | MyOldFlame117 CarryBack120 Julitta | 18 |

March 8 TrP 3-8 ft :37bg March 2 TrP 5-8 ft 1:02⅗b Feb 15 TrP 3-8 ft :38b

Notice again how a race for Maidens Special Weights is indicated by an apparently unimportant little "Mdn." You can also see how the race we saw earlier in the *Telegraph* as the Florida Breeders Stakes now shows up as a rather ordinary "SpwS" (Special Weight Stake), and Garden State's Cherry Hill Stakes becomes a colorless "AlwS (Allowance Stake). In other words, the *Telegraph* lists the stakes races by their full names, whatever they are—Kentucky Derby, Preakness, etc.—while the *Form* uses the appropriate racing paper abbreviation. The Kentucky Derby would appear in the *Telegraph* as just that, "Kentucky Derby"; in the *Form* the same race becomes "HcpS" (Handicap-Stakes).

About the *Telegraph's* technique of giving the full name for each stakes race—some stakes races have pretty long names, Belmont Park's Coaching Club American Oaks, as an example—the result is that such a name gets pretty well abbreviated due to the very mechanics of the thing. If you don't have some idea of what the race is in the first place, you may go crazy wondering what all those apostrophes stand for.

About the *Form's* technique of reducing great races to SpwS, AlwS, HcpS, etc. If some fine day you should get all the various conditions for such races all sorted out and catalogued mentally, then you will have become quite a file cabinet of rather useless information.

In the race of 11Mar60, the fact that Noble Turn was the favorite is shown by the small black triangle after his odds, thus: "1e▲."

Another item I'll mention is a practice that is employed by both the *Form* and the *Telegraph*. The three horses listed to the right of the speed rating are the first-, second-, and third-place horses in that particular race. If the horse under scrutiny happened to win the race, then his own name appears first, as witness Noble Turn's race of 22Apr60. Finished 1³. The first three finishers are then listed: Noble Turn, Corvus, and Seminole Cadet. On 2Nov60, when Noble Turn finished second by a nose, the first three finishers (the *Form* calls these horses the "Best Company Line") are listed: Lou Pelton, Noble Turn and Count Rose.

I will condescend at this juncture to make a comment or two about the speed rating figure we have mentioned earlier since the example as shown by Noble Turn is to my advantage. Had it been to my detriment, we would have skipped it altogether.

On 22Apr60, when Noble Turn won his race by 3 lengths, you will notice his speed rating figure is given as "100." That "100" means he tied the track record, 5 furlongs in 59 seconds flat. How nice. His next race illustrates just how earth-shaking such a feat was. In the first place his odds went from 5-1 to 32-1, which means that quite a few people didn't think too much of his chances. He lost the race by 28 lengths and finished next to last in a fifteen-horse field. Sad. And now, note the winner's final time in this race: 5 furlongs in 59⅘ seconds, or ⅘ of a second *slower* than our track record hero had previously run the same distance. Using time as the singular factor of importance, and not the fact that the horse went from non-winners to stakes competition, he should have been out there and winging—or if not out there winging, at least up there somewhere in the bunch and not dragging along next to last.

And, yes, I'm cognizant of the fact that the race track changed from Gulfstream Park to Garden State. I'm even aware of the fact that the track condition changed from "good" to "sloppy" and that Noble Turn has no mud mark after his name.

Well, in the first place, it may come as a shock to you to learn that changing the track condition from "good" to "sloppy" is changing from a *slower* track to a *faster* one, and not vice versa, as many would believe. And secondly, I see in his Past Performances where he ran in an Allowance Race at Garden State, and this time on a "slow" track (mud). He lost the race by only 6 lengths and not by 28. And so he did not do badly in his AlwS Race because he can't run well in the mud; he did badly because the other horses got up and ran away from him—"100" speed rating or no.

A couple final tidbits and you'll know all about how to

read a racing paper. Occasionally around the race track two or more horses hit the finish line at the same time, i.e., they finish in a tie. Such a state of affairs is called a dead heat. The *Form* notes such an occurrence thus:

Tries Hard $2^2$ $2^1$ $2^1$ $1^1$ † CulmoneJ
†Dead heat.

The *Telegraph* notes the same thing thus:

Tries Hard 3 $2^2$ $3^4$ $4^4$ $4^5$ JCulmone b 110♠
♠Dead heat.

As shown, the dead heat does not necessarily have to be for first place, might be for 6th.

Many times a horse is entered in a Claiming Race, is eligible to be claimed, and is. The *Form* notes this by placing a small "c" in front of the Claiming Price for that race. Thus: c1250. The *Telegraph* signifies the same thing by placing a small black diamond in front of the Claiming Price. Thus: Clm ♦1250.

Other eventualities may at times be seen in subscripts below the race:

†Disqualified and placed last.
†Disqualified and placed second.

---

**Mosby** **$9,000** **Dk gr g, 5, by Endeavour II—War Candy, by Great Wa**
**L. Weinberger M. J. Rosenthal**

| | | | | | | | | | | | | | |
|---|---|---|---|---|---|---|---|---|---|---|---|---|---|
| 3Mar61–3Hia | fst 6f | $.22\frac{4}{5}$ | $.46\frac{3}{5}$ | $1.12\frac{2}{5}$ | Clm | ♦5000 | 6 | 3 | $2^1$ | $3^{nk}$ | $4^{2\frac{1}{2}}$ | $5^{7\frac{1}{4}}$ | WHartack |
| 8Feb61–3Hia | fst 7f | $.23\frac{1}{5}$ | $.46\frac{3}{5}$ | $1.25\frac{2}{5}$ | Clm | 8000 | 7 | 6 | $5^{3\frac{1}{2}}$ | $5^{5\frac{1}{2}}$ | $7^9$ | $7^{8\frac{1}{2}}$ | SBoulmetis |
| 24Jan61–5Hia | fst 6f | $.22\frac{4}{5}$ | $.46\frac{3}{5}$ | $1.12\frac{1}{5}$ | Clm | 8500 | 12 | 6 | $5^{1\frac{3}{4}}$ | $4^{1\frac{3}{4}}$ | $6^{3\frac{1}{4}}$ | $6^{6\frac{3}{4}}$ | WHartack |
| 5Jan61–8TrP | fst 6f | $.22\frac{2}{5}$ | $.45\frac{2}{5}$ | $1.10\frac{4}{5}$ | Clm | 12500 | 1 | 7 | $4^{2\frac{1}{4}}$ | $5^5$ | $6^7$ | $5^{3\frac{1}{2}}$ | RFlanigan[5] |
| 20Oct60–6Bel | sf*2 | Hurdles | | $3.54\frac{2}{5}$ | NYTrfWrH | | 4 | 2 | $1^h$ | $8^{15}$ | Pulled up | | SRiles |
| 7Oct60–3Bel | fm*2 | Hurdles | | 3.46 | Allowance | | 3 | 4 | $2^1$ | $1^h$ | $3^5$ | $5^{20}$ | APSmithwic |
| 27Sep60–3Bel | fm*1⅞ | Hurdles | | $3.25\frac{2}{5}$ | Allowance | | 1 | 6 | $4^{2\frac{1}{2}}$ | $1^{2\frac{1}{2}}$ | $1^{10}$ | $1^{20}$ | APSmithwic |
| 24Sep60–2FH | fm*1¾ | Hurdles | | 3.13 | Md Sp Wt | | 1 | 5 | $5^{2\frac{1}{4}}$ | $1^{1\frac{1}{2}}$ | $1^4$ | $1^8$ | APSmithwic |
| 5Sep60–9Aqu | fst 7f | $.23\frac{1}{5}$ | $.46\frac{4}{5}$ | $1.24\frac{3}{5}$ | Clm | 10000 | 9 | 3 | $1^{\frac{1}{2}}$ | $1^{1\frac{1}{2}}$ | $1^{\frac{1}{2}}$ | $4^3$ | IValenzuela |

**LATEST WORKOUTS Feb 22 Hia 3f fst $.35\frac{2}{5}$ h Feb 3 Hia 6f fst 1.16 b**

2Nov60 Placed second through disqualification.
5Apr60 Awarded fourth purse money.

We have now covered everything except the two classes of horses which we may look upon as representing the dregs of the thoroughbred racing world.

At times a horse which has been competing in jump races and doing rather well will desert the ranks of the jumpers and try his luck racing on the flat. His attempts in the running races are, as a rule, pretty dismal. Here are the Past Performances of an erstwhile jumper turned runner as presented by the *Form*:

**Mosby** **110** Dk. gr. g, 5, by Endeavour II.—War Candy, by Great War.
Breeder, Mrs. M. E. Lunn. 1961 4 0 0 0 (——)
Owner, Leo Weinberger. Trainer, M. J. Rosenthal. $9.000 1960 14 2 1 1 $4,540

| | | | | | | | | | | | | | | | |
|---|---|---|---|---|---|---|---|---|---|---|---|---|---|---|---|
| Mar 3-61$^{3}$Hia | 6 f 1:12⅖ft | 8-5 | ▲118 | 2$^{1}$ | 3$^{nk}$ | 4$^{2½}$ | 5$^{7¼}$ | Hart'kW$^{6}$ | c5000 | 76 | P'ceW't'y118 | B'lchise116 | Rise andS've | 7 |
| Feb 8-61$^{3}$Hia | 7 f 1:25⅖ft | 8 | 112 | 5$^{3½}$ | 5$^{5½}$ | 7$^{9}$ | 7$^{8½}$ | Boul'tisS$^{7}$ | 8000 | 74 | Delm'go112 | Ram'aR'de117 | Br'fEnc't'r | 12 |
| Jan24-61$^{5}$Hia | 6 f 1:12⅕ft | 2 | ▲118 | 5$^{1¾}$ | 4$^{1¾}$ | 6$^{3¼}$ | 6$^{6¾}$ | Hart'kW$^{12}$ | 8500 | 77 | WhiteLabel 115 | Rory113 | SweetDaddy | 12 |
| Jan 5-61$^{8}$TrP | 6 f 1:10⅘ft | 86 | 107* | 4$^{2¼}$ | 5$^{5}$ | 6$^{7}$ | 5$^{3½}$ | Flan'nR$^{1}$ | 12500 | 84 | Airide 115 | Tile Son 108 | Nero | 9 |
| Oct20-60$^{6}$Bel | a 2 3:54⅖sf | 6 | 133 | 2$^{h}$ | 8$^{15}$ | Pull'd up. | | RilesS$^{4}$ | HcpS[H | | Nautilus 143 | Greek Brother 134 | Nala | 8 |
| Oct 7-60$^{3}$Bel | a 2 3:46 fm | 1-2e | ▲151 | 4$^{2}$ | 1$^{h}$ | 3$^{5}$ | 5$^{20}$ | Sm'ckAJ$^{3}$ | Alw [H | | Nautilus144 | Palladio151 | GreekBrother | 8 |
| Sep27-60$^{3}$Bel | a 1⅞ 3:25⅖m | 7-5 | ▲151 | 6$^{3¼}$ | 1$^{2½}$ | 1$^{10}$ | 1$^{20}$ | H'hw'kAP$^{1}$ | Alw [H | | Mosby 151 | Sunny Celt 140 | Auriate | 8 |
| Sep24-60$^{2}$F.H | a 1¾ 3:13 fm | | 152 | 5$^{3¼}$ | 1$^{1½}$ | 1$^{4}$ | 1$^{8}$ | Sm'ckAP$^{4}$ | Mdn [H | | Mosby 152 | Gowran 136 | Me Broke | 9 |
| Sep 5-60$^{9}$Aqu | 7 f 1:24⅗ft | 12 | 118 | 1$^{½}$ | 1$^{1½}$ | 1$^{½}$ | 4$^{3}$ | Val'z'lal$^{9}$ | 10000 | 84 | Sp'dyContessa115 | Trock124 | VanQuest | 13 |

**Feb 22 Hia 3-8 ft :35⅖h** **Feb 3 Hia 3-4 ft 1:16b** **Jan 30 Hia 3-8 gd :36⅗b**

Below is the same horse as presented by the *Telegraph*.

Notice the *Telegraph* spells it right out for you: "Hurdles," while the *Form* uses the symbol [H. Note also the

**(Mrs. M. E. Lunn)** **110** 1961 4 0 0 0 ——
1960 14 2 1 1 $4,540

| | | | | | |
|---|---|---|---|---|---|
| b 118 | *1.65 | 76–15 | Prince Whitney 118$^{½}$ Belchise 116$^{3¾}$ Rise and Survive 119$^{2¼}$ | Used up | 7 |
| b 112 | 8.00 | 74–21 | Delmargo 112$^{¾}$ Ramona Rode 117$^{¾}$ Brief Encounter 113$^{2½}$ | Tired | 12 |
| b 118 | *2.95 | 77–24 | White Label 115$^{1}$ Rory 113$^{3}$ Sweet Daddy 112$^{½}$ | Wide all the way | 12 |
| b 107 | 86.15 | 84–19 | Alride 115$^{2}$ Tile Son 108$^{no}$ Nero 111$^{no}$ | Raced evenly most of way | 9 |
| s 133 ‡ | 5.90 | —— | Nautilus 143$^{20}$ Greek Brother 134$^{6}$ Nala 162$^{3½}$ | Speed, stopped | 8 |
| s 151 ‡ | *0.50 | —— | Nautilus 144$^{8}$ Palladio 151$^{7}$ Greek Brother 145$^{1½}$ | Speed, tired | 8 |
| s 151 | *1.35 | —— | Mosby 151$^{20}$ Sunny Celt 140$^{14}$ Auriate 135$^{3}$ | Had speed in reserve | 8 |
| s 152 | —— | —— | Mosby 152$^{8}$ Gowran 136$^{½}$ Me Broke 136$^{¾}$ | Drew clear with ease | 9 |
| b 118 | 12.50 | 84–11 | Speedy Contessa 115$^{¾}$ Trock 124$^{1½}$ Van Quest 119$^{¾}$ | Set pace, tired | 13 |

**Jan 30 Hia 3f gd .36⅗ b** **Jan 20 Hia 3f fst .35⅗ h**

long distances of these races: 1¾ miles, 1⅞ miles, 2 miles, etc. These long distances are indications of jump races. Note too the larger weights carried, upwards of 150 pounds. Weights of this magnitude are not carried by horses racing on the flat.

And so—when you see a Belmont Park horse, as this one is, who has raced in Maidens Special Weights and Allowance competition and has won impressively, as this one has, and who is entered today in a Claiming Race at a lesser track, as this one is—before you dash down to the betting area and start shoving all your money through the window, make sure that all those impressive races you saw in the paper were on the level. (Ouch.) Oh, well. Make sure the horse has been racing and not jumping; a jumper is a poor risk in a running race. Notice his odds when he turned up at Tropical Park in a Claiming Race for $12,500: 86.15-1.

And speaking of odds—we now have the one remaining classification of horses to consider: limbo. How do you know when a luminary from the County Fair circuit is entered at a bona fide race track? How is one to know when a horse is trying to raise his snoot up out of the abyss of limbo?

It's very simple. If the horse has been racing where there is no betting, then he will have no odds on his chances of winning. Now observe Mosby's race of 24Sep60 which was run at a race course abbreviated "FH." We have no racing paper abbreviation "FH" in our list of race courses and that is a clue that the horse *may* be from some strange place. But the test for whether or not a horse is up from limbo is not whether or not his race course abbreviation is in our list. Our list covers only Eastern Racing and therefore you will frequently encounter race course abbreviations which are not in our list. The acid test for confirming or denying whether or not a horse has come from some strange brand of racing is to notice whether or not he had betting odds against his chances of winning. Look in the column of approximate odds for Mosby's race of 24Sep60 and you will see there aren't any. No odds = no betting. No betting = limbo.

As a last-glance observation, we will make the comment that the abbreviation "FH" in the above example stands for Far Hills Hunt, New Jersey. Notice that a horse from limbo does not necessarily have to be from Pennsylvania or Virginia or some other state where betting is illegal. Racing states such as Maryland and New Jersey also have some racing without betting.

One other note—the *Morning Telegraph* indicates in its Past Performances races which were solely for the females. All races, of whatever type, exclusively for fillies, or fillies and mares, are now designated as such by the symbol "f." Examples: f-Allow, Allowances (fillies); f-2500, Claiming $2,500 (fillies); f-M4000, Maidens. Claiming $4,000 (fillies); f-Md. Sp. Wt., Maidens Special Weights (fillies); f-Ladies, Ladies Handicap (fillies and mares), etc. And so—if you should see some of these "f" symbols in the Past Performances of a *colt*—you'd better keep your eye on that rascal; he's pretty shifty.

And there you have it, friends. Now you should be able to read a racing paper and know what all the little marks mean. Well, maybe not *all* the little marks; when we get into the next chapter on handicapping, we will weed out a lot of those little marks which we don't really need. This chapter dealt with *how* to read a racing paper; the next chapter deals with *what part* of it *to* read.

### ADDENDA

The following changes have been made in the racing papers since this chapter was written:

1. The single dagger (†) indicating a mutuel field, the double dagger (‡) indicating an entry, and the diamond (♦) indicating a claim—all formerly used by the *Telegraph* —have been discontinued. Now *both* racing papers indicate a mutuel field by placing a small "f" after the odds, an entry by placing a small "e" after the odds, and the fact that a horse was claimed by placing a small "c" in front of the Claiming Price. Examples: 13.00f, 3.00e, and c4,000.

2. Both papers have changed the manner in which they reveal the age of a horse. Instead of giving the actual figure, they print instead the year in which the horse was foaled. Then to find the animal's age, simply subtract this figure from the current year. There, that's much better. I think we'll all agree with that.

# 8th. HANDICAPPING

FIRST we should define handicapping. *Webster's New Collegiate Dictionary* defines handicapping as a transitive verb meaning to place at a disadvantage. We will immediately chuck that version because if there is anything we do not want to do, it's to place ourselves at a disadvantage—although I once heard a cynic remark that the prime purpose in reading a *Racing Form* is to give yourself something to do in between races. There's always a wise guy.

We'll take a look at the *Morning Telegraph's* definition, which suits our purposes and which is rather all-encompassing:

*Handicapping:* Study of all factors in past performances determining relative qualities of horses in a race. These factors include distance, weight, track conditions, riders, past performances, breeding, idiosyncrasies of the horses, etc.

This is a most comprehensive, omnibus definition and just to allow for any loose ends, the "etc." was added. We'll make our own definition and make it shorter and to the point: *Handicapping*: Studying the past performances of a group of horses and deciding which one, if any, you believe to be superior to the others.

As in most matters of great import, there are two schools of thought as how to best deal with the problem. And here I do mean *thought*; I don't subscribe to the notion that tacking the list of entries up on the outhouse wall and throwing a dart at it is competently dealing with the problem. Neither is the hatpin technique, or any other by-guess-and-by-God procedure.

The first method of attacking the multiple problems involved is to use the time factor as the basis for all computations. This method is based strictly on speed, and adherents to this school of thought are referred to as speed boys.

I'm sure that using time as the significant figure for handicapping has some merit. I'm also sure that there are days when the speed boys cash a lot of tickets and yours truly is anxious to get the entries for tomorrow. I suppose their methods will grind out the anticipated 30% winners, as will mine. I am also sure that they will have winning streaks and losing streaks, good days and bad days. I'm very sure that they have fun kicking their speed figures around and that they assume a sickening smirk when a standout "speed" horse bears out the figures and wins easily at 10-1. I'm also sure that now and again their "speed" horse finishes away up the track and, to their way of thinking, for no apparent reason. And I'm absolutely sure that nothing I ever say here will cause them to junk their speed figures for another line of approach.

Now then, with all of that objectively stated introduction out of the way, I want to make the other side of the discussion known (which, as you may have gathered by now, represents my viewpoint). I have one statement to make that should alienate roughly 60-85% of all horse players. Up until now when I distinguished the front end of a horse from the back end, it was hard to dispute such a statement. And when I pointed out that a furlong was ⅛ of a mile, 220 yards, or 660 feet, it was hard to find fault with that. But, as we proceed along and opinions and conclusions must by the very nature of the topic become more subjective and slanted, we must at times set down some "principles" which are going to raise a hue and cry from among those of conflicting views who hold certain cardinal truisms to be sacred. Therefore, knowing full well that many people are going to disagree, I would like to make the statement: Time as a factor in handicapping a horse race doesn't mean a damn thing—nothing. (There will be a slight pause now while all those who disagree stop shouting.)

To repeat: Time as a factor in handicapping a horse race doesn't mean a damn thing—nothing. And for many reasons. First, *if* all horse races were run on concrete instead of on soils of various textures, then time as a factor could *possibly* be looked upon as having some significance. Better go back and make that "dry concrete" instead of just "concrete," since if we had varying degrees of wetness or dryness even with the stable base, we would again be trying to equate dissimilar factors. With a large field of well-shod horses swinging into a turn on wet concrete, the winner could very well turn out to be the one who managed to stay upright.

But horse races aren't run on concrete; they're run on dirt —all kinds of dirt: hard dirt, soft dirt, sandy dirt, etc.— all kinds. So what does that mean? Here's what it means.

In the preceding chapter you saw some figures listed in the Past Performances as "Latest Workouts." Basically there are three different kinds of workouts indulged in by the horses: breezing, handily, and driving. (There are others, but they serve only to confuse the issue.) "Breezing" means that the horse moved at a brisk pace, but with much speed in reserve. "Handily" means the horse was extended, but not to the utmost. "Driving" means the horse was "set down" to run about as fast as he can go.

Now with that information assimilated, I want to pass along a little tidbit of interesting racing wisdom that you can file away somewhere in the recesses of your vault of racing knowledge. To wit: A competent horse, when in form, and when on a fast track, should work out ⅛ of a mile in 12 seconds, handily, and should be able to maintain that pace for four furlongs. Thus:

| | |
|---|---|
| ⅛ | 12 sec. h. |
| ¼ | 24 sec. h. |
| ⅜ | 36 sec. h. |
| ½ | 48 sec. h. |

And then, since the horse is an animal and not a machine, the final figure for a good workout of ⅝ mile is 1:01, and not a flat 60 seconds, or 1 minute. Even a horse is given some leeway.

Knowing that, the next point is that fractional running

times in actual races are all faster than the workouts—a statement which makes much sense; the horse moves faster against competition than he does when running against a stop watch. As an example, we'll look at the fractional times given in Noble Turn's winning effort at 5 furlongs:

> At the ¼:   22⅘   (And not 24)
> At the ½:   46   (And not 48)
> 5 Furlongs:   59   (And not 1:01)

In this particular race the 59 seconds flat tied the track record. And now here's the point of all this background material: Out in California, where the real "pasteboard" tracks are, horses can *work out* 5 furlongs in 58 seconds, or even less. In other words, given a hard enough racing surface, one group of horses can record faster times during their morning practice sessions than a second group can record during their actual competition. Are the horses in California that much better? I think not.

Using a California track for comparison took us outside the scope of Eastern Racing for a moment. California was chosen, since the race courses out there when compared to those in the East show the greatest variations in times. But there are also differences among the many tracks in the East.

And then there's the weather. At times it rains. Then the sun shines. The upshot of these meteorological phenomena is that a "good" racing strip in the morning, through the medium of a hot July sun, may dry out 2 seconds' worth between the first and the seventh races. And so, comparing times of different horses at the *same* track is likewise folly.

And then there's the work angle. Most horse players

are inherently very lazy. They do not choose to labor and toil. They always want a system, some effortless, mechanical, thoughtless process whereby they drop a series of figures into a computing device (possibly a cocked hat), turn a crank, the name of the winning horse pops out, and they wind up with money all over the floor. Sad, but true, things just don't work out that way. However, and again it's a big however, I see no point in intentionally putting work into something that was meant to be fun in the first place. Using time and speed and speed ratings is too much work for me.

For instance—to give you some idea as to how much work and sweat the speed boys must expend, we'll take a peek at their methods. First off, they note the distance of today's race; we'll take 6 furlongs as an example. Then they find the fastest time recorded by each of the entrants for 6 furlongs. (The *Form* saves them some time here by listing this information at the beginning of the Past Performances for each race, as noted in the preceding chapter. The fact that one, or two, or half, or all of the horses entered may never have raced 6 furlongs before may complicate things right here at the outset, but such contingencies are to be expected around a race track.) Having found the horse's best time for 6 furlongs, which may have been run 2 months ago, they then proceed to give a speed rating figure for each fractional time and a final speed rating figure found by adding the first three. Naturally, the faster a horse runs, the higher his speed rating, and the final choice for the race is the horse with the largest figure. The exact figures as to just how much speed is worth how many points is the deep, dark secret of the speed boys themselves, and they guard their little black books of figures with about the same secrecy and care the Norden bombsight received during World War II, which is certainly their privilege.

To return to our example—they find the fastest race ever run by the horse at 6 furlongs; note his time during this race for the $\frac{1}{4}$ mile. This time figure is worth "X" number of points. Then the figure for the $\frac{1}{2}$ mile is noted and another "X" number of points is recorded. One final tabulation for the final time of the race; then all three figures are added together and there is that horse's "speed rating" for that race.

Where does all the work come in? Well, the time at the $\frac{1}{4}$ mile is listed as 22$\frac{4}{5}$ seconds—at which time the horse under consideration was running 5th by 5 lengths. Remember, the 22$\frac{4}{5}$ seconds applies only to the horse that was running *first*. This horse is not first; he is 5th and is 5 lengths behind. What is his time for the $\frac{1}{4}$ mile? Well, don't despair; it's all been figured out. Add $\frac{1}{5}$ second for each length the horse is behind. Time of front runner: 22$\frac{4}{5}$ seconds. Speed horse is 5 lengths behind; add $\frac{5}{5}$ seconds—1 second. The time of the speed horse at the quarter mile is 23$\frac{4}{5}$ seconds. When this figuring is done, you have one fractional time for one horse; each horse has 3 fractional times; there are as many as 12 horses in each race, 8 or 9 races a day.

Now there is the "speed boy" with all his figuring done; his eyes are all bloodshot; he has writer's cramp; he's gone through 2 pencils and 4 tablets. But, he's ready. He's out at Bowie just itching for action. He's got a horse in the first race with a speed rating of 857, and the closest rating to that figure is a measly 710. The fact that all his speed rating figures for his standout horse were computed on a race run 2 months ago at Tropical Park, which is a fast track, and today we are at Bowie, which is a slow track, and the fact that the speed horse earned his rating while carrying 109 pounds and today is toting 122 pounds, and the fact that the speed horse raced his previous "speed" race over a fast track and the track today is listed as being "good," and the fact that the "speed" horse has raced at Bowie only once before and finished a distant 9th, and the fact that the speed race was a Claiming Race for $2,500 and today's race is a Claiming Race for $3,500, and a few other extraneous details—all mean nothing. The speed boy wants speed, and this horse has shown just that—speed. Even when the speed horse finishes away up the track, the speed boy is sure there must have been a mistake in his arithmetic—his speed horse just couldn't have been that bad. Besides that he has a horse in the 2nd race just as good as the one he had in the 1st race.

I'll even go back and make some concessions to the speed horse. This time the track will be the same, the track condition will be the same, the weight carried will be the same; everything will be the same as the day he compiled his speed race—with one exception. His speed race must have been a Claiming Race for $2,500, and today's race must be a Claiming Race for $10,000. And once again there is no doubt in my mind that Mr. Speedball is going to finish away up the track, whatever his standout speed figure may have been.

I'll cite one example. One morning up in Suffolk Downs a $5,000 Claimer shook the cobwebs out of his system by working out ½ mile in 47 seconds, driving. That's racing time at Suffolk. The trainer got carried away by such a display of speed and entered the horse in an Allowance Race against some of the best horses on the grounds. The Plater ran true to form; he started off last, held his position, and finished right there. He struggled in a distant last—beaten 33 lengths. I don't know what his speed rating figure was on that particular race since he was being timed through the final furlong with an eight-day clock. Nothing unusual about that; he had no business being in such a race in the first place. But what was unusual about the race was that the time for the first ½ mile was 47 seconds. Now how could a horse work out ½ mile in 47 seconds, and then run in an actual race in which the first ½ mile was clocked at 47 seconds, and not be running first? Or, if not running first, at least running up there somewhere in contention, anywhere but flat last. To finish the example—the horse's next start was in a Claiming Race for $5,000 and he win by 2, making it look easy all the way. Or, in other words, the gist of the thing is that how fast a horse can run in one particular race or during one isolated workout is not nearly as important as is his *proper placement* in racing competition.

Or—to look at it from another angle—if a horse is in form and is ready to run his race and is properly placed so as not to be hopelessly overmatched, then he can be expected to perform to advantage. Now the problem is still what it was in the first place—how does one know when a horse is properly placed? Or, in the vernacular of the $2 punter, "What in the hell horse is gonna win?"

·One method of determining the answer, as we have already stated at some length, is to use time as the measuring device. Which horse runs the fastest? And, again, to my way of thinking, this approach is founded upon fallacy.

Well, if time is unimportant and useless in handicapping horses, what is important? What is the yardstick of comparison? The answer is "class." What is "class"? Well, every other turf authority has defined class at one time or another, and I may as well take my crack at it. *Class*: The inherent ability of a superior horse to win over a group of inferior horses.

To illustrate: A $2,500 Claimer running in a Claiming Race for $1,750 would be the class of the race. Conversely, a $3,000 Claimer racing in a Claiming Race for $6,500 would be outclassed.

Now that makes everything relatively easy to pick a winner—all you have to do is determine which horse has been running in the highest-priced races and doing the best, or which of the horses under consideration is in form and possesses the most class?

Of course, a second survey may reveal the problem to be a bit more complex than initially estimated. For instance, that little part "which horse has been running in the highest-priced races" is a bit of a pitfall in itself. And, friends, the whole proposition goes back to the chart of race tracks on page 49. If you do not have some kind of working knowledge with that chart, then you are never going to know what's going on when you visit your local oval. If you do not know that the horses campaigning at Churchill Downs are inherently superior to those racing at Miles Park, and that a $3,500 Claimer from Charles Town is overmatched in a Claiming Race for $3,500 at Saratoga, and that a losing horse from Hazel Park commands new respect when he steps out on the track at Weymouth Fair, and a few hundred other possibilities of stepping "up" or "down" in class, even at the same Claiming Price level, among all the various tracks—then you are never going to know what's going on. And when you do go out to the races, I suggest you take only a few dollars and look forward to an afternoon of laughs and a few beers, and, as a necessary corollary to such levity, plan on forfeiting your few dollars—by default. And even if you should luck onto a big-paying winner, your plight will only be worsened, since you will then be comparable to the 100+ golf duffer who quite unexpectedly smacks a 4 iron 170 yards to within 1-putt distance of the cup. After a momentary flush of accomplishment his whole game progressively goes from bad to worse as he labors around over the course trying to figure out how he ever pulled off such a shot.

About here I would like to cite another quote from *Across the Board* to let it be known that I do not stand alone in this relegation of time to the role of an unimportant sidelight:

Among handicappers one of the greats, if not the greatest, for my money, is Fred Keats. . . .

There are two basic schools of handicapping. One uses time and the other class. Time handicappers, or speed chart men, argue, "What else can you adopt as a basis for class except time?" But Keats answers that a horse who will run in fast time against cheap company will lose in slower time in better company. Also, an ordinary horse that is in form and has won over the track will beat a better horse that is out of form and hasn't been over the track. Horsemen grade horses according to their value in dollars, and that may range from as little as $100 to more than $100,000.

As a member of the class handicapping school of thought, I would like to call particular attention to the statement: "A horse who will run in fast time against cheap company will lose in slower time in better company." That's true. Very true.

But how can it be that a horse can run 6 furlongs in 1:11 and win for $4,000, and then come back and run in a Claiming Race for $7,500 and lose when the winner's time was 1:11⅖? This apparent paradox brings us to the factor of *pace*. Or, "It isn't what you do; it's the way that you do it." And pace is the manner in which a race is run.

To show how pace represents the way in which something is done and not how fast it was done, we will abandon the horses and the races for a moment and investigate a hypothetical race and some hypothetical time trials, or workouts. This is to be a footrace between 2 boys; one boy is muscular and strong for his age, the other one is on the dinky side. Both are preparing for a race in which each will carry a 100-pound dumbbell a distance of 100 feet.

In his final pre-race tune-up little "Sickly," with much huffing and puffing, made the 100-ft. distance in a sparkling 20 seconds. His final stride was a desperation-like lunge to get the dumbbell over the finish line before it threw him down.

The second entrant in his final practice session flipped the dumbbell up on his shoulder and read a comic book as he loped along. Even this casual tempo was slowed down even further when he stopped to chat with some friends. His final "workout" was a lengthy 2 minutes.

And now comes the race. Which one to bet on? One has a final workout of 20 seconds; the other has a final workout of 2 minutes. Easy to pick the winner.

The race was run and as impossible as it may seem, little Sickly was never a factor at any stage of the contest. He lost rather convincingly. The winner's final time in the race was 30 seconds, or 10 seconds slower than little Sickly had done in practice. Sickly's final time in this race? I guess we'll never know, since the dumbbell became too unwieldy during the heat of competition, fell on his toe, and made him limp off the track a beaten man in more ways than one. He hasn't finished yet.

And it's the same with horses. You do not need to be concerned with how fast they have worked out or with how fast they have happened to run in one particular race a couple of months ago. What you do need to know is where they have been racing and for how much. Should a $2,000 Claimer try to match strides with a $6,000 Claimer, at some point during the race, the big horse is going to look the little horse in the eye and say, "OK, Cheapie, now that we have the feel of the track, let's run a while."

And little Cheapie shamefacedly retorts, "You tomfool idjit, I *am* running!"

At which time the class horse says, "If that's the case, Cheapie, then I have but one thing to say to you: 'Adios!' "

And away he goes—regardless of whatever their previous comparative times may have been. "It isn't what you do; it's the way that you do it."

And so, you see, the ridiculously easy task of determining which horse has the most class and has been doing the best is not as all-fired simple as a preliminary examination may have led you to believe. Assuming that you do know the relative merits of the different types of races run— Claiming, Allowance, Handicap-Stakes, and Non-winners —and assuming that you can correlate these different types of races with the different-caliber race tracks, Major and Minor—there are still some enigmas to overcome. That little phrase, "which horse has been doing the best" is also fraught with puzzlement.

For instance, you are out at Atlantic City and the race in question is a 6-furlong Claiming Race for $5,000. Two horses which figure well up in the race are:

> #1   Consistency Plus
> #2   Dropping Down

Here is an abbreviated Past Performance line showing the lastest race of each:

Consistency Plus
    Atl   6f   Clm 3,500   1   $1^1$   $1^2$   $1^4$   $1^4$   Easily   12
Dropping Down
    Atl   6f   Clm 7,000   5   $5^2$   $5^3$   $7^4$   $7^7$   No mishap   12

Which horse has been racing in the highest races? That's easy. Dropping Down has been racing for $7,000 while Consistency Plus has been competing in the $3,500 ranks. Which horse has been doing better? There's the joker. Is it better to win for $3,500 or to run in the middle of the bunch for $7,000? This is always and forever the riddle for the horse player to unravel. Is it better to gamble on a winning horse that is moving up, or is it better to gamble on a losing horse that is dropping down? As you sit there impaled on the horns of the dilemma, you may seek deliverance via an old backstretch proverb, to wit: "The same horses win and the same horses lose." Knowing that, the problem is quickly resolved and you are ready to go buy a hatful of tickets on good ol' Consistency Plus. About halfway down to the ticket window, you suddenly remember another, conflicting backstretch proverb which is just as authoritative and just as reliable as was the first, to wit: "Class will tell." And there you are—right back where you were, up a stump. Which one to pick? If you do pick one, you are more or less guessing and you will soon learn that such a racing selection was another thing the man had in mind when he said you could beat a race, but you couldn't beat the races. You may guess correctly in this race and then guess incorrectly in the next ten races. Your winning percentage of guesses should hover around 30%, which seems kind of low since with only two possibilities you should do better than that—say 50%. But it may surprise you to learn that there are going to be some few races in which *neither* of your last two choices wins. There *are* other horses in the race.

I will add this little thought to aid you in your deliberations regarding the poser as to whether it is better to bet on a winning horse moving up the equine scale of values, or whether it is better to risk your chances on a losing horse that is dropping down the scale: A horse who won his last race figures to win any race he is entered in today. After all, the horse can't improve on a winning effort; he did all that was asked of him. Therefore, if he won his last race, whatever the value, then he figures in today's race, whatever the value. Albeit, just how well he figures to win in today's race may be infinitesimally small.

And then, we can apply the antithesis of the above generality. A horse who ran last in his latest effort *may* not figure to win at any price. Finishing last is most assuredly not much of an indication of merit—whatever the value of the race. Here are examples to illustrate the different situations:

Today's race: Clm 3,500
Big Winner
　Clm 3,000　　2　$1^1$　$1^2$　$1^4$　$1^4$　Easily　12

Big Winner certainly figures well up in today's race. He ran and won easily for $3,000; today's race shows an increase in value of only $500, and $500 shouldn't break his back, although it might. Some high jumpers clear 6 feet by 6 inches of daylight, then raise the bar ½ inch and can't get over it to save themselves.

Today's race: Clm 3,500
Just Made It
　Clm 1,500　　2　$1^1$　$1^{\frac{1}{2}}$　$1^h$　$1^{nk}$　Long hard drive　10

Now you can see that Just Made It may not figure seriously in today's Claiming Race for $3,500. In his $1,500 race it was a struggle from flag fall to finish. Today the ante has been upped $2,000, and such an increase may represent an insurmountable obstacle. Then, on the other

hand, it may not. To return to the high-jumping event—
some jumpers clear 6 feet by ½ inch, raise the bar an inch,
and still clear it by ½ inch. Just where their true "breaking
point" is, is hard to tell. And so, if you did bet against
Just Made It in today's race and he again triumphed in a
long, hard drive, you couldn't look back at his last race,
another winning effort, and honestly say he had no chance.
Can't improve on finishing first.

Today's race: Clm 7,500
Way Back
Clm 8,000    8   9$^2$   10$^6$   12$^{10}$   12$^{12}$   No speed   12

Way Back just finished 12th in a 12-horse field. Poor.
Dropping down $500 worth for today's race is not signifi-
cant. It's going to take more than a drop of $500 to make
him a contender. But—suppose today's race had been
Clm $2,000? How now, brown cow?—or horse, as the
case may be. Now we have to hedge a bit. Is he now properly placed and able to win? Or is he actually a horse that
has "gone bad" and isn't going to win at any price?

The examples given here made no reference to a specific
race course, a generalized "phantom track" was sufficient.
But in reality, when the tracks themselves and their relative
merits are brought into play, wider extremes can be reached
—in both directions.

For example—a winner for $1,500 at Sunshine Park can
be looked upon as having no chance in an Allowance Race
at Hialeah. And a horse chronically running last for $7,000
at Belmont Park who suddenly pops up at Shenandoah
Downs running for $2,000 may not figure to run last.

About here you may be getting discouraged. Too many

tracks, too many races, too many horses, too many everything. The horses shift all around and create chaos. An Allowance horse at Cranwood isn't an Allowance horse at all when he is entered in an Allowance Race at the Big "A." High-priced Claimers out of Gotham move down to Delaware and give some of the best horses on the grounds a fit. A Maiden from a big track may find himself going postward as the betting favorite at a lesser track. Can't even use time as the great equalizer, since cheap horses will perform in commendable time against cheap competition and then finish nowhere against better horses—when the winner's time was slower than they had run previously. Is nothing sacred?

Isn't there some kind of quick and easy way to get a line on the entries in a race? Some short cut to separate the contenders from the garbage without too much effort and sweat? Isn't there some mechanical method to aid the novice? Some gambit to allow even a first-time visitor to have some indication as to what's going on?

And the answer is "Yes." It's as easy as copying numbers out of a book. In fact, that's exactly what you do—copy numbers out of a book.

In Baltimore there is a firm called the Montee Publishing Co., publishers of a monthly Turf magazine called *Turf and Sport Digest*. The magazine, in my opinion, has many features—some good, some not so good, some indifferent. However, in the back of the book there is a department which by itself makes the whole thing worthwhile, especially for the neophyte handicapper about to receive his baptism of fire from the deadly pari-mutuel machines.

*Turf and Sport Digest* features a "Rating Department." These ratings, basically, are very easy to use. If one works at it diligently, however, he can make their application to the races a most complex ordeal. The lazier horse players and/or the more experienced, who do not put too much credence in them anyhow, have no such problem. These two groups strive to keep the implementation of the ratings and their concomitant arithmetic at a minimum. Let's keep a day at the races a day of fun.

The rationale of the ratings is very simple. The best horse in the whole country is given the highest rating—145 or thereabouts. The second-best horse in the whole country is given the second highest rating—144 or so. And on down the line. At times, of course, there will be many horses with the same rating—115 as an example. Down from the 140 class to 130, 120, 110, 95, 85, 75, bottom.

Now the purpose here is not to go into a long dissertation on the use and application of *Turf and Sport Digest* ratings; however, a few items about them will be mentioned. We'll make up a horse and call him Whiz-Bang, since that sounds like a good name. We will then use Whiz-Bang to illustrate a *Turf and Sport Digest* rating, and since we like to think that Whiz-Bang is a pretty fast-stepping horse, we'll give him a rating of 130 (pretty good).

You will recall that there are short races called Sprints and then there are long races called Routes. With that in mind—if Whiz-Bang happened to be a Sprinter, his rating would appear in the book as 130S. If a Router, 130R. And now I have to digress again.

When I was younger, *Turf and Sport Digest* had the same

distance symbols, "S" for Sprinter and "R" for Router. When using the ratings, if a horse happened to be misplaced as to his proper distance preference, then an adjustment was made in his rating—on the debit side. Also the versatility group had recognition—horses which can race well at whatever the distance asked. Such horses had the symbol "A" after their names, thus: 130A. Such a horse held his rating whether the distance today was 5 furlongs or a mile and a half. And again, to lend symmetry to the various distance classifications, horses which couldn't do well at any distance were tabulated by omission from the list.

But we must progress. And *Turf and Sport Digest,* as a twentieth-century organization striving for perfection, junked such a fine premise and introduced an improvement in the name of progress. And so—the symbol "A" has been scrapped; nothing superseded it; it has simply been cast away. The ratings henceforth decided that no one horse could do well at all distances. Exterminator must tremor in his sepulcher to learn that members of his aristocracy here in the age of specialization must train and point for only one distance classification. But I digress.

The result of it all is that a new symbol has been put into vogue: "M." (I think this stands for Muddled.) And now the distance symbols for *Turf and Sport Digest* ratings mean:

S:   Horse does well in distances up to and including 7 furlongs.
M:   Horse does well in distances up to and including $1\frac{1}{16}$ miles.
R:   Horse does well in distances of $1\frac{1}{16}$ miles and over.

There is no penalty for a horse that is obviously misplaced as to his proper distance. You just pays your money and you takes your chance. I will mention that of the two misfits, a sprinter in a long race and a router in a short race, the sprinter asked to go a distance has the better chance of success. For this reason—the early speed, fleet-footed sprinter, if he has any worth at all, will be in front at one stage of the race anyhow. He should immediately go to the front, open up a long lead, and get out there winging. Then as to whether or not he can hold off the late-charging plodders is doubtful. He'll be backing up through the stretch, but he may make it. The slow-starting router, on the other hand, has almost no chance in a short race. About the time he gets running smoothly and is ready to make his late surge to the wire, the race is all over and the speedsters are easing up and turning around for the unsaddling procedure.

Many uninformed handicappers at times note that a router is usually in front for a mile or so in his long races only to falter and finish 9th or 10th. The theory is to play such a horse when he drops into a short race—at the same class figure, Claiming $3,000 as an example. And sure enough, there's ol' Pace Setter in the very first race, a sprint of only 6 furlongs. Today he'll make it all the way for sure.

And then much to their astonishment, Pace Setter breaks last, passes a tired horse or two in the stretch, and again finishes 10th. Where did all that front running early speed go? Well, Pace Setter's early speed didn't go anywhere; he didn't have any. In long races the early stages are waiting games of pace and position; any slow-footed also-ran can sprint to the front and cut out the pace. However, at about the ¾ pole the race starts in earnest. It's time to run.

And right about here is where Pace Setter's troubles began. At the ½ mile pole he would suddenly falter; at the ¼ pole he was in reverse, and through the stretch he was looking for a place to sit down. Therefore, to place him in a short race, where the race starts with the first jump out of the gate, his inability to win a horse race for $3,000 will only be brought into focus more quickly and more positively. The window dressing of his being in front for a while is abandoned. He's an also-ran and shows it immediately.

This reasoning *does not apply* to a *sprinter* who has been running with the front runners in his *sprints* only to weaken and finish 4th or 5th. This horse is running with the speed from the beginning in a speed race. Assuming he is not a *chronic* quitter, which would show in his Past Performances, this horse has simply been a little short but is coming to form and is getting ready to crack down, especially if he drops down the scale a bit.

It is not impossible for a horse to lay off the pace a bit in a short race and then make a late rush; not all sprinters run full blast from start to finish. And we already know that many horses will be making a late rush in a long race. With that in mind, we will point out that everybody likes to have as his betting choice the horse who suddenly looms up into contention in the run down the stretch. The "Beetle-baum" who up until this point hasn't gotten a call, but who is now passing one horse after another as he makes his belated bid to nip them all right at the wire. I know of no greater thrill than to see my personal choice come from "out of the clouds" and pass all the tiring front runners in a stirring stretch drive, especially when the price is right.

However, as thrilling as it is, the rush of a stretch-running horse is not the best betting risk.  Such a horse has many disadvantages to overcome—the front runner may have kept a little something extra in reserve; traffic problems on the homestretch turn and through the stretch may hinder the late charger and nullify his finest effort; he may try to come through on the rail and get shut off; he may be forced to take the "overland route," the extreme outside, and simply not have enough time and distance left to catch the front runner.  Many things can happen.  So, when choosing between a stretch runner and an early speedster, the odds are in your favor with the front runner.  He has nothing between him and the finish line except space; all he has to to do is hold on.  Unfortunately, there is nothing more disgusting than to have to stand there and watch your front-running speedster quit cold in the stretch.  You see the advantage of your horse over the second horse getting smaller and smaller.  You look up to the finish line and it looks like it's one hell of a way up there; maybe somebody moved it back.  Frustration, there's nothing you can do but stand there and watch your choice lose—inch by heart-rending inch.  Damnation.  Next time play the stretch runner.

So much for distance.  Another important factor is weight.  The ratings in the book are "raw" ratings and have to be refined commensurately with the amount of weight the horse is being asked to carry.  The formula for the weight adjustment is not too complicated:  In sprints, races up to and including 7 furlongs, subtract 1 point for each 3 pounds over 100 the horse is to carry.  In routes, races

1 mile and over, subtract 1 point for each 2 pounds over 100 the horse is to carry.

Now, you see, with this weight adjustment the horse with the highest rating initially may not wind up in the final analysis as the highest-rated horse. Example using a route of 1⅛ miles:

| Horse | Rating | Weight | Weight Adj. | Final Rating |
|---|---|---|---|---|
| Lead Lugger | 132R | 130 | —15 | 117 |
| Whiz-Bang | 130R | 110 | —5 | 125 |

Even though Whiz-Bang started out 2 points in arrears, he wound up with a bigger rating due to his 20-pound weight advantage.

A few words about the ratings—Each month *Turf and Sport Digest* magazine contains what is known as the Master List of ratings. During the course of a month, however, some horses will get better in their efforts and others will get worse. Revisions, therefore, must be made in the Master List. The publishers cope with this shifting-sands situation by then publishing a weekly revision list. This is a small paper called the *Turf Flash,* or—as it's better known around the track—the "Green Sheet," since for some reason it's green (possibly because green is a favorite color among horse players). And for the discriminating player, it is even possible to get daily rating revision service in lieu of monthly or weekly, just as a definitive precaution against slip-ups.

The very fact that the ratings change all the time only shows up their basic weakness. And many times the latest list of revisions only louses things up. For example, a horse has a rating of 125. He runs and loses. Loses again, and again. His rating will be lowered if he persists in this display of mediocrity. Now his rating is only 110, and then he suddenly runs true to his original rating and would have been the rating pick had it not been for his penalizing revision. It works both ways. Another horse has a rating of 90. Wins. Wins again, and again. Now he is rated 112. Now that his rating figure has caught up with him, he has passed his cycle of peak form and has tailed off—stale. And now this stale horse becomes the rating choice, when he wouldn't have been with the old rating list.

The rating revision lists are most helpful in that they assign ratings to horses which may have been omitted entirely from the Master List. A horse which hasn't raced in six months is dropped from the list; hence, in the spring you will have many fine horses returning to the racing wars —but they have no ratings. Weekly and daily additions and revisions remedy this shortcoming. A horse in today's entries, therefore, who has no rating at all, either has been idle for at least six months or hasn't raced well enough to earn a rating.

Another factor noted in the ratings is the horse's mud-running ability. And in this respect there are only two possibilities: good or bad. The horse is either a good mudder whose chances increase on an "off" track, or he dislikes running in goo and his performance is apt to be dull. Therefore, if the racing strip is muddy and a horse is noted as being a good mudder, his rating is increased 5 points. If the track is muddy and the horse is noted as being a poor mudder, his rating is decreased 5 points. If the horse has neither symbol, good or bad, then it is assumed that the presence or absence of mud will have no effect on his running ability.

What is an "off" track? Picture if you will a race track under a hot summer sun. Hasn't rained in weeks. This is a fast track. If fast enough, a track record or two may be broken. Weather clear; track fast.

Then comes a summer rainstorm—short, quick, thorough. The racing surface is now under water. But—underneath that temporary veneer the track is still hard and firm. This racing surface is called sloppy, and all the term "sloppy" rightfully means is a fast track with water on it. The horses will be splashing a lot of water around and it wouldn't be too clever to stand too close to the rail in your Sunday-go-to-meeting suit. However, such a track condition has NOTHING to do with mud or with mud-running ability. All you need is a horse that isn't afraid of getting his feet wet. The times for races run on sloppy tracks will be very good—may tie a track record or two.

Then the next day it rains again, and again—a slow, steady downpour. The hard, firm racing surface is now soft and gooey but good. This is mud. The track condition is now termed muddy. Times for today's races will be very slow; may be a spill or two; footing is treacherous.

The rain is over; the sun is shining. The track is starting to dry out; albeit, it has a long way to go. The track is now said to be slow. Again, this is an "off" track and your selection must show some mud-running preference or ability.

In a day or two the mud is abating and now the track is said to be heavy. Still on the slow side—still need some mud-running ability.

More sunshine and the track is almost dried out. Now it's called good. All of the horses should now be able to stand up and the non-mudders in the ranks stop being at a disadvantage. With a little more sun the track will return to being fast, and it is precisely at this time, this drying-out interlude, that a track may speed up 2 seconds' worth between the 1st and 7th races.

Summary:

> Fast: Mud-running ability not a factor.
> Sloppy: Mud-running ability not a factor.
> Good: Mud-running ability no serious factor.
>
> Heavy ⎫
> Slow  ⎬ "Off" tracks; mud-running ability needed.
> Muddy ⎭

And lest I forget:

> Frozen track: Ice skates recommended.

And don't take the management's opinion as the gospel truth regarding the present track condition. (The current track condition will be posted in the infield.) If the sign says "sloppy" and you have reason to believe it's "muddy," you're portable; walk down to the rail and take a look. If they say the track is "good" and you hear horses squishing their way to the paddock for the first race, be suspicious; go look; it's free. The powers that be have an overwhelming tendency to minimize the existence of an "off" track. Instead, they glory in the ol' cliché: "Weather clear; track fast," even if it stopped raining only this morning after a prolonged two-week deluge. Off tracks are tantamount to "off" attendance and betting figures, and if there is anything the management does not want, it's declining attendance and money figures. That's show biz, too.

Since a horse player doesn't have enough irregular variables and elusive intangibles to plague him, race tracks have introduced a few more unknowns by staging races on the grass. Turf course track conditions are three in number: hard, firm, and soft. Hard corresponds with fast; firm with good, and soft with all the off track conditions. Now just how much significance is to be attached to the fact that a horse with a mud mark is about to race on a soft, grass course, whose squishy, waterlogged lack of resiliency may resemble the nether reaches of Okefinokee, is anybody's guess. So—lotsa luck.

How does the presence of mud affect one's handicapping technique? The answer is, "Damn little." You proceed in a perfectly normal fashion and arrive at what you believe to be the best horse, and then, *and only then,* do you check his mud-running ability. If the horse has a mud mark after his name, or if he shows a winning race or a creditable "off track" race in his Past Performances, then his selection stands. If his chances are apparently jeopardized by the presence of mud, then you muster up all the strength of your convictions and utter the two most difficult words in a horse player's vocabulary, "I pass." And in 20 minutes or so there will be another race.

To work the problem backwards is bordering on lunacy. To make some glue-footed, outclassed, down-in-the-mouth chronic also-ran your choice solely on the basis of a mud mark after his name makes no sense—at least not to me. Granted there are many "form reversals" in which an habitual loser suddenly runs a smasher in the mud. But a hopelessly misplaced horse isn't suddenly going to make like Man o' War just because it rained last night. Not for my money he isn't. For my money the horse is going to have to figure to win and then, *and only then,* demonstrate *in addition* some mud-running ability, and not be some rank outsider who suddenly becomes the choice solely on the basis of the fact that he has a mud mark after his name.

And about those mud marks in the racing papers—there will be times when you see a horse labeled by the *Form* and/or *Telegraph* as a mudder and yet all his races on off tracks as shown in his Past Performances, to put it mildly, leave a lot to be desired. Finished way back. From experience I have found that most likely in all of those races in which horses with mud marks finished way out of it when racing in the mud, they most likely would have also finished way out of it had they been racing on a cloud. So you acquiesce and go along with the racing papers' decisions. Do *not* alter or try to censor their allocations of mud marks. If they say he's a mudder, he's a mudder. And you believe it.

In the next chapter, which deals with betting, you, as a student, will be given an assignment to carry out on your first day at the track. And since this assigned task does not represent what we might call a "full day," here is another little supplemental chore I want you to do. For one race on the program, and it doesn't matter a whit which one, I want you to secure as a vantage point to view the race a location as near the homestretch turn as you can get. Stay off the track; you don't have to get that close;

I don't want you to wind up trampled under the thundering herd. But I do want you up at the head of the stretch so that you can observe the field of horses as it swings around the turn and heads for home. And yes, I know that in your poorly chosen "railbird" position you won't be able to see who wins, but that's beside the point. I want you to see how those flighty, high-strung, hard-headed thoroughbreds battle it out through the final turn—the last chance to gain position—from here on in it's RUN, you cotton picker! Watch how the front runner labors to hold his advantage; notice the lead jockey employing all the "tricks" at his command to keep his tiring mount up front—whether it be hand riding, whipping, offsetting the horse's tendency to lug in to the rail, preventing the horse from drifting out wide on the turn, or whatever. Note the second horse. He has been second for a while and is now trying to head that last horse; or, he has been second for a while, is running out of gas himself, and is now in a struggle to salvage second place. Ditto for the third horse. Other horses will have been off the pace up to this instant and are now being set down for the drive to the wire. No more dillydallying; there's no time. And then there's a "Beetlebaum" or two who up until this point have been away out of it—and their attitude is that *all* of those front runners will come to naught because they have been waiting for this precise moment ever since the race started. Listen to the jockeys as they chastise their mounts to make them run just a little bit faster; listen to the whips smacking against genuine horsehide, the hooves pounding, the roar of the crowd.

And then I want you to discount all the grunt-and-groan

effort you have just witnessed and rest assured that you already know which horse will win—#3. And why #3? Because some turf expert sitting at a desk back in Baltimore gave #3 a *Turf and Sport Digest* rating of 95, and the nearest thing to that figure was a little ol' 93. The eventual outcome was a foregone conclusion all the time. Doesn't make much sense, does it?

With all that introduction in mind, I want you to be fully aware of the fact that *Turf and Sport Digest* ratings are only adjuncts to handicapping and not a final, cut-and-dried, sure-fire, winner-producing system. The fact that an expert, or a board of experts, rated one horse 95 and the others 93 or less does not mean that an easy victory for the highest-rated horse is a certainty. Hardly. There are many factors, and the horse's rating is only one of them. However, if one of the horses in the race is rated 112 and all the rest are wallowing around in the 90's, then that one horse most surely at some time, somewhere, must have done something and his chances of success in today's race should be investigated.

Here is an excerpt from *Turf and Sport Digest* magazine under the heading: "How To Read *Turf and Sport Digest* Ratings and How To Use Them":

You will soon learn to proceed with a further analysis of the relative merits of each horse, the playability of the race, the rider, distance ability, and other determining factors . . . and *you'll be doing your own thinking* . . . not blindly following someone else's opinion.

In other words, the Montee people want to be as honest as possible. They say something to the effect, "Here are our ratings and they are as good as we can make them; albeit, as good as they are, they too are a little short. Take them for whatever they're worth. And remember; they are meant to be a help, not a panacea."

And now for a few comments on the positive side about *Turf and Sport Digest* ratings. Many horse players when they reach a certain age of turf maturity begin to desert the supposition that a day at the races is meant to be a day of fun. They haven't been having too much fun anyhow, dropping all those defunct mutuel tickets all around the premises and littering up the place. Too many sawbucks have been sacrificed on the altar of entertainment; too many well-backed steeds of their choice have finished in the ruck; too many photos went the wrong way; too many trips have been made to the well only to come up empty. In fact this horse player's entire campaign at the local oval is now bordering on the brink of being a complete financial calamity, and the whole rotten spectacle of a bunch of horses going around a track has degenerated into being about as funny as a busted crutch. The awful truth is that this punter's eagerly sought after Midas touch has now taken on most cursed overtones. In short, this man is up against it.

But is he discouraged? Never. He'll see that ticket seller in hell first. He now takes on what we might call the "Also-Ran Syndrome." He sets his chin at an obnoxious angle, always surveys his environment through a somewhat mesmerized stare, and if he ever laughs, it always comes out sounding like the confidence inspiring chuckle of a Digger O'Dell.

For this man's sake I hope he gets some winners—but actually he isn't interested in winners anymore; he's interested in *losers,* and how to avoid them. Since latching onto winners can be a painstaking, trying task, the avenue of thought to increase his over-all percentage of winners per selection is to avoid all those discomforting and bankroll-reducing clusters of losers. Such a bit of reasoning is fundamentally very sound. To skip off to another sport again— the great Tommy Armour, after years of the keenest competition, pointed out in one of his instructional golf books that the margin of victory in golf tournaments was not how many *good* shots a player could hit during the course of a round, but rather, how many *bad* shots he did *not* hit during the course of a round. The aspiring links champion would not be called upon to exhibit some sort of golf wizardry by successfully playing a ball which was lying under 2 inches of water if he hadn't hit the damn thing into the water in the first place. The whole wretched mess could have been so much easier if he just hadn't hit that heart-rending, round-house slice that plopped the ball into the water. And by golf tournament here we do not necessarily make reference to the Masters; the same line of reasoning applies to all golfing echelons—right on down to the Sunday Morning Duffers Club.

And so our mythical horse-playing friend here is starting out on a program dedicated to the proposition that all losers must be avoided. And he sets out to implement this program with rules—all kinds of rules. Each rule is designed to eliminate some quantity of what were heretofore most hazardous risks, which have demonstrated rather unfailingly a tendency to wind up in the lost column.

Rule 1: Do not bet on jump races. A most sensible rule. God knows there are enough uncertainties in a horse race already without the horses having to jump over fences and/or hurdles. Since this book deals only with thoroughbred *running* races, such hedge-hopping contests were not even considered in the first place.

Rule 2: Do not bet on any untried 2-year-olds. Nothing to go by here in the way of Past Performances, and the whole thing is reduced to a guessing game of the first order.

Rule 3: Do not bet on any horse that has been idle for six months. Anything may have happened in six months. The horse most likely will return to the races a little "short" and is a poor risk.

Rule 4: Do not bet on any Maidens. The reasoning here is that since the horse has never won a race in his life, there is little or no reason why he should win today.

And on and on. Our friend can make all the rules he wants. If he applies himself diligently, he may succeed in ruling himself right out of action. At least then he will have eliminated all those troublesome losers. There is nothing wrong with making rules. Before this chapter is over, I too will make a list of what I call simply "Horses to Avoid."

But here's the point to all this build-up about rules—it's the ratings again. The very beauty of it all. With the ratings you can play any race you choose, no limitations, except—and it's a big "except"—there will be many instances of many races and many horses where the ratings indicate "No play." For instance, all the horses which were the target of the preceding list of rules as set down by our disgruntled loser have already been weeded out and nixed by the ratings. Jumpers have no ratings; untried 2-year-olds have no ratings; horses which have been idle for six months have no ratings; Maidens *may* have a rating. Should the Maiden in question be entered in a Maiden race, then we can proceed as usual; if the Maiden in question is not entered in a race for non-winners, then his rating will indicate whether he has any chance or not.

Besides enlightening the beginner as to what races to shun altogether, the ratings also let you know just what kind of race horses you are handicapping during any one particular race. For example, if the highest-rated horse in the race being studied has a rating of 73, that's a pretty weak bunch of horses. Could have been worse, though, you understand, there will be races when none of the horses has *any* rating. If the horses are rated in the 90's, then you know they are a bit more expensive and a bit more reliable. Should the mean rating be in the 100's, you are getting up into the horses. All horses rated over 100 are OK. When the mean figure has risen to the teens and to the 120's—you are handicapping a horse race. Damn few horses will have a rating over 120, because by the time they have picked up enough raw rating to reach 130 and beyond, they will have also picked up enough lead from the racing secretary to bring their ratings back down due to the weight adjustment dictated by the use of the ratings.

And remember this—whatever you do—the ratings are an adjunct and not a Utopian vestige.

Another comment about *Turf and Sport Digest* ratings—away back there in the chapter dealing with jockeys I mentioned that there was a way to get an index as to the capabilities of the various jockeys. This too is done by *Turf and Sport Digest* magazine. The jockeys are also rated. And why not? If you can assign numerical ratings to an assortment of horses, you ought to be able to afford the same service to a group of hard-working men. And 'tis done. All the jockeys have been assigned ratings which serve as an index to their proficiency. And these figures too will fluctuate. Jockeys too have good months and bad months, hot streaks and cold streaks. Any jockey not listed in the ratings hasn't ridden well enough or long enough to earn one.

One final comment about *Turf and Sport Digest.* It will be a trite observation, but nevertheless it must be said. I have no affiliation with the Montee Publishing Company nor with *Turf and Sport Digest* magazine. The truth is, I don't even have a subscription to the periodical, but I *do* buy a copy now and again.

Of all the fund of information given by the racing papers in the Past Performances, what part of it is pertinent and important to the problem at hand? Here again is the Past Performance record of Promoters Dream, and this time when we run through it we will differentiate what information counts and what information is interesting but useless. A bit more than that—this will be a one-race, one-horse example of just how one goes about handicapping.

Here is the problem: On the 16th of March, 1961, Promoters Dream was entered in:

1ST RACE GULFSTREAM PARK
7 FURLONGS (Hornbeam, April 2, 1947, 1:22⅗, 7, 120.)   Out of

Chute. Purse $3,000. 3-year-olds. Claiming. Weight 121 lbs. Non-winners of two races since Feb. 8 allowed 2 lbs., in 1961, 4 lbs., a race, 6 lbs. Claiming Price: $4,000.

Which horse, of those entered for this race, can win a 7-furlong sprint at Gulfstream Park when the competition consists of 3-year-olds valued at $4,000?

The conditions of the race item by item:

1st Race Gulfstream Park: A very important item. We know immediately that we are dealing with a Major League track and with Major League horses. Horses that can't win here may be able to win somewhere else—in some lesser, more modest form of racing. The chances of some "big" horse being wheeled in from some "bigger" track are minimal since we are already in a fine level of racing; Gulfstream Park is the scene of the $100,000 Florida Derby—as an example. The horses here will be able to hold their own wherever they campaign; or, to put it another way, a $4,000 Claimer here will be a $4,000 Claimer anywhere, possibly more.

We now know that any horse we select to win this race will also have to be a Major Leaguer; or, if not, then his racing record is going to have to be bordering on the sensational side, 5 starts, with 4 wins and a second, or thereabouts. Any "speedy cheapie" up from Sunshine Park or Jefferson Downs, or any other lesser track, is going to have two strikes against him right here at the outset.

That's a good bit of information to assimilate just by reading the heading of the race in question.

7 FURLONGS: Very important. The length of the race. We need a sprinter who can carry his speed ⅞ of a mile.

An early speedster who is fleet but fainthearted won't do. A plodder who needs 6-7 furlongs to get started just won't do either. We want a horse that can break alertly and get right to the front, or one that can break alertly and pace himself just off the leader and then have some speed in reserve for his drive to the wire.

Hornbeam, April 2, 1947, 1:22⅗, 7, 120. Useless. Status-seeking. And who in the hell is Hornbeam? If he has a horn, let him go blow it. I'm not interested in what happened in 1947; I'm concerned with what's going to happen today. (This record no longer stands anyhow.)

Out of chute: Semi-important. This lets me know that the horses in the outside post positions, 9-10-11-12, will have an adequate chance to get to the front because they will have a long run on a straightaway and will not be eliminated by the fact that the field must immediately swing around a turn and thus leave them stranded on the outside rail. If the horse I choose is in the middle or on the inside rail, then the presence or absence of a chute should make no difference.

Purse $3,000: Useless. I don't own any horses and so the amount of loot put up by the track to be distributed amongst the winning owners does not interest me. I won't get any of it—no matter how much it is.

3-year-olds: Important. In this particular race since all of the entrants are 3 years old the possibility of your having to bet a 3-year-old against a 5-year-old (boy vs. man) is eliminated. No specification is made regarding sex, however, and the likelihood of betting a filly against a colt (girl vs. boy) is present. Three-year-olds will defeat older horses occasionally, and fleet fillies will at times best slow-footed colts, but any time you bet on such a supposition, there is the possibility that you are opening up an avenue of miscalculation. Try to keep all the percentages on your side.

Claiming: Very important. Now we know just what kind of race at a Major League track we are trying to handicap, a Claiming Race—or one of the many races offered for the cheapest horses on the grounds. The term "Claiming" should alert us to watch out for members of the Allowance ranks who are tired of chasing better horses and today are dropping down to meet weaker opposition. I don't think there will be any losers from the Handicap-Stakes classification. From Handicap-Stakes to Claiming $4,000 wouldn't be a drop; it would be more in the nature of a catastrophic plunge. If there are any entries in today's race who are coming off *winning* efforts in Allowance Races, then these Allowance Races must be of the Minor League variety and will have to be evaluated accordingly. A "speedy cheapie" is on the premises and is entered right where he belongs— in a Claiming Race. Either that or the horse has broken a leg since his latest effort.

Weight 121 lbs. Non-winners of two races since Feb. 8 allowed 2 lbs., in 1961, 4 lbs., a race, 6 lbs.

This information is not important. Except in this particular race and then only in an indirect way. These are the final conditions of the race as drawn up by the racing secretary. He is putting weight on winners and taking it off losers, penalizing the successful horses and aiding the failures. The exact formula for the weight assignments is not important—

whenever the racing secretary gets it figured out, the trainers of the individual horses will comply and the correct weights will be printed right on your program. You will have enough to worry about, so let those running the show worry about the precise weight assignments.

However, notice in these conditions that the word "Maidens" does not appear. Maidens are referred to only indirectly. This race is NOT designed specifically for Maidens. The conditions of this race allow the entry of both winners and non-winners. As you will recall, even our losing, out-for-blood friend, whom we discussed earlier, learned to shy away from Maidens—especially when they were entered against winners. Therefore, the result is that any horse we select in this race should show a winning effort *somewhere* in his Past Performances—even if it's been a long time ago. Any Maiden we consider will have to be convincing us pretty strongly that all of those failures of his were really not his fault and that today it will all be different. Or, like the "speedy cheapie" in today's race, all Maidens also have two strikes against them. Perhaps one type Maiden we might consider is the horse who has been up against it in races for Maidens Special Weights. A Claiming race for only $4,000 is a pretty cheap Claiming Race here at Gulfstream Park and hence a horse dropping down out of the "Handicap-Stakes" ranks for non-winners could conceivably be dropping down far enough to win. Albeit, if we bet on such a horse and then he goes out there and gets beaten and makes a rather sorry spectacle of himself in the process, we may be muttering to ourselves as we discard the worthless mutuel tickets, "Why did I ever bet that damn thing?"

Claiming Price: $4,000: Very important. This lets us know where we are in the type-of-race scheme of things, a Claiming Race for $4,000. It could have been cheaper— $3,500 or $3,000, and that's all the cheaper at Gulfstream Park. And it certainly could have been a hell of a lot more —up to $50,000. We are down in the lower strata of Major League racing. All we need to win this race is a so-so Claimer that can win on the Major League level for $4,000.

Summary:

> 1st Race Gulfstream Park
> 7 Furlongs. Out of chute.
> 3-year-olds. Claiming.
> Claiming Price: $4,000.

And those are the conditions of the race; or, as the man said, "Them's the conditions that prevail."

Now, friends, you *must* read the conditions of a horse race *before* you start doing any handicapping. Don't go looking through the Past Performances willy-nilly seeing which horse ran second the last time out, which one ran fourth, which one ran last, or any other factor you may deem significant, until *after* you first know exactly *what qualifications the winning horse must possess.* Trying to pick the winner of a horse race without first knowing what kind of horse race it is, is ludicrous and absurd.

Now that we know what kind of horse race we are trying to win, we will again look at a one-line version of the Past Performances of Promoters Dream and separate the relevant information from the trivia.

**Promoters Dream** $4,000  Ch g, 3, by Big Money—Exploitation
Arbywood Stable      M. A. Buxton
7Mar61–2GP   fst 7f .22⅘ .46  1.25⅖ Clm   5000  9  1  3² 3²  2²  54¼ JCulmo

Promoters Dream: Name of horse. Important only in an aesthetic sense. I guess it's sad but true, but with the advent of the pari-mutuel machine betting system, horses, like most modern people, progressed into a realm of quasi-anonymity. Now the horse too has a number. And the cry of yesteryear, "Up and at 'em, Aristides!" has now become a more mundane, "Come on, #4."

Promoters Dream has no mud mark after his name, but this is unimportant for today's race since the track is fast anyhow.

$4,000:   Today's Claiming Price. Very important. The horse is entered to be claimed for $4,000.

Ch:   Color of horse. Chestnut. Unimportant. I wouldn't care if a horse was purple, as long as he could run. About the only significance attributable to a horse of such a gaudy hue would be that he may forsooth be that horse of another color I've heard about so often.

g:   Sex. Gelding. Semi-important. With this horse we won't have a filly running against colts.

3:   Age. Unimportant in this race. The conditions of the race have made it mandatory that all the entries be 3-year-olds.

by Big Money-Exploitation, by Sky Raider: Pedigree. May be interesting but not too reliable—many high powered horses have sired many low-powered lemons. And as to just how fickle the fingers of genetic fate can be, it

y Sky Raider            **115**    1961   4   M   0   0    $100
        (H. G. Jones)         1960   0   M   0   0   ———
116   14.05   82–12   Miss Standish 106$2\frac{1}{2}$ Colonel Hastie 116$^1$ Arctic Pilot 115$\frac{3}{4}$    Tired 12

must only be remembered that Man o' War had a full younger brother who wasn't worth a damn.

Arbywood Stable:    Owner.

M. A. Buxton:    Trainer.    These two items can be important.    At all levels of racing there are owners and trainers who year in and year out get more than what we might call their "fair share" of winners.    In racing, as in anything else, the rich get richer and the poor play bingo. If you select a horse and then see he is trained by one of the leading trainers at the meeting, that's fine; that's another factor in your favor.    But don't turn the thing around and pick a horse only because he is trained by Henry Fine-touch of Moneybag Stables, Inc.    Even these big successful stables have been known to send out a loser now and then.

(H. G. Jones):  Breeder.  Unimportant.  The name of a high powered horse farm here (when studying a cheap Claiming Race—as this race is) means only that said high-powered horse farm decided to unload a lemon.

115:    Weight to be carried in today's race.    Very important.    We do not want to select any horse who has been "weighted out" by the racing secretary.    Exactly what we mean by a horse who has been "weighted out" will be touched upon when we make up our list of horses to avoid.

1961  4  M  0  0

1960  0  M  0  0:  A composite summary of the horse's racing efforts for the past two years.  Very important.

We will want to know the horse's in-the-money consistency rating and how many races he has won in the last two years. One word of caution about this "box score" summary—if the horse hasn't raced in two or three years, or even if he hasn't raced this year, the racing papers will simply publish in this space the summary of the horse's last two years of activity—whenever they were—two years ago, four years ago, or whenever. So—before using these figures for *anything*—make sure they refer to *this* year and *last* year. If a horse hasn't raced this year, then his in-the-money consistency rating becomes 00% for today's race, in spite of whatever he may have done two or more years ago.

$100:   Amount of money earned this year. Interesting. This figure can serve as another indication of the caliber of racing in which the horse has been engaging. One horse may show no wins and yet has earned $30,000, while another horse may show 5 wins and $4,000 earned.

7Mar61:   Date of last race. Important. This horse ran less than two weeks ago and we can assume he will run to his currently exhibited form.

2GP:   Race and track at which the horse ran his last race. THE SINGLE MOST IMPORTANT ITEM IN THE HORSE'S PAST PERFORMANCES. We now know *where* he has been campaigning—at a Major League track. In this instance, the very same locale as today's race. Fine.

fst:   Track condition when he ran his last race. Important, and it's the same as today's.

7f:   Distance of his last race. Important. Same as today's.

.22⅕  .46  1:25⅖:  Fractional times and final time of *winning* horse. Doesn't mean a damn thing. HERESY! HERESY!

Clm 5000:  Type of race and its exact value. Most important. Claiming Race. Claiming Price: $5,000. Compare to today's race: Claiming $4,000.

9:  Post position. Unimportant.

1  3²  3²  2²  5⁴¼:  A running description of the horse's latest effort. Most important. On the good side, it shows that he can get out there in a hurry. However, it also shows rather conclusively that he has a tendency to "die" in the stretch. He backs up pretty good. Seven furlongs may be too far.

And remember, when reading Past Performances, the superscript numbers indicate how far the horse was behind the *first* horse. The 5⁴/¼ means Promoters Dream finished 5th, 4¼ lengths behind the *winner*. That's important. To illustrate—here are the finish positions of two horses in two different races:

| #1 | Illusion | Clm 4,000 | 2⁶ |
| #2 | Up Close | Clm 4,000 | 4½ |

Which horse came closer to winning? That's easy; Illusion, because he finished second while Up Close was clear out of the money. Or did he *really* finish nearer the winner? Taking the generally accepted length of a horse as being 8 feet, we see that Illusion lost his race by some 48 feet. Up Close, on the other hand—in spite of finishing "clear out of the money"—lost his race by only four feet, ½ length.

So don't discount a horse's effort too quickly because he finished "out of the money"—see by how far he *actually* lost the race. And one more time . . . What's been said here does *not* apply when reading charts. And one other loose end that is kind of dangling—in reading Past Performances, since the superscript numbers indicate how far the horse is behind the lead horse, I might mention that in case the horse in question happens to be running first himself—then the superscript number indicates how far he is ahead of the second horse. Example: $1^1$ means the horse is running first and is one length ahead of the second horse.

JCulmone: Jockey. Just interesting. The substitution of a hotshot apprentice for an established jockey might mean something. Today's program shows us Promoters Dream will be ridden by William Hartack, so we certainly won't be lacking in the jockey department. I always like to assume that a trainer who is smart enough to get his horse ready for a winning effort will also be smart enough to secure the services of a competent jockey. And I know for absolutely damn certain that *no* jockey is going to win if he doesn't have enough horse under him.

b: Blinkers. Unimportant—unless you wanted the horse to wink at you on his way to the post.

116: Weight carried in his last race. Important. Compares favorably with the weight assigned today. Today we have 1 less pound to carry.

14.05: Betting odds to the dollar. Interesting. This figure points out the general public's opinion of the horse in his last race. Today's odds, as seen on the infield "tote" board, are only 3-1, which indicates the horse has picked up a lot of support.

82-12: Speed rating and track variant. Nothing. Heresy!

Miss Standish 106²½  Colonel Hastie 116¹  Arctic Pilot 115¾: Best Company line. Gives us the names of the first three horses on the day Promoters Dream finished 5th. Interesting.

Tired: Comment. Can be useful. Such observations as "Tired," "Weakened," "Close gap late," etc., may be obvious from looking at the description of the race; however, other happenings will not show in the running description. For example, you may see this: 1  1¹  1½  1½  4². This horse quit through the stretch after having led all the way. This looks very damaging to his character until you read the comment: "Lost whip." When barreling down the stretch and things are getting tough, it's no time to be losing your whip. Of course it is also possible that this horse may have quit cold and finished out of the money even if his rider had had two whips.

A winning effort may actually be marred by the comment: Example: 4  3³  2¹  1¹  1². A very good race. Win easy. Good show. And then comes the disturbing comment: "Finished lame." A poor risk in today's race; such a horse may not even make it around the track. Big win or no.

12: Number of horses entered in Promoters Dream's last race. This innocent little number too can be important.

After seeing in which position your horse finished, always make sure you note how many horses were in the race. Promoters Dream just finished 5th in a 12-horse field; that's pretty good; he beat most of 'em. But you may see a situation like this:

|  | Finish Position | Starters |
|---|---|---|
|  | $6^{20}$ | 6 |
| Mr. Also-Ran | $12^{12}$ | 12 |
|  | $12^{8}$ | 12 |
|  | $12^{15}$ | 12 |

Here is a horse, whom we've aptly named Mr. Also-Ran, who has been demonstrating an unerring ability to finish away out of it. Persists in running 12th. And then in his latest race he suddenly "improved," finishing 6th. A closer examination, however, will show he didn't improve a damn bit—the only reason he finally finished 6th instead of 12th was because in his last race there were only 6 horses running. Further, taking into account his total lengths off the leader, we now see that he actually did *worse* than usual in his latest effort. He had been staying within 10-12 lengths of the winner, but today he lose by 20.

LATEST WORKOUTS: Time trials. Nothing. Heresy.

Here is the Past Performances record of Promoters Dream in an abbreviated form; all extraneous material has been deleted:

## Promoters Dream    $4,000    115

| | | | | | | | | | |
|---|---|---|---|---|---|---|---|---|---|
| 7Mar61–2GP | fst 7f | Clm 5000 | 1 | $3^2$ | $3^2$ | $2^2$ | $54\frac{1}{4}$ | JCulmone |
| 1Mar61–4Hia | fst 6f | Md Sp Wt | 5 | $4^5$ | $6^9$ | $10^{18}10^{19}$ | | NBarnardo |
| 18Feb61–2Hia | fst 6f | Md Sp Wt | 6 | $5^5$ | $7^{10}$ | $9^{14}10^{13}$ | | EMonacelli |
| 28Jan61–3Hia | fst 6f | Md Sp Wt | 2 | $42\frac{1}{2}$ | $9^9$ | $9^{13}$ | $5^{17}$ | EMonacelli |

We can now study and evaluate this pertinent information and begin to estimate the chances of success of Promoters Dream in today's race. Does he meet the specifications as set forth in the conditions of the race? Is he the one horse we believe to be superior to the others?

First we will turn to the March issue of *Turf and Sport Digest* magazine and find his rating. Damnation. Promoters Dream isn't even listed. His program of being chosen as our selection just got started off on a sour note. The experts back in Baltimore are of the opinion that as of this date Promoters Dream hasn't done anything noteworthy enough to merit his inclusion in the list of rated horses. A sorry start. However, we won't condemn the horse as being an incorrigible only because he is unrated; horses without ratings have won before. It would be nice if he had a rating, but he doesn't have one, and that's the way things are. We must be cognizant, however, that already Promoters Dream may be standing on sinking ground.

Next we'll check to see how many races he has won this year: Zero. Zip. A bubble. Last year? Another bubble. He has those two damn "M's" in his two-year record. He hasn't won any races, anywhere, at any time. This horse is a loser running against winners and is quickly losing my favor.

What is his in-the-money percentage? There it is for the

| g, 3, | | | 1961 | 4 | M | 0 | 0 | $100 |
|---|---|---|---|---|---|---|---|---|
| Arbywood Stable | M. A. Buxton | | 1960 | 0 | M | 0 | 0 | — |
| 116 | 14.05 | Miss Standish 106²½ Colonel Hastie 116¹ Arctic Pilot 115¾ | | | | | | Tired 12 |
| 118 | 92.85 | Spartan Dip 118²¼ Camp Royal 118½ Fleet Together 118²¼ | | | | | | Tired 12 |
| 118 | 49.10 | Swing Span 118¹¾ Creswood Paul 118³ Fleet Together 118¹¼ | | | | | | No sp'd 12 |
| 118 | 121.85 | Silent Trade 118⁶ Outrigger 118⁴½ Commandeer 113⁵ | | | | | | Tired 11 |

whole world to see: 00%. More bubbles. No seconds. No thirds. No nothing. And this factor is very important because I distinctly remember hearing somewhere that the same horses win and the same horses lose.

The likelihood of this horse becoming our choice is fading like a $2.00 shirt; his entire semblance of superiority is falling apart like a house of cards.

But—we won't be narrow-minded; there are still two sides to everything. Let's remember the power of positive thinking; let's look at the good side of things—assuming there is one.

First off—*where* has Promoters Dream been campaigning? Florida. And not only Florida, but Hialeah—the #1 track of Southern Racing. That one little item alone raises his stock somewhat.

Secondly—what *kind* of races has he been running in? And there it is in black and white: Md. Sp. Wt. These first three races of Promoters Dream prove only that he had no business running with the best non-winners on the grounds. He demonstrated very clearly that he simply could not keep up with the fleet-footed steeds who have notions of joining the Allowance ranks ("several hundred others which are fair"), or perhaps even going on to the Handicap-Stakes division ("20 or 30 which are really good"). Promoters Dream could do no better in three tries than to get within 13 lengths of the winner. "Tired." "No speed." "Tired." But *do* note, and *do* take care to observe that in one of those races he finished 5th in an 11-horse field; or, in other words

—he actually *beat most of them*. Now when you combine that fact with the fact that he was racing at the #1 track in the South, in the toughest kind of race to win (for non-winners)—you can rest assured that on some fine day, at some race track, against weaker, cheaper opposition, Promoters Dream will find himself a bunch of horses he can beat. Have no fear.

So damn those races for Maidens Special Weights. Let's move on to Gulfstream Park and try something else. Have to try somewhere and Claiming $5,000 sounds like as good a place as any. Now note all the improvement. Broke on top; assumed 3rd place only 2 lengths off the leader; was actually second for a while. "Tired." Finished 5th, only 4¼ lengths off the winner. Never finished that close before. And read the type of race again; that's simply Claiming $5,000 and not *Maidens* Claiming $5,000. Promoters Dream was running against *winners* in the $5,000 classification—and doing rather well too.

Today Promoters Dream is dropping down $1,000 worth —from Claiming $5,000 to Claiming $4,000. That Claiming price of $4,000 represents the cheapest race he has ever been entered in—more improvement is expected—how much? Can he get out there today and go all the way? Can he actually *win* this race? And the big question: Would you *bet* on it?

Well—here's the way it all turned out. Here is a subsequent line from the Past Performances of Promoters Dream: (I will not show a chart.)

| | | | | | | | | | | | | | |
|---|---|---|---|---|---|---|---|---|---|---|---|---|---|
| 16Mar61–1GP | fst 7f | .23 | .45⅘ | 1.26⅗ | Clm | 4000 | 2 | 5 | $1^{1}$ | $1^{3}$ | $1^{4}$ | $2^{nk}$ | WHartack |

Damnation. Gollllllly damnation. That horse blew a 4-length lead in the stretch; that's the worst kind, the very worst. As a matter of fact—after leading in the stretch by 4, he wound up in a three-horse photo finish and almost lost second money. Notice his advantage over the third horse. However, when you consider him as a loser running against winners, you'll have to admit he did pretty well, as the comment put it: "Just missed."

Since Promoters Dream seems to have come a cropper against a horse called Pegs Lad, perhaps a look at the Past Performances record of Pegs Lad would be in order. And here it is:

**Pegs Lad** **$4,000** **Dk b or br c, 3, by Solar Slipper—Pegeen, Mrs. G. H. Emick G. Stutts**

| | | | | | | | | | | | | | |
|---|---|---|---|---|---|---|---|---|---|---|---|---|---|
| 11Mar61–4GP | fst 7f | .23 | .46⅗ | 1.25⅖ | Clm | 7500 | 7 | 3 | $7^{7\frac{3}{4}}$ | $8^{10}$ | $9^{13}$ | $9^{9\frac{1}{2}}$ | JLRotz |
| 27Feb61–4Hia | fst 6f | .23 | .46⅘ | 1.12⅗ | Clm | 7000 | 6 | 6 | $5^{5\frac{1}{2}}$ | $5^{8\frac{1}{2}}$ | $4^{7\frac{1}{2}}$ | $5^{7\frac{1}{2}}$ | WChambers |
| 14Feb61–4Hia | fst 6f | .23 | .46⅖ | 1.11⅗ | Clm | 7000 | 2 | 9 | $9^{7\frac{1}{2}}$ | $8^{10}$ | $7^{12}$ | $6^{11}$ | WChambers |
| 4Jan61–4TrP | fst 6f | .22⅗ | .46⅖ | 1.11⅗ | Clm | 8000 | 5 | 9 | $9^{7\frac{3}{4}}$ | $8^{6\frac{1}{4}}$ | $5^{8\frac{1}{2}}$ | $4^{8}$ | CBoland$^{5}$ |
| 29Dec60–6TrP | fst $1^{70}$ | .46⅗ | 1.12⅕ | 1.43⅗ | Clm | 10000 | 4 | 4 | $6^{6\frac{1}{2}}$ | $8^{14}$ | $8^{16}$ | $8^{19}$ | HHinojosa |
| 10Dec60–6TrP | fst $1^{70}$ | .47⅖ | 1.12⅘ | 1.45⅘ | Clm | 9000 | 6 | 5 | $5^{5\frac{1}{2}}$ | $7^{7\frac{1}{2}}$ | $6^{5}$ | $3^{1\frac{3}{4}}$ | BBaeza |
| 10Dec60—Placed second through disqualification. | | | | | | | | | | | | | |
| 24Nov60–4TrP | fst 6f | .22⅗ | .46⅕ | 1.12 | Allowance | | 1 | 10 | $10^{11}$ | $9^{13}$ | $9^{11}$ | $9^{13}$ | JCulmone |
| 7Nov60–4Spt | gd 6½f | .22⅘ | .47 | 1.22 | Clm | 7000 | 2 | 7 | $6^{6}$ | $3^{3\frac{1}{2}}$ | $2^{\frac{1}{2}}$ | $1^{2}$ | SLeJeune |
| 19Oct60–2Spt | fst 6½f | .22⅖ | .46 | 1.18⅗ | Clm | $7000^{0}$ | 10 | 4 | $4^{5\frac{1}{2}}$ | $4^{7}$ | $5^{9}$ | $6^{7\frac{1}{4}}$ | BWalt |

**LATEST WORKOUTS Mar 10 GP 4f fst .50⅗ b Feb 26 GP 3f fst .37⅘ b**

The first big difference we can note between this horse and Promoters Dream is that this horse doesn't have those "M's" out there in his two-year record. This horse is not a loser running against winners; this horse has won before. Last year's record discloses 2 wins, and one of those two winning efforts shows in his Past Performances. The "Spt" is not in our list of race tracks because it is not an Eastern track; it's Sportsman's Park in Cicero, Illinois. We can be assured the unfamiliar "Spt" does not refer to limbo by the fact that there are odds given against the horse's chances

15 3.10 80–20 Pegs Lad 115nk Promoters Dream 115nk Mt. Hood 1101 Just missed 12

of winning. The very fact that Pegs Lad was running at "Spt" in Claiming Races for $7,000 shows that it must be a fairly decent track because we already know by now that a small-time "bush" track doesn't card Claiming Races for $7,000. Why? Because any horses there worth $7,000 would be running in its Saturday afternoon feature race—the Potato Sack Purse.

And so, without having any idea what track or what type of racing is represented by "Spt," we can correctly surmise that wherever it is, it offers a fair brand of racing. This supposition is borne out by the fact that Pegs Lad uncorked a 3rd by 1¾ at Tropical Park for $9,000—and was actually

| | | | | | | | |
|---|---|---|---|---|---|---|---|
| **Shannon II.** (B. N. Linder) | **115** | 1961 | 4 | 0 | 0 | 0 | $100 |
| | | 1960 | 10 | 2 | 1 | 0 | $4,050 |

| | | | | |
|---|---|---|---|---|
| 14 | 31.00 | 76–14 | Summer Rain 115½ Jazz Player 1172½ Soups On 114¾ | Had no speed 10 |
| 10 | 12.65 | 74–25 | Newsmonger 1191¼ Crafty Marine 1165 Cosmic Sucre 112h | Evenly 9 |
| 11 | 13.00 | 76–17 | Fort C. 1132¼ Thygold 1146 Musical Prince 112no | Never a factor 12 |
| 07 | 58.15 | 76–22 | Rebakline 1122 Mays Landing 1103 Henry County 1173 | Rallied 11 |
| 17 | 7.45 | 60–20 | Noble Union 1153¾ Prophets Call 113½ Borreraig 1102¼ | Stopped 8 |
| 11 | 5.45 | 66–21 | Roneil 106no d–Noble Union 1131¾ Pegs Lad 111no | Made late rally 8 |
| 17 | 18.50 | 69–20 | Little Tipper 1141¼ Scratch Off 1112 Count Rose 1141 | No speed 10 |
| 11 | 17.10 | 74–24 | Pegs Lad 1122 Mon Reve 109½ Major Scale 1111½ | Was going away 10 |
| 12 | 40.60 | 84–10 | Ditch Road 1173½ Energize 1141½ Val Hawley 1121½ | Early foot, tired 10 |

**Feb 11 GP 4f fst .50 b** **Feb 6 GP 4f gd .50⅖ b**

even bothered in the process, having been moved up to second.

Look at the winning effort of Pegs Lad:

| *Track* | *Race* | *Finish* |
|---|---|---|
| Spt | Clm 7,000 | $1^2$ |

If "Spt" is a mystery track, note his race of 10Dec60:

| *Track* | *Race* | *Finish* |
|---|---|---|
| TrP | Clm 9,000 | $3^{1\frac{3}{4}}$ |

And now look at today's Claiming Price: Clm $4,000.

Nowhere in the Past Performances of Pegs Lad do we see a race as cheap as Claiming $4,000. This horse is dropping way down. Now let's see what the experts back in Baltimore say about Pegs Lad. We'll look him up in the March issue of *Turf and Sport Digest* magazine. There he is: Pegs Lad 113S, with the weight adjustment: 108S. Rated well over 100—this just might be a hoss.

And so, after all this discussion about Promoters Dream and Pegs Lad, the moral is: When doing your handicapping, before you hurriedly discount the chances of success of an unplaced* Maiden (Promoters Dream) or a horse who ran next to last in his latest effort and who has a current in-the-money consistency rating of 00% (Pegs Lad), don't be too hasty and do be as objective as possible. Weigh all the facts and evaluate *where* the horse has been racing and in what kind of races he has been running there. Of course, to do this you are going to have to know one race track from another and the relative merits of the different types of races run. If you know neither one race course from another nor one type of race from another and if you choose not to acquaint yourself with these two factors, then you too must be content to limit your "handicapping" to noting which horse finished second his last time out. As an unavoidable sequel to such limited effort, you will never experience the thrill of seeing your personal choice, "a rank outsider overlooked in the betting," score handily at odds of 10-1 or beyond because you won't be betting on any Maidens, or on any horse who finished last or close to it in his latest race, or any horse who failed to finish within

*Unplaced means the horse has never finished first, second, or third.

3 lengths of the winner in his latest effort—or any other such odds-restraining rule. And by such logic I do not mean to imply that the correct way to handicap a horse race is to suddenly turn the whole process upside down and start looking for the worst horse in the race. Never, never. But I do mean that I believe a chimpanzee, with a little coaching, could learn to put his finger on the horse who finished second in his latest race. In one of his bridge books, under the heading of "Slam Bidding," Charles Goren remarked that just because he could teach a poll parrot to say "Four no-trump," it did not necessarily follow that he would like to have the bird for a playing partner. There's a bit more to it than that. And in horse racing too, you still get out of it only what you put into it. F. L. Emerson made the following very apropos remark: "I'm a great believer in luck. The harder I work, the more of it I seem to have." And you might apply that bit of homespun philosophy to whatever it is you may be doing—whether it's handicapping a horse race or selling ribbon at the ribbon counter.

And now I'm afraid it may come as a surprise to you to learn that our discussion of handicapping is almost concluded. You may be reading away, waiting for the doctor to tell you how to glance over the Past Performances of a group of horses and spot the winner in a burst of inspiration—something akin to the "Eureka!" yarn. Just how does the doctor sift out the one superior horse? Or—as the punter wants to know: "How in the hell do you know which horse is gonna win?" Well, friends, I'm afraid I can't answer that one for you. If I knew a flawless answer to that poser, I could junk this typewriter, a dental drill, some Xylocaine carpules, and all the other bits and pieces of a dentist's armamentarium, and dash out and make a bundle.

For instance, I could say something concrete and specific like, "In a 5-furlong race, run on the side of a hill into the wind, always bet on the horse that has a white nose." And then I could show a chart of just such a race and sure enough—there would be the winner with a white nose. But then some yardbird or some die-hard would say something like, "Oh, I don't know; I've always been kind of a brown-noser myself." And then he would go get a chart of a 5-furlong race that was run on the side of a hill into the wind and there would be the winner with a brown nose. And so it goes. Then I would have to get two more charts. And then he would go get some more, and where it would all end, I don't know. Probably have to call a truce when someone produced a chart of such a race and the winner turned out to be gray.

If you are against thinking as a matter of principle and if you regard it as a degrading waste of time—then I'm sure your handicapping technique will be only cursory and haphazard anyhow. With that in mind, I'll give a very brief rule of thumb to follow. Before putting any money down, set the following as standards to be met by the horse of your choice:

1. Must have a good *Turf and Sport Digest* rating, over 100 after the weight adjustment and within 4 points of the highest-rated horse. (If you are going to bet on horses that are not within 4 points of the highest-rated horse, you may as well discard the ratings.)

2. This year's in-the-money consistency rating must be at least 60% or over. (Even here you are going to have troubles. The horse may have raced only once this year and finished 3rd—that makes his in-the-money consistency rating 100%. Kind of a fluky 100%. What now? You'll probably have to pro-rate that in-the-money consistency rating of 100% commensurately with last year's figures. Or something. I'm afraid you're just going to have to do some thinking. It looks like there's just no way out.)

No set of numbers or any combination of sets of numbers can be used continually to profitably grind out winners. It's still a problem of learning to spot a horse who is favorably placed according to the conditions of the race and who is currently in form. And the real art of the matter is to spot such a horse when his proper placement is not obvious. In other words, he did not run second the last time out, or third, or within 3 lengths of the winner—or anywhere else of such obvious accomplishment. In his last race he did manage to show up at the right place at the right time and made it around the track without falling down. That was last time. This time when he cracks down against weaker, cheaper opposition and becomes a wire-to-wire winner at 18-1, that's his moment of glory. And your moments of glory will come when you have learned to anticipate such examples of "form reversals." It's not easy, friends.

In the interest of avoiding losing streaks and of avoiding losers in general, I will next list what I call "Horses To Avoid." Here again, if you can master only this list of horses, you will know more than most of the patrons out there at your local oval. And from what I've seen—you will also know more than many, or most, of the "experts" who make a living picking horses for the racing papers. Although in fairness to the experts I'll add hurriedly that they are beset with deadline problems and with the impossible task of picking all the winners at all the tracks—quite a job. About all they could have time to note is which horse finished second his last time out.

After you have finished your handicapping procedure, whatever it is—speed figures, ratings, a hatpin, or whatever, and are of the opinion you have selected the one superior horse, keep the following list of horses in mind, and if your noble steed happens to fall into one of these categories— then you had better look again. And I'll be the first to admit that there will be times when members of the following list will win a race. That's horse racing. But we are concerned here with the selection of winners and the avoidance of losers. Therefore, since things are risky enough already, we must always try to keep all the percentages possible on our side. And accordingly, although members of this "deadhead" list will occasionally stagger across the finish line first —the chances are very much greater that they will not.

### HORSES TO AVOID

1. The Ancient Maiden. Fourteen times is the limit. Any horse who has raced fourteen times and still hasn't won a race becomes a member of the Ancient Maiden set. I don't care how far he is dropping down in class today; I don't care what transfer in track locations he may be making— Aqueduct to Maumee Downs, Belmont Park to Waterford

Park, or anywhere to anywhere—if he hasn't found a bunch of horses he can beat in fourteen tries, he and I are finished. I don't even care if he ran second the last time out. During the course of fourteen attempts he may have been second on other occasions—and then never ran back to his good effort.

You may be thinking that advising you to steer clear of such losing horses is superfluous. After all, who would bet on such an habitual loser? Well, friends, many times a horse who has tried 20, 25, 28 times or more, and who is still winless, will go to the post not only with some few dollars bet on him, but is actually sent off as the betting favorite. Imagine that. What a beautiful stiff favorite— just what a horse player is always looking for.

And right about here we'll mention our old friend Major Chips one more time. When Major Chips was chosen at random in our sample race, it marked his eleventh (11th) attempt to win a race. In this chapter on handicapping we saw the result of that race and again Major Chips was not listed as being among those who finished first, second, or third. Major Chips now has three remaining chances to win himself a horse race or he and I are done, finished, through. Three more failures on his part, and sad but true, it's a case pure and simple of, "Goodbye, Mr. Chips."

2. The Oldster. Nine years of age is the limit. Bet no 10-year-olds and up. A horse hits his prime at the ripe old age of 5, so you can see that going along with 9-year-olds is stretching a point a bit. No bets on horses older than 9; don't want to back an 11-year-old, see him break down, and

then have to wonder, "Why did I ever bet that ol' bastard?"

3. The Has-Been. Here is a very abbreviated Past Performances record of a horse we've called Has-Been:

| Race | Finish | Best Company Line |
|------|--------|-------------------|
| HcpS | 1$^{nk}$ | Has-Been$^{nk}$ Tom Fool$^1$ Donor$^{\frac{1}{2}}$ |
| HcpS | 3$^2$ | Stymie$^1$ Noor$^1$ Has-Been$^2$ |
| Alw | 1$^4$ | Has-Been$^4$ Swaps$^{\frac{1}{2}}$ Sea Biscuit$^2$ |
| Alw | 1$^{no}$ | Has-Been$^{no}$ Coaltown$^{nk}$ Ponder$^1$ |
| HcpS | 2$^2$ | Count Fleet$^2$ Has-Been$^1$ Nashua$^1$ |

Quite a record. Necked out Tom Fool. Third behind Stymie and Noor, ran away from Swaps and Sea Biscuit, nosed out Coaltown, and finished a good second behind Count Fleet. All Handicap-Stakes and Allowances Races. Very good. So what's the problem? Well, the problem is that today Has-Been is entered in a Claiming Race for $2,500. And one other little item—all those high-powered races were run three years ago. What in the hell happened in the interim? Break a leg? I don't know if he broke a leg or not, but he certainly has gone bad. Even his owner now thinks he is worth only $2,500. What to do with such a horse? Again there are two schools of thought. The first backstretch proverb says; "They never come back." Even Citation was just another horse when he tried to make a comeback. He performed in an ordinary win one, lose one routine (still in Handicap-Stakes, however, not in Claiming Races). The other opinion states: "They always have one race left." That may be true. But when is the Has-Been going to exhibit his "one race left"? Today? Next week? Next month? Next year?

If you bet on a Has-Been, either due to his sparkling Past

Performances record or just due to sentimental reasons, he'll do nothing and may even go lame in the process. And then you'll wonder why you ever put real money on such an old broken-down relic. However, if you bet against him, he'll waltz home by about 5 lengths and make it all look so easy, and then you'll wonder how you could be so dumb to miss such an obvious winner. Imagine, a conqueror of Tom Fool running for $2,500, and you bet against him. The best thing to do when a Has-Been shows up in a race you intended to play is to just keep your money in your pocket and watch. It will be interesting to see if the ol' bastard makes it. Keeping your money in your pocket is your most direct, effective method of letting the management know that you wished they would keep such beat-up ol' hides off the Major League tracks.

Not all Has-Beens are as dramatically apparent as was the illustration used here. A used-to-be $7,000 Plater entered in a Claiming Race for $1,000 is the same thing.

4. The Lead Lugger. Bet no horses which may be weighted out of contention. The weight limits: Bet *no* horse carrying 126 pounds or over, unless—There is always an unless. Unless *all* the horses in the race are carrying 126 pounds or over. If all the entrants are carrying 126 pounds or over, then your particular choice will be at no weight disadvantage. Example: Belmont Stakes, all colts carry 126 pounds.

Bet no Allowance horse in a sprint when the assigned weight is over 124 pounds. Bet no Allowance horse in a route when the assigned weight is over 122 pounds. Bet no Claimer in a sprint when the assigned weight is over 122 pounds. Bet no Claimer in a route when the assigned weight is over 120 pounds.

| *Race* | *Maximum Weight Limit* |
|---|---|
| Any horse—any race | 126 pounds |
| Alw or HcpS Sprint | 124 pounds |
| Alw or HcpS Route | 122 pounds |
| Clm Sprint | 122 pounds |
| Clm Route | 120 pounds |

And remember—your Allowance and Handicap-Stakes horses at the Minor League tracks are actually moderately priced Claimers.

5. Backsliders. Bet no horses which are in reverse with respect to the type of race scale of values. To explain what is meant by "in reverse"—A horse coming off a winning effort for $5,000 should be entered today for $6,000 or even $7,500. If not elevated in class, then he should at least be holding his own at his winning level, namely, $5,000. The horses to shun are those going backwards, winning for $5,000 and entered today for $4,000, or even $3,500. These horses are as stiff as a board, as a rule, and should be avoided like the plague. The owner and trainer didn't think much of their horse when he won for $5,000 and if they don't think much of it, then I don't think much of it either. These Backsliders will be going to the post as odds-on favorites and will be eliminated as our betting choice on another count when we get to the next chapter on betting. These horses too make beautiful false favorites.

6. The Close Consistent Loser (abbreviated CCL). Of

all the exasperating, nerve-racking horses the horse player has to contend with—this eight ball takes the prize—the Close Consistent *Loser*. The important word there is *loser*. Keep in mind we are trying to avoid losers, and in spite of his many fine showings and in spite of his heart-rending string of near-misses—this joker is still a loser. It's hard to keep from betting on the beast; he always finishes well up; he's forever getting necked out, or beaten by a nose; he's dropping down in class today and will surely make it . . . Only he never does. His in-the-money consistency rating is a gaudy 80%, but his *win* percentage is a complete bust: 00%.

| This year | 10 | 0 | 3 | 5 |
| Last year | 22 | 1 | 8 | 9 |

That one win showing there in last year's record came about when the horse who beat him on that particular day had the misfortune to be disqualified.

Here is an example of a CCL who can't miss today, but will.

Horse CCL    Weight 112 pounds
Today's race: 7 Furlongs.  Clm 3,000

CCL's last race (At the same track—wherever it is.)

| | | *Str.* | *Fin.* | | |
|---|---|---|---|---|---|
| Clm 3,500 | 6f | $4^3$ | $2^{no}$ | 118 | Closed fast. |

Now everything is in his favor. Dropping down $500 worth. Six less pounds to carry. One more jump in that last race and he would have made it. Today he has a whole extra furlong to make up the distance of one nose; he "Closed fast." Today he can't miss. But he will; have no fear. He'll find some way to lose it.

The CCL does serve one useful purpose. He too makes a beautiful false favorite. After all—he did run second his last time out. Also the time before that—and the time before that, third the time before that and second again the time before. Only one thing wrong with all those close finishes and all those fine races—he didn't *win* any of them. Not a one. He'll goof it again today, too.

And I certainly do not want to imply that any horse who finished second in his last race and third the race before that is some kind of a hard-luck, close and almost chronic loser. Many fine horses finish close up a time or two before they finally hit their winning stride. But watch out for the horse who has what we might call an abnormal number of near-misses among his list of finish positions. Once you suspect him of being a CCL, check his box score for the year, and if your suspicions are warranted, his tough luck habit will be there for the whole world to see. After you've made a few trips to your local oval, you'll get to know these hard-luck Louies by their names; there aren't too many.

And here's something to put a bug in your ear. It's one of the many things which causes horse players to be a little glassy-eyed periodically. The CCL's have a knack of *winning* the first time they are entered in a race in which they don't figure to do *anything*. That ought to give you something to worry about.

7. The Anemics. This category includes all the lightly campaigned mature horses. Example: Weak Knees (4-

year-old colt). Two-year racing record:

| This year | 3 | 1 | 0 | 1 |
| Last year | 4 | 1 | 1 | 0 |

This horse has run seven races in 2 years, or an average of about three per year. His record, what there is of it, is very good—but—there surely must be some basic weakness in his makeup. He must really be held together with chewing gum and string. Any horse that is sound enough to make it to the post only three times a year isn't sound enough to represent my racing interests. But he'll be entered, and apt as not, he'll figure to be there or thereabouts. This racing enigma is comparable to the Has-Been as to whether you should bet on him or against him.

8. Tip Horses. You won't make many trips to any race track without soon getting a hot tip—a real inside sure thing. The hot tip might come from the butcher, the baker, the garbage man, a jockey, trainer, stable swipe, your grandmother, Uncle Ned—anybody. And via any conceivable means of communication: telephone, telegraph, orally, a letter, smoke signals, or perhaps up out of Mexico via ox cart. I've said before that anyone's percentage of winning selections will hover around 30%; however, with "tip" horses it's all different. My exposure to tip horses has revealed them to be consistent to the phenomenal degree of 100%—every damn one of them finished clear out of the money. That's the record of tip horses over a twenty-year period, not a one of them could get as close as third. So the next time someone gives you a hot tip, thank him, and then eliminate that horse from any further consideration. The

number of horses you now have to evaluate has just been reduced by one.

And now, friends, it's time to put it all together. Up to this point you have been absorbing some racing background, some racing facts, and some racing "know how" in bits and pieces. But when you are out there fighting the iron men and the horses start going around in circles—bits and pieces just won't do. When your American dollar bills start going into the machine, the time to know what's going on is here and now.

Therefore, there follows a list of ten actual races. And since the conditions of races deal largely with dates and pounds, I will add that all ten races were carded for the racing schedule of May, 1962. All ten races, that is, except one; one race in the group was not run in 1962. This juxtaposition of another time element was not done to create confusion—but rather to instill in you the habit of checking the dates in the Past Performances with the date of *today's* race. When evaluating what a horse has done in the past, we want to be sure we are examining current form and not an abbreviated capsule comment of ancient history. In addition to knowing what a horse has done and where he did it, we want to know *when* he did it. Accordingly, the first item given in the ten problem races will be the date of the race—just as a racing paper you may be reading at some future date will have the date at the top of the page.

After the date of the race and the conditions of the race, as seen in the *Form* or *Telegraph,* there follows the Past Performances of one horse entered in that race. Your problem then is to read the conditions for the race and then study the Past Performances of the one horse shown and decide in a "Yes" or "No" fashion as to whether or not the horse shown has an above average chance to win. To possibly set your mind at ease, I will make known now that the list contains four winners. And then I'll hurry to add that your reputation as one knowledgeable about horses will *not* stand or fall depending upon whether or not you select the right four horses. As a matter of fact, one of the winners shown is actually a bit of a dog, but was included to enhance the verisimilitude of actual racing problems and pitfalls. In addition such an inclusion will serve to bring home the thought that the horses are still animals and not a sect of well-disciplined automata. And when you think about it—how could you be expected to select the "one superior horse" in our sample races when only one horse is shown? If you pick the four winners, that's OK. If you miss 'em, that may be OK, too—as long as your misses had a reasonable chance to win and were not hopelessly misplaced or chronic losers. And so—whether or not you happen to hit upon the four winners is not important. What is important? The fact that you read the conditions for the race and then compared the horse's capabilities against those conditions. *That's* the important thing. In other words—if you decided "No," you had a reason. And if you decided "Yes," you had a reason. The outcome of your decision took some thought and was not arrived at by the random placement of a hatpin. And the most important thing of all—as you were dealing with the ten presented problems—possibly without your even knowing it—you were dabbling in handicapping real horse races. And think about it for a minute—when you began the book, you weren't overly certain which end of a horse was the front end!

A few final words and thoughts before you get to the races—just what it is you are trying to do. As you read the following list, you should be able to classify each race mentally as: Major League, Minor League, sprint, route, cheap race, fair race, good race, great race—races for non-winners—good, fair, highly mediocre.

To have any success in your racing endeavors, you must not only be able to evaluate the different types of races, but also be able to do it through the complexities of changing sites, Major League and Minor League double standards, and the graduated calibers of the various race courses. How can you possibly hope to have winning selections if you don't know what it is your selections are trying to win? And the beauty of it all is that when you can catalogue and grade the different races at the different race tracks, you will already know more than the majority of people out there, most of whom are betting via a hatpin and going home thoroughly confused, regardless of whether they won or lost, and with the laws of combination and probability being what they are, I sort of imagine it would be lost.

In reading over the races, then, if you grasp the meaning and the worth of the presented examples, that's fine. You're in there pitchin'. If, however, these ten races and their Past Performances are just a mish-mash of racing terms, then you had better flip back to page 16 where it says "This is a horse" and start all over.

DATE OF RACE: MAY, 1962.

## 1st Suf

**1 MILE & 70 YARDS. (Dare Do Well, May 6, 1961, 1:40⅖, 3, 113.)**
**Purse $2,000. 4-year-olds and upward which have not won a race at a mile or over since Feb. 12. Claiming. Weight, 120 lbs. Non-winners of three races in 1962 allowed 3 lbs.; two races, 5 lbs.; a race, 7 lbs. Claiming price, $2,000.**

### Great Caesar
**113** Dk. b. g, 8, by Roman—Hushaby Baby, by Questionnaire.
Breeder, H. F. Guggenheim. 1962 2 0 0 0 (——)
Owner, A. Georgopoulos. Trainer, J. Allen. **$2,000** 1957 11 5 1 1 $12,085

Apr26-62[2]Suf 6 f 1:13 ft 37 115 12[13]11[20]11[20]11[21] FisherRM[2] 2000 62 PittsburghGus115 FairEf'rt115 Ahead 12
Apr18-62[1]L.D 5 f 1:02⅗ft 18 116 12[12]12[12]12[19]12[15] FisherRM[8] 2500 60 Homew'dAngel 116 St'pAtor116 Ouran 12
Dec19-58[2]TrP 6 f 1:10⅘ft 20 110 86¼ Broke down. GibbG[7] 2500 Barina 112 FleetArgo 115 Declaration 12
Apr 2-58[1]Jam 6 f 1:13⅘ft 13 113 7[7] 7[9] 7[10] 7[16] BolandW[3] 3500 62 PromHall 119 ElliottsDream113 Yarn 7
Oct29-57[8]Jam 1 1/16 1:47⅕ft 1 ▲119 2[1½] 1[h] 1[h] 1[nk] BolandW[2] 5000 74 Pre-pat113 Papa willPlay116 Byroon
Oct16-57[2]Bel 1 1/16 1:46 ft 3-2 ▲116 6[4½] 6[3¼] 2[½] 1[2½] BolandW[5] 5000 78 Mt.C'mel 113 Myth'ker116 B'by'sBabe 9

**April 17 LD 1-2 ft :53b** **April 11 LD 1-2 ft :52bg**

DATE OF RACE: MAY, 1962.

## 3rd Pim

**5 FURLONGS. (Itsa Great Day, May 20, 1960, :59, 2, 118.)**
**Purse $3,000. Maiden 2-year-olds. Claiming. Weight, 118 lbs. Claiming price, $10,000.**

### East Echo
**118** Ch. c, 2, by Decathlon—Fleur d'Amour, by Ardan.
Breeder, Miss M. W. Woolwine. 1962 2 M 0 0 $150
Owner, Hickory Tree Stable. Trainer, Charles W. Shaw, Jr. **$10,000**

Apr19-62[3]Lrl 5 f 1:00⅖ft 13 118 2[2] 3[3½] 5[6½] 6[11] CorleRE[1] Mdn 87 Pep 118 Ten Wins 113 Cathelle 12
Apr 6-62[3]Lrl 4½ f :53⅖ft 13 118 3 3[3½] 3[2½] 4[7] TeagueD[5] Mdn 94 YouR'calYou118 D'dyDulin118 Nirboy 10

**May 4 Pim 1-2 ft :50⅘b** **April 26 Lrl 1-2 ft :54b** **April 15 Lrl 5-8 gd 1:05b**

DATE OF RACE: MAY, 1962.

## 7th CD

**6 FURLONGS. (Benedicto, May 13, 1961, 1:09⅕, 6, 117.)**
**Jet Pilot Purse. Purse $4,500. 4-year-olds and upward, non-winners other than optional or claiming in 1962. Allowances. Weight, 122 lbs. Non-winners of $5,000 other than claiming in 1961-62 allowed 3 lbs.; $3,100, 6 lbs.; $2,275, 10 lbs.**

### Coon Hollow
**112** Ch. g, 4, by Model Cadet—Lindy, by Lovely Night.
Breeder, E. W. Richmond. 1961 10 3 1 3 $7,050
Owner, Mrs. G. Imorde. Trainer, J. H. P. Richards. 1960 11 2 4 2 $4,380

Aug26-61[8]Tdn 1 1/16 1:54⅖hy 2 120 2[½] 3[1] 6[6] 7[11] KaelinF[3] HcpO 32 Col.Wil'mP.119 S'rra'sCl'd116 Mr.Sag 8
Aug14-61[8]Tdn 6 f 1:11⅗ft 4-5 ▲120 3[½] 2[½] 1[½] 1[½] KaelinF[2] Alw 92 CoonHol'w120 J'nieG.109 M'dy'sBr've 7
Aug 5-61[8]Tdn 6 f 1:09⅘ft 4 114 4[4] 3[4] 3[4½] 3[2½] KaelinF[4] HcpO 98 L'dyManneq'n118 GoG'd116 C'nHol'w 8
Jly 29-61[8]Tdn 1 1/16 1:44⅘ft 11 112 1[h] 1[h] 2[h] 2[nk] KaelinF[1] HcpO 91 H'ryHome118 C'nHol'w112 L'dyLaRue 8
Jly 22-61[8]Tdn 6 f 1:14⅖sl 8-5 ▲112 3[6½] 3[5] 3[½] 3[1¾] KaelinF[1] HcpO 76 Top'r-J'n112 C'l.Wil'mP.108 C'nH'l'w 9
Jly 8-61[8]Ran 6½ f 1:17 ft 6 105 3[1] 2[h] 2[h] 3[nk] ClarkH[3] HcpO 96 Old Cash 118 Sir Tom 120 Coon Hollow 8
Jly 1-61[8]Ran 6 f 1:10⅕ft 5 117 4[nk] 2[½] 2[h] 4[1½] KaelinF[3] Alw 95 ParlezVous 103 Mr.Tip 111 Zorach 8
Jun21-61[8]Ran 6 f 1:14⅕sy 6-5 ▲113 1[½] 1[1] 1[2] 1[1¾] KaelinF[3] Alw 77 CoonHol'w113 PureVil'ge117 Rol'gR'm 6
Jun15-61[8]Ran 6½ f 1:19⅖gd 2 ▲112 1[½] 1[3] 1[4] 1[10] KaelinF[5] Alw 84 C'nHol'w112 Roy'lM'ney121 D'dym'n 10
May30-61[8]Ran 6 f 1:11⅖ft 16 112 3[nk] 2[h] 1[½] 3[3]† ShermanA[7] Alw 88 Gay's Pal 117 Mems 117 Coon Hollow 7

†Disqualified.

**May 2 CD 5-8 m 1:04b**

DATE OF RACE: MAY, 1962.

## 5th Aqu

**7 FURLONGS (chute). (Rare Rice, May 24, 1960, 1:22, 4, 120.)**
**Purse $5,000. 3-year-olds and upward. Claiming. $20,000, 3-year-olds, 114 lbs.; older, 124 lbs.; 2 lbs. for each $1,000 to $18,000. Non-winners of three races since Jan. 16 allowed 3 lbs.; of two races since then, 5 lbs.; of a race since then, 7 lbs. (Races when entered to be claimed for $16,000 or less not considered.)**

### Fauve *
**109** Ch. g, 3, by Beau Max—Blind Frenzy, by Bimelech.
Breeder, King Ranch. 1962 4 1 1 1 $3,880
Owner, King Ranch. Trainer, M. Hirsch. **$20,000** 1961 11 M 1 1 $1,280

Apr20-62[4]Aqu 1 1:36⅗ft 5¾ 122 6[4¾] 5[6] 4[8½] 3[8½] BolandW[4] Alw 76 Excl'siveNashua115 Vitality110 Fauve 6
Apr 9-62[6]Aqu 1 1:37⅗m 20 115 4[3½] 5[5½] 4[7½] 6[10] BolandW[1] Alw 70 DesertKing 117 Comic 117 LordQuillo 9
Apr 4-62[8]Aqu 6 f 1:12⅗ft 2½ ▲122 4[5] 2[3] 2[h] 1[h] YcazaM[4] Mdn 82 Fauve 122 BrotherGolden 122 OldFool 10
Mar28-62[1]Aqu 6 f 1:12 ft 18 111 3[4½] 3[3½] 3[1] 2[h] MellonS[7] Mdn 85 Benaghazi 114 Fauve 111 KingDenny 13
Mar 10, Columbia, S. C. Trials, ft 4f :48⅕. Won by 4 length.
Oct31-61[8]Lrl 6 f 1:12⅗ft 16 108 2[1] 2[½] 2[1½] 3[5½] CorleRE[6] 12000 86 GetS'eM're113 Lev'niaPr'ce114 Fauve 7
Oct13-61[5]Aqu 6 f 1:12⅗ft 33f 122 8[9½] 7[12] 8[7½] 9[5] BolandW[3] Mdn 77 BF'sFav'te122 Bl'napl'n122 Sc'nicS'th 14
Oct 2-61[5]Bel 6 f 1:12 ft 107 122 10[11]12[10]10[15]10[16] BolandW[12] Mdn 71 Toot theFlute122 Nahum122 Melanion 12
Sep26-61[4]Bel 7 f 1:26⅕ft 27 117* 3[2½] 4[4] 6[11] 7[16] MellonS[1] Mdn 60 DoctorH'nkK.122 Sh'testWay122 Zab 10
Sep23-61[3]Bel 7 f 1:26⅖ft 25 115* 8[9¾] 7[4] 8[11]11[14] MellonS[4] Mdn 61 West'nW'rior120 Keyl'sue120 OldFool 12
Jly 22-61[3]Aqu 5½ f 1:05⅕ft 17 122 5[3½] 4[3½] 4[5½] 4[3¾] BolandW[5] Mdn 90 Sc'resville122 Str'gSal'nt122 Os'geR'd 8

**May 4 Bel trt 3-4 sy 1:16⅗h** **May 1 Bel 1-2 ft :47⅘h** **April 28 Bel 1m ft 1:43b**

5. DATE OF RACE: MAY, 1962.

# 8th Race Charles Town

**Leddysmaun** — Ch g, 5, by Saggy—Milos, by Ladysman
W. G. Sims — L. Messaris

| | | | | | | | | | | | | | | |
|---|---|---|---|---|---|---|---|---|---|---|---|---|---|---|
| 15May62–5Pim | fst | 6f | .24 | .47⅗ | 1.13⅕ | Clm | 5000 | 2 | 4 | $3^{\frac{1}{2}}$ | $3^{2\frac{1}{2}}$ | $2^{2}$ | $1^{no}$ | LReynolds |
| 9May62–8Pim | fm | $1\frac{1}{16}$ | T. C. | | 1.43⅕ | Allowance | | 6 | 3 | $4^{2\frac{1}{2}}$ | $5^{6}$ | $6^{12}$ | $7^{12}$ | CGonzalez |
| 23Apr62–6Lrl | fm | 1 | T. C. | | 1.37 | Clm | 15000 | 5 | 2 | $2^{1\frac{1}{2}}$ | $5^{4}$ | $5^{6}$ | $5^{7\frac{3}{4}}$ | MBeneito |
| 20Mar62–8Bow | fst | $1\frac{1}{16}$ | .48⅕ | 1.13 | 1.45 | Allowance | | 1 | 1 | $2^{1}$ | $4^{2\frac{1}{2}}$ | $7^{3\frac{1}{4}}$ | $7^{12}$ | CShaw |
| 5Mar62–8Bow | fst | 7f | .24 | .47⅕ | 1.26⅖ | Allowance | | 8 | 6 | $8^{15}$ | $8^{14}$ | $8^{14}$ | $8^{11}$ | CShaw |
| 15Feb62–8Bow | gd | 7f | .23⅘ | .47⅗ | 1.26⅘ | Allowance | | 2 | 3 | $6^{2\frac{3}{4}}$ | $7^{11}$ | $7^{15}$ | $7^{25}$ | CShaw |
| 10Feb62–8Bow | sly | 5½f | .22⅗ | .46⅕ | 1.06 | BurchH | | 2 | 3 | $5^{4}$ | $4^{4\frac{1}{2}}$ | $8^{4\frac{3}{4}}$ | $9^{3\frac{1}{2}}$ | CShaw |
| 31Jan62–6CT | fst* | 4½f | .21⅖ | .45⅗ | .49⅖ | Allowance | | 6 | 3 | | $6^{3\frac{1}{2}}$ | $7^{9\frac{3}{4}}$ | $8^{9\frac{3}{4}}$ | CGambarde |
| 28Sep60–7Bel | fst | 1⅝ | .47⅖ | 1.12⅖ | 2.40⅘ | Law.Riztn | | 8 | 1 | $1^{h}$ | $8^{17}$ | $8^{25}$ | $8^{34}$ | CShaw |

6. DATE OF RACE: MAY, 1962.

# 1st Race Garden State

**Billingsgate** $4,000 — Ch g, 4, by Billings—Away East, by Airway
Williscroft–Costanzo — W. Tronco

| | | | | | | | | | | | | | | |
|---|---|---|---|---|---|---|---|---|---|---|---|---|---|---|
| 18May62–4GS | fst | 6f | .23⅕ | .47 | 1.12⅘ | Clm | 4000 | 8 | 5 | $3^{nk}$ | $3^{nk}$ | $3^{nk}$ | $2^{\frac{3}{4}}$ | LLefebvre |
| 9May62–8GS | fst | $1\frac{1}{16}$ | .48⅕ | 1.13 | 1.45⅘ | Clm | 3500 | 8 | 2 | $2^{h}$ | $12^{13}$ | $12^{24}$ | $12^{29}$ | GGlassner |
| 24Aug61–2Atl | my | $1\frac{1}{16}$ | .47⅘ | 1.14 | 1.49⅕ | Md | 4500 | 8 | 6 | $9^{14}$ | $12^{26}$ | $12^{29}$ | $12^{29}$ | WBlum |
| 12Aug61–2Atl | fst | 6f | .22⅗ | .46 | 1.11⅕ | Clm | 4000 | 4 | 9 | $9^{5\frac{1}{4}}$ | $9^{9\frac{1}{4}}$ | $7^{8\frac{3}{4}}$ | $6^{9\frac{1}{4}}$ | WBlum |
| 15Jly 61–5Mth | sl | 6f | .22⅕ | .45⅘ | 1.12 | Clm | 5000 | 3 | 6 | $6^{5\frac{1}{2}}$ | $7^{15}$ | $7^{14}$ | $6^{19}$ | KKorte |
| 8Jly 61–3Mth | fst | 6f | .22⅕ | .45⅕ | 1.11 | Md | 6000 | 10 | 1 | $4^{1\frac{1}{4}}$ | $5^{7\frac{1}{2}}$ | $8^{17}$ | $8^{14}$ | BFrazier |
| 29Jun61–4Mth | fst | 6f | .21⅘ | .45⅕ | 1.11⅕ | Clm | 6000 | 3 | 10 | $9^{4\frac{1}{2}}$ | $10^{9\frac{3}{4}}$ | $11^{8\frac{1}{2}}$ | $11^{11}$ | KKorte |
| 21Jun61–4Mth | fst | 6f | .22⅗ | .45⅗ | 1.11⅖ | Md Sp Wt | | 7 | 11 | $9^{6\frac{1}{4}}$ | $11^{11}$ | $11^{13}$ | $10^{15}$ | KKorte |
| 10Jun61–5Mth | sl | 6f | .22 | .46⅕ | 1.12⅕ | Clm | 7000 | 1 | 11 | $8^{7\frac{1}{2}}$ | $8^{10}$ | $9^{9\frac{1}{2}}$ | $10^{18}$ | KKorte |

7. DATE OF RACE: MAY, 1962.

# 9th Race Charles Town

**Star Breeze** × $1,200 — B g, 6, by Fleeting Star—Valley Tthel,
Mrs. A. K. Frank — A. K. Frank

| | | | | | | | | | | | | | | |
|---|---|---|---|---|---|---|---|---|---|---|---|---|---|---|
| 15May62–9ShD | my | $1\frac{1}{16}$ | .48⅕ | 1.15⅘ | 1.51⅗ | Clm | 1250 | 8 | 1 | $1^{6}$ | $1^{8}$ | $1^{6}$ | $1^{3}$ | CGamb'della |
| 30Apr62–9ShD | fst | $1\frac{1}{16}$ | .47⅗ | 1.15 | 1.52⅖ | Clm | 1250 | 5 | 1 | $2^{1\frac{1}{2}}$ | $2^{4}$ | $2^{2\frac{1}{2}}$ | $3^{\frac{1}{2}}$ | CGambard'la |
| 23Apr62–5ShD | fst | 1 | .50⅕ | 1.16⅖ | 1.44⅖ | Clm | 1250 | 1 | 2 | $2^{1}$ | $2^{1}$ | $2^{1}$ | $2^{2}$ | RGHanson$^{7}$ |
| 23Apr62 | Dead heat. | | | | | | | | | | | | | |
| 21Dec61–7CT | sl | $1\frac{1}{16}$ | .51⅗ | 1.19⅖ | 1.55 | Clm | 1200 | 6 | 1 | $1^{2}$ | $1^{2}$ | $1^{2}$ | $1^{1\frac{1}{2}}$ | CGambard'la |
| 18Dec61–8CT | sly | $1\frac{1}{16}$ | .49⅘ | 1.16⅖ | 1.50⅗ | Clm | 1200 | 4 | 5 | $6^{15}$ | $6^{16}$ | $6^{19}$ | $5^{19}$ | RGHanson$^{5}$ |
| 11Oct61–9ShD | fst | $1\frac{1}{16}$ | .49 | 1.15⅖ | 1.49⅖ | Clm | 1200 | 2 | 3 | $4^{2}$ | $4^{3\frac{1}{2}}$ | $4^{7\frac{1}{2}}$ | $6^{9\frac{1}{2}}$ | JDavidson |
| 29Sep61–10ShD | fst | 1 | .49⅕ | 1.14⅘ | 1.43 | Clm | 1200 | 1 | 3 | $3^{1\frac{1}{2}}$ | $2^{3}$ | 2k | $2^{1\frac{1}{2}}$ | JDavidson |
| 14Sep61–9ShD | fst | $1\frac{1}{16}$ | .49⅖ | 1.15 | 1.49⅘ | Clm | 1200 | 9 | 8 | $9^{13}$ | $9^{20}$ | $9^{19}$ | $9^{18}$ | JDavidson |
| 24Aug61–7ShD | fst | $1\frac{1}{16}$ | .50 | 1.16 | 1.50⅕ | Clm | 1500 | 4 | 3 | $4^{7}$ | $6^{6\frac{3}{4}}$ | $6^{6}$ | $6^{3}$ | JDavidson |
| 9Aug61–9ShD | fst | $1\frac{1}{16}$ | .50 | 1.15⅖ | 1.48⅘ | Clm | 1200 | 3 | 1 | $2^{h}$ | $3^{2\frac{1}{2}}$ | $4^{5}$ | $5^{7\frac{1}{4}}$ | JDavidson |

**LATEST WORKOUTS** Apr 22 ShD 5f gd 1.04⅗ h

**6 1-2 FURLONGS. (Misty Lady, December 18, 1943, $1.18\frac{3}{5}$, 4, 107.)**
**Purse $2,000. 4-year-olds and upward. Allowances. The Silver Spring Purse. Non-winners of $975 other than maiden, starter or claiming since Dec. 15. Weight, 120 lbs. Non-winners twice since Mar. 1 allowed 3 lbs., once, 6 lbs., in 1962, 8 lbs., Oct. 2, 10 lbs.**

| (G.-W. G. Sims) | **117** | 1962 | 8 | 1 | 0 | 0 | $1,950 |
|---|---|---|---|---|---|---|---|
| | | 1960 | 16 | 5 | 1 | 1 | $19,570 |

| | | | | | |
|---|---|---|---|---|---|
| 116 | 3.70 | 84–17 | Leddysmaun $116^{no}$ Sun Tan Miss $113^{2}$ Heebie-Jeebies $112^{4}$ | Driving | 8 |
| 110 | 24.20 | 90— | War Council $114\frac{3}{4}$ Decline and Fall $103^{nk}$ Cyprian Cat $113^{4}$ | Tired | 10 |
| 115 | 13.30 | 81–11 | Isyurbuddy $112^{2\frac{1}{4}}$ Cyprian Cat $115^{1}$ Adorette $112^{2\frac{1}{2}}$ | Early foot | 7 |
| 112 | 47.20 | 76–14 | Billy Overman $109^{2\frac{1}{2}}$ Ray Tomroy $122^{nk}$ Gaghatur $105^{2}$ | Fell back | 7 |
| 113 | 20.40 | 70–14 | Billy Overman $112^{1\frac{3}{4}}$ Rich Greek $115^{no}$ Best Brother $116^{2\frac{1}{2}}$ | Trailed | 8 |
| 112 | 3.40 | 54–23 | Nirulla $115^{1\frac{1}{2}}$ Yeuxdoux $114^{1\frac{1}{4}}$ Invigor $120^{nk}$ | Dropped back early | 7 |
| 112 † | 18.70 | 85–19 | Vir-Marie $112\frac{3}{4}$ War Council $114^{h}$ Mr. Egotist $116^{h}$ | Speed, hung | 16 |
| 113 | 8.70 | 84– 9 | Silver Song $113^{2}$ School Caper $111^{2\frac{1}{2}}$ Our Bonnie S. $113^{no}$ | Fell back | 9 |
| 116 | 96.05 | 66–14 | Kelso $120^{4\frac{1}{2}}$ Tompion $123^{1\frac{1}{2}}$ Tooth and Nail $116^{5\frac{1}{2}}$ | Speed, stopped | 8 |

**6 FURLONGS. (I Appeal, May 21, 1955, $1.08\frac{4}{5}$, 4, 112.)**
**Out of chute. Purse $3,500. 4-year-olds and upward. Claiming. Which have not won a race since Mar. 3. Weight, 120 lbs. Non-winners of two races since Jan. 16 allowed 3 lbs., a race, 6 lbs. Claiming price $4,000. 2 lbs. for each $250 to $3,500.**

| (C. G. Raible) | **114** | 1962 | 2 | M | 1 | 0 | $700 |
|---|---|---|---|---|---|---|---|
| | | 1961 | 17 | M | 1 | 1 | $1,250 |

| | | | | | |
|---|---|---|---|---|---|
| b 114 | 73.00 | 79–17 | Inquisition $114\frac{3}{4}$ Billingsgate $114^{nk}$ Dix Dago $114^{1\frac{1}{4}}$ | Sharp | 12 |
| b 114 | 83.30 | 52–15 | Michelly $114^{4\frac{1}{2}}$ Bull Rose $117^{h}$ Lap Dog $117^{3\frac{1}{2}}$ | Stopped to a walk | 12 |
| b 112 | 26.60 | 36–24 | Chocolate Chip $115^{1\frac{1}{4}}$ Triple Five $122^{h}$ Coma Belle $113^{4}$ | No factor | 12 |
| b 112 | 27.70 | 80–11 | Oil Payment $114^{3}$ Ambeginning $112^{1}$ Jill Ganey $112^{1}$ | No factor | 12 |
| b 116 | 28.90 | 63–23 | Colonel Hastie $122^{1}$ Loft $116^{3\frac{1}{2}}$ Poky Nose $111^{7}$ | Never a factor | 7 |
| b 114 | 46.70 | 73–12 | C-Ace $114^{3\frac{1}{2}}$ Olien $114^{1\frac{1}{4}}$ Marlton Pike $114^{2\frac{1}{2}}$ | Bolted on final turn | 11 |
| b 114 | 107.70 | 75–14 | Joe Cave $118^{2}$ Four Circles $118^{1\frac{1}{4}}$ Stan's Song $113^{h}$ | Was never close | 11 |
| b 120 | 53.30 | 70–12 | Towson $120^{1\frac{1}{4}}$ Arbitrage $120^{1\frac{3}{4}}$ Wind Sweep $120^{1}$ | Raced far off pace | 12 |
| b 112 | 71.30 | 63–25 | M'selle Mill $117^{4\frac{1}{2}}$ Brass Knuckles $113^{5}$ Joe Cave $115^{3}$ | No factor | 11 |

**1 1-16 MILES. (Bright Fate, December 19, 1953, 1.44, 3, 113.)**
**Purse $1,200. 4-year-olds and upward. Claiming. Weight 120 lbs. Non-winners twice since Mar. 1 allowed 3 lbs., a race, 6 lbs., in 1962, 8 lbs. Claiming price $1,200.**

| by High Breeze (C. W. Black) | **117** | 1962 | 3 | 1 | 1 | 1 | $990 |
|---|---|---|---|---|---|---|---|
| | | 1961 | 24 | 3 | 1 | 2 | $2,990 |

| | | | | | |
|---|---|---|---|---|---|
| b 118 | 4.30 | 69–20 | Star Breeze $118^{3}$ Plymps Girl $107^{1}$ Loving Cup $107^{2\frac{1}{2}}$ | Easily | 10 |
| b 118 | 3.30 | 64–18 | Montego Bay $118^{nk}$ Beechley $108^{nk}$ Star Breeze $118^{no}$ | Sharp try | 9 |
| b 110 ♠ | 12.90 | 75–18 | Two Star Final $115^{2}$ ♠StarBreeze $110^{nk}$ ♠Hunter'sBay $109^{nk}$ | Gamely | 7 |
| b 115 | 27.90 | 45–46 | Star Breeze $115^{1\frac{1}{2}}$ Key Escort $112^{2}$ Une Heure $108^{6}$ | Hard ridden | 8 |
| b 110 | 10.50 | 48–33 | Russell Boy $112^{14}$ Lonesome Steve $115\frac{1}{2}$ Air Battle $118^{2}$ | No factor | 10 |
| b 117 | 2.20 | 70–13 | Hunter's Bay $117^{3\frac{1}{2}}$ Lilamme $117^{3}$ Loud Applause $117^{h}$ | Fell back | 7 |
| b 117 | 14.30 | 82–16 | Tip Sheet $114^{1\frac{1}{2}}$ Star Breeze $117^{2\frac{1}{2}}$ Dispend $117^{1\frac{1}{2}}$ | Made game effort | 10 |
| b 117 | 4.50 | 60–16 | Corn $115\frac{1}{2}$ Blue Boy B. $116^{nk}$ Sun Bolt $120^{2\frac{1}{2}}$ | Impeded on early turn | 9 |
| b 120 | 8.70 | 73–17 | Christie Lee $112^{nk}$ Iolanthe $113^{1\frac{1}{2}}$ River Gate $114^{no}$ | Fell back | 7 |
| b 114 | 3.70 | 76–10 | Hellaurora $117^{1\frac{1}{4}}$ More Music $114^{h}$ Loud Applause $117^{3\frac{1}{2}}$ | Tired | 8 |

**Apr 16 ShD 3f fst $.38\frac{2}{5}$ bg**

8. DATE OF RACE: MAY, 1959.

# 6th Race Belmont Park

## Sword Dancer * 

**Ch c, 3, by Sunglow—Highland Fling, by By Jimminy**
**Brookmeade Stable E. Burch**

| | | | | | | | | | | | | | |
|---|---|---|---|---|---|---|---|---|---|---|---|---|---|
| 16May59–8Pim | fst | 1 3/16 | .47⅕ | 1.11⅗ | 1.57 | Preakness | 7 | 6 | $5^{6}$ | $2^{h}$ | $2^{2}$ | $2^{4}$ | WShoemaker |
| 2May59–7CD | fst | 1¼ | .47⅗ | 1.11⅗ | 2.02⅕ | Ky.Derby | 14 | 4 | $4^{3}$ | 1½ | $1^{h}$ | $2^{no}$ | WBoland |
| 25Apr59–7CD | fst | 7f | .23 | .45⅖ | 1.22⅕ | Allowance | 1 | 5 | $1^{h}$ | $1^{h}$ | 1½ | $1^{1}$ | WShoemaker |
| 4Apr59–7GP | fst | 1⅛ | .46⅗ | 1.09⅘ | 1.47⅕ | FlaDerby | 9 | 2 | 2½ | $1^{3}$ | $1^{2}$ | 2¾ | SBoulmetis |
| 24Mar59–7GP | fst | 1 70 | .47⅖ | 1.11⅖ | 1.41 | Allowance | 3 | 3 | 2½ | 1½ | $1^{3}$ | $1^{2}$ | SBoulmetis |
| 11Mar59–7GP | fst | 6½f | .22⅕ | .44⅗ | 1.16 | Hutcheson | 5 | 9 | 76¾ | $5^{6}$ | 54½ | $5^{4}$ | SBoulmetis |
| 11Nov58–6Jam | fst | 1 1/16 | .47⅖ | 1.12 | 1.44⅗ | Remsen | 4 | 5 | $7^{5}$ | $7^{3}$ | 74¾ | 46½ | EGuerin |
| 25Oct58–7GS | sly | 1 1/16 | .46⅗ | 1.12⅘ | 1.46⅖ | GrdnState | 2 | 9 | 87¼ | $4^{7}$ | 33½ | $3^{2}$ | EGuerin |
| 18Oct58–8Suf | fst | 1 70 | .45⅕ | 1.11⅘ | 1.42⅘ | Mayflower | 14 | 11 | $11^{13}$ | $6^{5}$ | 11½ | 14½ | NMercier |
| 7Oct58–5Bel | fst | 6f | .22⅗ | .46⅗ | 1.12⅖ | Allowance | 2 | 3 | 31½ | $2^{1}$ | $2^{1}$ | $1^{nk}$ | MKay5 |
| 27Sep58–3Bel | sly | 7f | .22⅖ | .45⅗ | 1.24⅕ | Allowance | 2 | 4 | 43¼ | $5^{4}$ | $3^{2}$ | 32¼ | ENelson |
| 10Sep58–7Atl | fst | 7f | .21⅘ | .44⅕ | 1.23⅖ | World'sPla | 3 | 10 | 83½ | $10^{7}$ | $7^{7}$ | 42¾ | JChoquette |

**Nominated for Belmont Stakes. LATEST WORKOUTS May 27 Bel m.t. 5f**

9. DATE OF RACE: MAY, 1962.

# 5th Race Delaware Park

## Sand Spur

**Ch g, 2, by Woodlands—Cha-La Cha-La, by King Cole**
**H. C. Presnell M. Benson**

| | | | | | | | | | | | | | | |
|---|---|---|---|---|---|---|---|---|---|---|---|---|---|---|
| 14May62–1Pim | fst | 5f | .22⅘ | .47⅕ | 1.00⅖ | Md | 7500 | 1 | 4 | $1^{h}$ | $1^{3}$ | 11½ | $2^{h}$ | WDowns |

**LATEST WORKOUTS May 25 Del 5f sl 1.06⅖ b May 19 Pim 4f fst .53⅗ b**

10. DATE OF RACE: MAY, 1962.

# 1st Race Suffolk Downs

## Two Timing Lady * $2,500

**Br f, 4, by Double Jay—Perfidy,**
**L.-L. Stable J. McLoughlin**

| | | | | | | | | | | | | | | |
|---|---|---|---|---|---|---|---|---|---|---|---|---|---|---|
| 10May62–1Suf | fst | 6f | .23⅕ | .47⅘ | 1.13⅖ | Md | 2500 | 8 | 11 | 119¾ | $9^{11}$ | 45½ | $2^{3}$ | WSilva5 |
| 3May62–1Suf | my | 1 | .49⅖ | 1.16⅕ | 1.44⅗ | Md | 2500 | 2 | 6 | 46½ | $3^{4}$ | 21½ | $2^{1}$ | GRMunsell |
| 26Apr62–1Suf | fst | 6f | .23⅖ | .47⅗ | 1.13⅘ | Md | 2500 | 11 | 12 | 83¾ | $4^{4}$ | $2^{h}$ | $2^{nk}$ | GRMunsell |
| 16Apr62–5LD | gd | 1 1/16 | .50 | 1.17 | 1.52⅕ | Clm | 2000 | 8 | 9 | 86½ | 51¾ | $4^{5}$ | $4^{5}$ | GRMunsell |
| 7Apr62–8LD | gd | 7f | .24⅗ | .49 | 1.30⅗ | Clm | 2000 | 3 | 7 | 79½ | $6^{10}$ | 67¾ | 45¼ | HMcGuigon |
| 29Mar62–8LD | fst | 1 1/16 | .53 | 1.19⅕ | 1.54⅕ | Clm | 2500 | 1 | 2 | $3^{2}$ | $4^{3}$ | 42½ | 65¾ | TWolski5 |
| 26Mar62–6LD | fst | 5f | .23⅗ | .49 | 1.03 | Clm | 3250 | 11 | 11 | $11^{11}$ | $9^{10}$ | 68½ | 54¾ | TWolski5 |
| 9Mar62–3LD | gd | 5f | .23⅕ | .48⅖ | 1.02⅕ | Md | 3000 | 7 | 10 | 96¼ | 99½ | 68½ | 54¼ | RConnolley |
| 22Dec61–2TrP | fst | 1 70 | .46⅘ | 1.12⅖ | 1.44⅕ | Clm | 3000 | 1 | 4 | 64¾ | 66¾ | $7^{8}$ | 89¾ | GGibb |
| 13Dec61–2TrP | fst | 1 70 | .46⅘ | 1.12⅕ | 1.43⅘ | Clm | 3500 | 11 | 9 | 108¾ | 97¾ | $10^{10}$ | $10^{11}$ | JChestnut |
| 5Dec61–3TrP | fst | 6f | .21⅘ | .45⅖ | 1.11⅗ | Clm | 3750 | 11 | 10 | $11^{13}$ | $11^{12}$ | $10^{11}$ | 98¾ | JChestnut |

**LATEST WORKOUTS May 8 Suf 3f fst .38⅕ b Apr 14 LD 4f gd .53 b**

**1 MILE. (Count Fleet, October 10, 1942, 1.34$\frac{4}{5}$, 2, 116.)**
**Sixty-sixth running. THE METROPOLITAN HANDICAP. $100,000 added. 3-year-olds and upward. Handicap stakes. Scale of weights for May, 3-year-olds 113 lbs., older 127 lbs. By subscription of $100 each. $1,000 to start. The added money and all fees to be divided 65% to winner, 20% to second, 10% to third, 5% to fourth. Weights, Monday, May 25. Starters to be named through the entry box the day before the race at the usual time of closing. A trophy to winning owner, trainer and jockey. Closed Friday, May 1 with 49 nominations.**

**(Brookmeade Stables)** **114**

| | | | | | |
|---|---|---|---|---|---|
| 1959 | 6 | 2 | 3 | 0 | $80,875 |
| 1958 | 14 | 3 | 2 | 3 | $60,531 |

| | | | | |
|---|---|---|---|---|
| b 126 | 1.70 | 84–17 | Royal Orbit $126^{4}$ Sword Dancer $126^{3}$ Dunce $126^{2\frac{1}{2}}$ | Best of others 11 |
| b 126 | 8.80 | 96– 6 | Tomy Lee $126^{no}$ Sword Dancer $126^{2\frac{1}{4}}$ First Landing $126^{1}$ | Bore in 17 |
| b 122 | 3.60 | 99–14 | Sword Dancer $122^{1}$ Easy Spur $122^{1\frac{1}{2}}$ Silver Spoon $117^{2}$ | Driving 5 |
| b 122 | 3.90 | 97–10 | Easy Spur $122^{\frac{3}{4}}$ Sword Dancer $122^{9}$ Master Palynch $122^{1}$ | Gamely 9 |
| b 118 | 1.70 | 93–14 | Sword Dancer $118^{2}$ Noble Sel $108^{3}$ Dunce $114^{2\frac{1}{2}}$ | Speed in reserve 8 |
| 122 | 5.25 | 91–14 | Easy Spur $122^{2\frac{1}{2}}$ Pointer $114^{\frac{1}{2}}$ Octopus $122^{nk}$ | In close in drive 9 |
| wb 117 | *1.00 | 80–21 | Atoll $117^{4\frac{1}{2}}$ Rico Tesio $114^{h}$ Derrick $114^{2}$ | In close on backstretch 7 |
| wb 122 | 11.40 | 76–31 | First Landing $122^{h}$ Tomy Lee $122^{2}$ Sword Dancer $122^{3}$ | Game try 13 |
| wb 116 | 13.00 | 91–19 | Sword Dancer $116^{4\frac{1}{2}}$ Atoll $119^{1\frac{3}{4}}$ Open View $119^{1\frac{1}{2}}$ | Speed to spare 14 |
| wb 112 | 3.55 | 86–20 | Sword Dancer $112^{nk}$ Sir Salonga $115^{5}$ Principality $117^{1\frac{1}{2}}$ | Just up 14 |
| wb 118 | 5.30 | 84–13 | Hoist Away $118^{nk}$ Matinal $115^{2}$ Sword Dancer $118^{\frac{3}{4}}$ | Held on well 13 |
| wb 111 | 82.70 | 86–16 | Demobilize $119^{h}$ Intentionally $122^{2\frac{1}{2}}$ Pen Bolero $110^{h}$ | Closed gap 15 |

**fst 1.00$\frac{2}{5}$ h    May 24 Bel m.t. 7f fst 1.27$\frac{1}{5}$ h    May 21 Bel m.t. 4f fst .49$\frac{2}{5}$ b**

**5 FURLONGS. (Itsa Great Day, June 3, 1960, .57$\frac{4}{5}$, 2, 117.)**
**Purse $3,500. 2-year-olds. Colts and geldings. Maidens. Special weight, 120 lbs.**

**(H. C. Presnell)** **120**

| | | | | | |
|---|---|---|---|---|---|
| 1962 | 1 | M | 1 | 0 | $560 |

| | | | | |
|---|---|---|---|---|
| 118 | 5.20 | 93–13 | Flexer Foot $115^{h}$ Sand Spur $118^{no}$ Debbie Dares $115^{2}$ | Just headed 11 |

**May 12 Pim 4f fst .50$\frac{4}{5}$ b    May 9 Pim 4f fst .50 b**

**6 FURLONGS. (Appealing, July 26, 1937, 1.09$\frac{3}{5}$, 4, 117.)**
**Out of chute. Purse $2,100. 4-year-olds. Maidens. Claiming. Weight 118 lbs. Claiming price $2,500.**

**by Zacaweista**
**(J. C. Rader)** ***108**

| | | | | | |
|---|---|---|---|---|---|
| 1962 | 8 | M | 3 | 0 | $1,775 |
| 1961 | 12 | M | 0 | 0 | $257 |

| | | | | |
|---|---|---|---|---|
| 108 | *1.50 | 78–16 | Rustless $113^{3}$ Two Timing Lady $108^{1\frac{1}{4}}$ Internal King $113^{2}$ | Rallied 12 |
| b 113 | *1.00 | 53–33 | Sassy Marie $108^{1}$ Two Timing Lady $113^{9}$ Maryclare $117^{\frac{1}{2}}$ | Blocked 10 |
| b 113 | 4.70 | 79–19 | Lucky Basil $118^{nk}$ Two Timing Lady $113^{4\frac{1}{2}}$ Stepth $113^{h}$ | Sharp try 12 |
| 109 | 7.70 | 51–36 | Little Rumor $116^{2}$ Lin-Lo-Su $112^{2\frac{1}{2}}$ Sir Rascal $118^{\frac{1}{2}}$ | Hung late 11 |
| 113 | 8.70 | 64–31 | Jolly Harp $117^{2\frac{1}{2}}$ Field of Glory $117^{2\frac{3}{4}}$ Lee's Act $112^{no}$ | No threat 8 |
| 106 | 7.20 | 40–39 | Flossie G. $112^{1}$ Lisduff $115^{3}$ Rhumbaba $112^{nk}$ | Speed to stretch 7 |
| 107 | 17.20 | 68–37 | Undertime $118^{h}$ No Gravity $110^{1}$ Little Terrify $119^{\frac{3}{4}}$ | Rallied 12 |
| 115 | 12.40 | 73–28 | Dodgem $106^{no}$ Aureous Lady $112^{2\frac{1}{4}}$ Red Seal $107^{1\frac{1}{2}}$ | Passed tired ones 11 |
| 106 | 23.55 | 66–18 | Shade Land $112^{no}$ Three For Me $115^{1\frac{3}{4}}$ MovinHy$112^{2\frac{1}{2}}$ | Never a factor 12 |
| 111 | 134.95 | 67–19 | Sheer Delight $112^{1\frac{1}{4}}$ FalconFlight $113^{h}$ Commocrete $110^{3\frac{1}{2}}$ | No factor 12 |
| b 111 | 218.50 | 75–14 | Star Shower $109^{4}$ Vista Rose $116^{nk}$ Tirzah $111^{h}$ | Was never close 12 |

**Mar 25 LD 3f fst .38$\frac{3}{5}$ b**

RESULTS AND COMMENTS

1. Loser.   This horse is a "Has-Been." Five years ago he was winning for $5,000 on the New York circuit. His first start the following year was a dismal effort—ran last by 16 lengths and this time under a Claiming tag of only $3,500. His next effort in December of the same year at Tropical Park was the living end—"Broke Down" altogether. Four years passed and he tried it again, this time at Lincoln Downs (Minor League) for $2,500. Last. Away last—last by 15 lengths. His latest effort at Suffolk Downs, April, this year—down to $2,000—next to last, beaten 21 lengths. This horse has "gone bad."

And just as apt as not on some fine day at Suffolk Downs, or Lincoln Downs, or Narragansett, or somewhere, ol' Great Caesar will uncork a smasher and win easily at a real boxcar mutuel. And the guy sitting beside you will exclaim, "Hot damn! I've got three tickets right on his nose!" And then you, in a mixture of disgust and bewilderment, will turn to him and ask, "How in the hell can you bet an ol' hide like that who has been finishing last and next to last all the time?" And without even batting an eye he'll be glad to inform you, "Just a little while back that horse was winning $5,000 races at Belmont Park. And you know what they say, 'They always have one race left.'" About the only thing left for you to do is to congratulate him on the fact that his money held out until Great Caesar finally "hit it."

2. Winner.   The 3-2 favorite went all the way and win by 4. Here we have a horse who has shown speed when entered against the best non-winners on the grounds being

dropped into a Maiden Claiming Race. All the way, and it looked so easy.

3. Loser. And for two reasons. First, this horse has been idle since August of last year. Second, we find he is a Minor Leaguer trying to bridge the gap up to the big time—from Randall Park and ThistleDown up to Churchill Downs. And so in spite of his many fine showings in Allowance Races and Overnight Handicaps, we have to nix this horse in today's race.

That's one side of the coin; now we'll look at the other side. Last year's in-the-money consistency rating: 70%. The year before, even better—73%. And keeping in mind "The same horses win and the same horses lose," we'll keep a watchful eye on this little gem of consistency. Today he finished 3rd, losing the whole race by 2 lengths and a nose.

4. Loser. This is a tough one, a $20,000 Claiming Race at the "Big A." Fauve shows all Md. Sp. Wt. races (including a winning one) and Allowance Races—all except one. That one is a $12,000 race at Laurel, and although that race is a good one, he lost, and lost by some 5½ lengths. To figure prominently in today's race, that $12,000 race at Laurel should have been a big win—certainly not a loss. We would not want to back a horse running for $20,000 at Aqueduct when he has already raced and lost when entered for $12,000 at Laurel. And today we figured correctly— Fauve at @20-1 finished next to last, "Couldn't keep up."

5. Winner. The successful $5,000 Plater from Pimlico drew out through the stretch to win the Silver Spring Purse by a length. He had a couple of things to recommend him besides his photo-finish win. For example, I see where he

lost the Burch Handicap at Bowie by only 3½ lengths—and yes, I know he was 9th. But never mind that 9th-place finish—how close did he actually come to winning the race? But perhaps this horse's greatest claim to fame is shown in the Lawrence Realization at Belmont Park—he actually outbroke Kelso (horse of the year, 1960, 1961, 1962). All right, so he stopped and finished flat last by 34 lengths; what did you expect for a 96-1 shot, a miracle?

6. Loser.   The Ancient Maiden loses again. This horse has tried it 19 times up to today's race, and I wouldn't want to bet that today is going to be the day. And yes, I see he finished second his last time out; most likely during the course of 19 attempts he has finished second a time or two before. The comment on his latest effort as seen in the *Telegraph* is "Sharp." Well, today he wasn't so "sharp"; today he finished a well-beaten, ordinary 9th.

7. Loser.   This is an example of a big winner in reverse —out there by 6 and 8 lengths and win "Easily" by 3 when entered for $1,250. And now today he comes back entered not for $1,750 or $1,500, but for $1,200. In other words—he went the wrong way. Got beat. Finished second—which surprised me, most of these "Backsliders" finish away back.

8. Winner.   And for no particular reason; I just wanted you to see a Kentucky Derby and Preakness horse in action. And—I also wanted to show you that any "backstretch proverb" can have a bad day. In this particular instance: "Never bet a 3-year-old when he is entered against older horses." Quite a few people liked Sword Dancer's chances; he paid only $7.20 to win.

9. Loser. I do hope you didn't pick this one. His one and only effort was a good one, "Just headed." But he lost. And he lost against a field of Maiden Claimers—and not very highly priced Maiden Claimers either, only $7,500. Now if he can't beat moderately priced Maiden Claimers, he sure as hell isn't going to suddenly find the inspiration and the speed to defeat the best non-winners on the grounds. This horse is just the reverse of the example shown in race #2. At 5-1 odds, Sand Spur "also ran."

10. Winner. Yes, that's right—a winner. Here's an Ancient Maiden who finally made it. It took a long time—21 starts. (At least 21 starts—the horse's record as a 2-year-old does not show in the Past Performances.) Just goes to show you that when you are down here amongst the dregs of the thoroughbred racing world, 4-year-old Maidens valued at $2,500, anything can happen. And today it did; today the favorite at $1.30-1, Two Timing Lady, was just that when she came all the way from last place to win by ¾ of a length. Some days nothing goes right.

# 9th. BETTING

FROM Col. Matt Winn's autobiography, *Down the Stretch*:

Pierre Oller, who ran a perfume shop in Paris, was creator of the pari-mutuel method of wagering. Oller was a horse player. One day, in 1865, after a prolonged losing streak, he denounced the bookmakers, asserting they owned horses in secret, and ran them in ways that were most beneficial to themselves—and most disastrous to the players.

Oller then proceeded with the invention of his system. This called for selling tickets on the different horses in each race, all receipts going into a common pool. After the race was run, Oller deducted 5% for his time and effort—he made all early sales in his perfume shop—and the balance then was divided among the holders of the winning tickets. If only one player had a ticket on the winner, he received the entire net pool. If two tickets were sold, the pool was split two ways, and so on.

Oller called his system pari-mutuel, the "pari" in French meaning "to wager," and "mutuel" meaning "between ourselves."

And there you have it. It all started in a perfume shop. All of which still goes to prove that a rose by any other

222

name . . . As an afterthought, I do wish that "mutuel" had meant "among ourselves."

For some few of you, all the information given in the previous chapters was merely necessary background material for this chapter on betting. The proposition that racing is a sport to be enjoyed as such has become lost somewhere in your lust for dollar bills. Or as John D. Rockefeller put it when he confided to a friend his thoughts on the pleasures of life:

"Do you know the only thing that gives me pleasure?" asked Rockefeller, looking up with a fashion of guilessness, at once sly and bland. "It's to see my dividends coming in," he whispered; "just to see my dividends coming in!" And as he said it he made a drawing, scraping motion across the table with his scooped hand, as though raking in imaginary riches.*

A tiny little world. And if your trips to the track are motivated only by a desire to see your dividends come in, then for your sake, I do hope your astuteness and your handicapping acumen parallel your monetary ambition. I have a feeling, however, that you may have to learn the art of losing gracefully, that your unwavering avariciousness may of necessity be tempered by a series of slow-moving horses, and lastly, that unlike John D., your imaginary riches will remain just that—imaginary. Things aren't easy out there, friends.

Go to the races to have fun. And if you're not having any fun, then, for everybody's sake, don't go. But let me quickly add this—it's much more fun out there when the

---

* John K. Winkler, *John D., A Portrait in Oils,* Blue Ribbon Books, New York, 1929, pp. 105-106.

horses are running in your favor. Damn little happiness radiates from my quarter when I'm watching my horse struggle in 9th or 10th. And damn few huzzahs emanate from my seat in the grandstand when I'm ankle-deep in defunct mutuel tickets. And just to keep everything on an even keel—neither do I slash my wrists amid adversity.

And so, friends, you do not pick winners just to have someone pat you on the back and say, "Nice going." The rewards of winning selections are much more material and much more tangible than that. For, you see, these racing establishments actually have men in their employ whose sole purpose in life is to give money away. Better check that—they really don't "give it away"—you have to earn it. And you earn it by making correct selections and then backing these said "correct selections" with some money of your own. In other words, by investing, or betting, or gambling, or whatever you may choose to call it.

Now that you have chosen a trusty steed which you believe to be the one superior horse—just how do you go about backing up your selection with money? Even the betting process has some ramifications which must be understood. The betting possibilities on any one particular horse race are four in number:

> Win (Straight, or "On the nose")
> Place
> Show
> Combined (Across the board)

Betting a horse to win means just that—before you win, the horse must win, i.e., your particular horse must finish first.

Betting a horse to place means that before you win the horse must finish *at least* second.

Betting a horse to show means that before you win the horse must finish *at least* third.

Remember the italicized "at least" in the above. If you bet a horse to place (to run second) and he wins, that's OK. That's fine. You're right in there pitching. If you bet a horse to show (to run third) and he runs third, or second, or first—that's OK too. Start looking for the cashier windows.

What isn't OK is when your horse finishes *farther back* than you had anticipated. If you bet a horse to win and he runs second, that's too bad; that wins nothing. If you bet a horse to place and he finishes third, that's a loser. If you bet a horse to show and he finishes fourth or worse, that's a dud. "But two tickets to next week's production," as the man used to say.

Should you be inclined to bet one horse in all three positions: win, place, and show, such a bet can be made through the purchase of a single ticket, a combined ticket. And since you are betting the horse three different ways, then you will pay three times as much for this one ticket. If your horse wins when you are holding a combined ticket, then you collect everything he pays: win money, place money, and show money. If he runs second, you collect place money and show money. If he runs third, you collect show money. And if he runs fourth or worse, you are a 3-time loser. Remember that.

The tickets sold on the competing horses come in various denominations, the minimum wager being $2. Do not go out to your local oval and start looking for the 50c window. If you do, you are going to have one hell of a long look. Besides the minimum $2 ticket, there are also $5 tickets, $10 tickets, $50 tickets, and $100 tickets. All combined tickets cost three times as much as the single unit ticket. The minimum-priced combined ticket, then, is $6: $2 win, $2 place, and $2 show. In the lingo of the race track—$2 across the board. Thus, as we've said, the minimum-priced combined ticket is $6, unless—There is always an unless. Unless you happen to be at a track which sells a bobtailed version of the $6 combined ticket—a $4 combined ticket. The $4 combined ticket gives you $2 to win and $2 to place; the show wager is omitted. There are also higher-priced combined tickets. Example: the $15 combined: $5 win, $5 place, and $5 show. Now frankly, I don't buy combined tickets and do not know the top limits of this increasing insanity. Conceivably there could be such a thing as a $300 combined: $100 win, $100 place, and $100 to show—just to cater to any lunatic fringe that may be present.

Now you can see that with four different betting positions, 1st, 2nd, 3rd, and combined, and with multiple ticket size possibilities—there are many ways to bet a horse: $2 win, $2 show, $5 show, $6 combined, $10 place, $20 win, $50 show, $200 win (What ! ! ! !), etc.

With all of this money going into the machines, just what part of it comes back to the players? Or at least what are the possibilities of some of it coming back to you? Such a question brings up the subject of odds. Out there in the infield there is a glittering monster of a machine which flashes odds on the various horses. I will not go into a detailed explanation of the pari-mutuel betting system any more than has already been given in the *Down the Stretch* quote. The prime thing to know is that the more money bet on any one horse, the lower his odds. And also, you *must* know that all the money bet by the crowd to win, place, and show is kept in three different betting "pools." And— the odds shown on the tote machine are the odds to *win* only. To explain: you may feel that Ol' Gluefoot may not win at 20-1, but at those odds he is a good bet to run third. But the odds on Ol' Gluefoot to run third may be only 2-1. No odds to place or show are posted. At the larger tracks the actual amount of money bet to place and show will be posted—but not the odds. At the smaller tracks even this information is not given.

Another drawback to betting Ol' Gluefoot to show is this: when you bet a horse to win, you know what the odds are and how much you will get in return if he wins. Under the pari-mutuel betting system all the people who hold tickets on the winning horse divide up the win pool, (after the race track and the zombies have deducted an aggregate 15-18% of the total, of course).

But—when you bet a horse second and he finishes second, you have the situation where there are now "2 sets" of winners. Other bettors in the crowd bet the *winning* horse to place and hence they won too. Now you can see why the place pool must be divided more ways.

Moving on to the show pool, things get compounded adversely, only more so since there are now "3 sets" of winners. The show pool must be divided among many more winning ticket holders. Getting it distributed to all the winners spreads it out pretty thin. And especially so if one of the 1-2-3 horses in Ol' Gluefoot's race was a very short-priced favorite. Such a well-backed horse will bring the show price down to almost nothing—regardless of the initial enticing odds of 20-1. Now if you can arrange it so that all the well-backed horses finish out of the money and the race is won by a 30-1 shot and the place horse is 50-1 and *then* comes Ol' Gluefoot at 20-1, then your show price will perk up considerably. All such arranging is putting many factors into the hands of the fates.

One thing more to understand about pari-mutuel betting —you are not betting against the race track. The race track management doesn't care which horse wins. You are betting against and are in competition with all the other people who are betting. Keep your eye on that dear sweet little ol' grandmother down there a few rows—she's trying to win all of your money. And that's why it's nice to know something about what's going on, to have some kind of an "edge" going for you. Don't discourage the "blind stabbers" and the "hatpin pickers" too much; their thoughtless expenditure of money is helping to establish the odds.

To illustrate the odds given on the tote machine to what they mean in money: A horse that wins at 50-1 pays $102— to win. What he pays to place and show is uncertain. It depends upon how much money was bet on him to place and show and what the odds were on the other horses who finished in the money. And remember—the odds as posted in the infield are *approximate* odds. Up among the longer-priced horses: 20-1, 30-1, 50-1, etc., the actual mutuel payoff has a tendency to be higher than what was posted.

Example: A 70-1 shot may pay $149 to win and not the expected $142. (You won't have too many of these.) And while we're talking about longshots, I'll add that the tote machine posts odds up to only 99-1. When you see odds of 99-1 on a horse, you know the odds are at least that high, possibly more; may be 300-1.) As the odds come down to earth they get more accurate. A 10-1 winner pays $22. Ten dollars for each dollar you put up—and your $2 back. Here are some sample odds and what they would pay for $2:

| | |
|---|---|
| 8-1 | $18.00 |
| 5-1 | 12.00 |
| 9-2 | 11.00 |
| 7-2 | 9.00 |
| 3-1 | 8.00 |
| 5-2 | 7.00 |

Here are samples of some other odds you will see posted from time to time, and they are included only as a matter of passing interest:

| | |
|---|---|
| 2-1 | $6.00 |
| 9-5 | 5.60 |
| 8-5 | 5.20 |
| 3-2 | 5.00 |
| 6-5 | 4.40 |
| 1-1 | 4.00 |
| 3-5 | 3.20 |
| 1-2 | 3.00 |
| 1-5 | 2.40 |

Don't worry too much about these short prices because any horse with such low odds is not to be considered for betting purposes anyhow. To repeat: 5-2 is the absolute, rock-bottom, minimum betting odds acceptable. Bet no horses that are 2-1 or less. Some horse players will not even accept 5-2; they may stop at 3-1, or 4-1, or even 5-1.

Assuming a winning percentage of 30% on your selections, you can see that if you bet 10 horses and have 3 winners at $7, you will have a profit. Very small, $1, but it's there. If you dare dip below 5-2, you cannot show a profit with 30% winners. So right away you figure what the hell—why not set 10-1 as the minimum betting price and then the 30% winners will show a much bigger profit. The hitch is that as the mutuel payoff goes up, the percentage of winning selections has a tendency to fade out— may even be cantankerous enough to vanish altogether. The 30% can be maintained with a minimum price of 5-2. The small profit as shown above assumed there were no winners over $7, and there should be since this figure represented the minimum and not the maximum odds, and that a flat bet of only $2 was made. Upping the ante can up the profit. However, many losing horse players offer as an excuse for failure that they didn't have enough money: "Couldn't cover themselves," or some such bit of hokum. The sad truth is that if you are betting dollar bills and losing, then betting ten dollar bills isn't going to help matters any. Before increasing the size of the bets can increase your take-home pay, there most surely must have been *some* profit in the first place. And them's also the conditions that prevail.

Here then are the betting rules to guide you in your battles with the pari-mutuel machines:

1. DO NOT BET EVERY RACE. I'll repeat that. DO NOT

BET EVERY RACE. Once more. DO NOT BET EVERY RACE.
Now I do hope that little tidbit sinks in. Friends, if you
insist on betting every race, then you are not even involved
in a game of chance because you don't have a chance. There
are going to be many races on many days when Divine
Guidance couldn't fathom which horse was going to win—
let alone mortal man. When such a puzzle comes up, you
just have to muster together all your courage and utter those
two most difficult words, "I pass." And such a test of
character brings us to that first day of racing assignment I
mentioned earlier. On your first day at the races I want
you to go in with all the races figured out to a T. You know
all the answers. And then I want you to have $120 cash
American money in your pocket. The $20 is for admission
and food and drink and rot like that. The $100 is to be
readily available small bills. And then your problem is
this—I want you to sit there and watch the racing card for
the day. See how your horses are doing. Betting? None.
Nothing. Just sit there and see how things go. Now, dear
heart, if along about the fifth race you suddenly find yourself standing in the $2 show line just to get a little "action"
or just to "have a horse in the race" or for any other reason
you may conjure up—then as a serious horse player you are
a flop and a failure. You haven't learned to sit on your
butt. If you can't learn to sit still, then you too had better
always go to the track for a few laughs and a few beers.
Learning to sit and watch takes some doing; many horse
players have been going to the track for years and haven't
mastered the fine art of sitting on their butts yet. Come on,
Hot Horse Harry, you've been situated on that broad back-

side of yours all week—can't you hold out 20 more minutes? So, you see, if you can learn to sit still on your first day at the track, you'll be way ahead. DO NOT BET EVERY RACE.

2. Keep your money "up front." That means—bet horses to *win* only. And remember our previous rule—no bets on horses whose odds are less than 5-2. The odds of 5-2 are kind of short, but I see nothing wrong with betting $20 on a solid horse and winning $50. When the odds are at the minimum of 5-2, however, the horse must be very solid—lest he blow when the big money goes down.

The payoffs in the place and show spots are simply not large enough to merit their play. And some other thoughts —when you bet a horse to run second, you are admitting to yourself that there is a better horse than yours in the race. When you bet a horse to run third, you are admitting to yourself that there are two horses in the race better than yours. And if there are two horses in the race better than yours, then you must be betting on the wrong horse. And leave the combined tickets alone; you tie up too much money in one horse, especially when ⅔ of your bet is linked to the place and show pools where the return is often only negligible. Combined tickets are for the thoroughly confused players who just don't know what they are doing.

To repeat: Bet all horses to win only, unless— There is always an unless. Unless the odds on the horse are 40-1 or higher. Then bet the horse first and second (win and place). A 40-1 shot running second and paying $20 or so is as good as a winner. (You won't be betting many horses whose odds are 40-1 or higher.)

If the odds on your horse are 80-1 or higher, then bet him first and third (win and show). An 80-1 shot running third and paying $20 or so is still as good as a winner. (And for your well being, I do hope there are damn few horses you play at odds of 80-1 and beyond.)

3. Select your horse and then check his odds and not vice versa. If you are going to look at the odds board and then pick a horse, you are really confused. To pick a horse from the odds board borders on lunacy—why be cheap? Why pick a 10-1 shot? Might as well pick a 40-1 shot, or a 50-1 shot. Such reasoning is idiotic. You pick the horse *first*—the one superior horse, in your judgment, and that's it. You sink or swim with that horse. If he's 5-2 or higher, that's fine; you've got a bet. If he slips to 2-1 or 9-5, no bet. None. Don't go picking another horse just because the odds on your first choice went to pot. If the price isn't right—no bet. And don't be scared off in the other direction. Don't let high odds influence you into discarding your original choice. If your horse opens at 15-1 and goes to 35-1, that's fine. That's when they pay big. I've heard people say, "I was going to bet ol' Boxcar Mutuel, but his price went to 50-1 and scared me off." Well, don't let big odds scare you off. It's your opinion against everybody else's; stick with it. How in the hell are you ever going to collect a big payoff on a long shot if you don't bet any? And what if he does run last? You'll have more losers than that before you're finished. At 35-1 he might just as well have finished second; he would still have been just another loser. And if he does run last, you'll soon learn that the next race will go off as scheduled; the world will keep on going around; the sun will come up the next morning—and, in short, things will go on just about as they were.

4. Don't bet too quickly. This is a touchy subject here.

You will have 20-25 minutes in between races to get your bet down, and the point to keep in mind is this: one wag once said that if horse players had 24 *hours* in between races, some of them would still get shut out at the windows. That's true. Very true. I do not mean that you should become an habitual Last Minute Louie and wind up getting no bet down at all. But—when the betting starts on any one race there will be odds posted on the infield tote board. And that's kind of peculiar, since we already know the odds are established according to how the money is bet on the various horses. Therefore, how can there be odds, if no money has gone into the machines? These early odds are called the "Morning Line" and are nothing more than one man's opinion as to what the real odds will be. As a rule the Morning Line is a very close approximation of the actual odds. However, and again it's a big however, there will be many horses in many races whose odds have been grossly misestimated. Your best bet of the day, ol' Hidden Sleeper, may be 8-1 on the Morning Line and apparently worth a sizable bet. Then on the first flash of the real odds he may sink to 5-2, and the next thing you know, you are hung with a short-priced favorite at 1-2. And—positively no refunds—1-2 and away he flew.

Don't bet without first knowing the real odds, and keeping that in mind, don't fiddle around and get shut out. I might mention that if you are pressed for time, you may avail yourself of the selling windows which aren't so crowded.

5. Hold all of your tickets until the race has been declared "Official." Ofttimes the zombies won't like the way

things turned out and will then proceed to rearrange the order of finish. Don't be found guilty of throwing away a winning ticket; clutch your ticket firmly in your hot little fist until all hope is gone. Hold all tickets until the race has been declared official and you see the payoff posted in the infield.

6. Increase the number and the size of your bets during a lucky streak and shy away when things have turned sour—and not vice versa. It's a peculiar observation, but most American gambling folk can stand to lose longer than they can stand to win. During losing streaks the average punter will start betting more often and heavier in an attempt to regain his losses all in one grand betting coup. (And there will be losing streaks.) Then on good days when manna is descending upon him from every possible angle, he wants to quit. Pour it to 'em during a hot streak; you're betting with other people's money anyhow. When everything seems to go wrong, shun the betting area until things have righted themselves. Do not increase your bets when you are plagued with a series of the "slows."

7. Avoid all betting progression schemes. About the only progressing you'll do is a steady march to the poorhouse.

8. When actually buying a ticket at the selling window, ask for the horse by his official program number—and then add the number of tickets you want. If you want two tickets on #4, don't walk up and say, "Two tickets on . . . " because by that time, you'll have a ticket on #2. Say, "#4, twice." And for heaven's sake, don't ask for the horse by his name. Such an occurrence may cause the ticket seller to have a stroke. He's been selling tickets for 38 years and

never knew those horses out there going around in rings even had names.

9. Don't bet too much on any *one* horse. Remember, it's only a game; and no matter how "certain" the outcome of any one particular race may appear to be, always keep in mind this favorite expression of the men along "shed row": "They gotta go 'round the track." And that's oh so very true; they sure do "gotta go 'round the track." And many, many things can happen during the running of any one particular horse race. As to just exactly how the mighty may fall—just remember that Citation and even Man o' War got beat.

Of course this rule is of a very personal nature—as to just what sum of money represents too much for any one bet. I suppose there are horse players to whom the immediate loss of a couple of "C" notes would elicit no response of woe or despair; theirs would be more of a savoir-faire. "How about that?" And, on the other side of the economic ledger, I'm very sure there are horse players to whom the loss of $10 all in one chunk could trigger financial chaos. You are out there with your money, betting on your selections. You know full well what your financial capabilities and limitations are (at least I hope you do), and knowing that—stay "in bounds." Make sure your racing outing is first, last, and always an outing of fun—not a long afternoon of cold sweat and panic. It's only a game.

10. Heed no hot tips. Nobody out there knows any more than you do.

11. And for the cynics in the crowd I'll add one more

rule: When going out to your local oval by means of public conveyance, always buy a round-trip ticket.

Those are the "do's" and "don'ts" for betting on individual races. However, there is still one large betting arrangement we haven't mentioned. And that's a thing called the Daily Double. There are 3 things I want to say about the Daily Double right here at the beginning:

1. The Daily Double is a sucker bet.
2. Bet it.
3. No matter how you bet it, you will bet it wrong.

The Daily Double is a sucker bet, no doubt about that. Your chances of winning a Daily Double are very slim. What is it? It's a betting arrangement conducted on the first two races. And the problem is to pick the winners of the first and second races. Only winners will do, second or third is no good.

If you think #6 will win the first race and #10 the second race, you plunk down $2; ask for 6 and 10, and you've got a bet. Of course picking the winners of the first two races is going to be a real puzzle. The management will see to it that there are 10-12 horses in each race, all very cheap, erratic, and practically unfigurable. A tough situation. What to do? Bet it. I say bet it because it's your best chance all day to get back a whole lot of money for just a little bit. One thing to understand—the Daily Double pool is a separate pool from the win-place-and-show pools of the first two races. (Incidentally, all of these pools and all of this money going around at a race track is called the "handle," most likely because it goes through so many hands before any of it comes back to the players. States' rights, State Racing Commissions, political debts, zombies.)

Therefore, the Daily Double payoff is independent of the mutuel prices of the first two races. Theoretically, that is. In practice the Daily Double payoff usually will closely parallel the odds of the winners of the first two races. In other words—if the favorite wins the first race and the favorite wins the second race, then the Daily Double payoff will be very small, $10—$20. The record low is $3.60. And with that emaciated mutuel in mind, we will add one more wagering rule to our previous list of eleven to arrive at a more symmetrical even dozen. This rule applies only to the Daily Double and states that when the two superior horses in the first and second races, in your opinion, are also the two superior horses in the majority opinion, then pass the Daily Double. Or, more simply, don't bet the two favorites in the Daily Double. The odds against your winning a Double are over 100-1 (the actual odds here, of course, depend upon the size of the fields present in the first two races), and with the deck stacked against you to such a prohibitive extent, when you play both favorites, you are accepting odds of 3 or 4-1—or less. That's a bad bet. Nix the Daily Double for that day, and tomorrow there will be another one. And the next day, and the next. One favorite? OK. Both favorites? Nup.

And again—don't stab at some other combination just because the odds on your first selection went to pot. Just say, "I pass." And I'll be the first to admit that such action is easier said than done.

If two medium-priced horses win the first two races, then the Daily Double will be medium-priced—$100 to $400. (All of these examples of Daily Double payoffs are for $2 —the minimum Daily Double wager at all tracks, at all tracks save one. In 1962 Tropical Park raised the minimum Daily Double wager to $3. Whether or not this awkward ticket innovation will remain is questionable.) If, however, the first two races go to long shots, then the payoff will be away up there—$500 on up to $5,000 or thereabouts. The record high for the U.S.A. occurred in 1939 at Washington Park in Illinois when the Daily Double paid $10,772.40 for $2. When you hear about these jackpot doubles and the lucky people who had them, you might wonder what would have happened had these lucky ones been scared off by high odds. Damn the high odds—that's when they pay big. When you pick a horse which you believe to be the "one superior horse," or as in the case of the Daily Double, the "two superior horses," then stand by your convictions and the hell with what other people think. You know as much as anybody out there.

Why will you always bet the Double incorrectly? Well, so far, as an example, we have established that you like #6 in the first race and #10 in the second race. So by asking for 6 and 10 and paying your $2, you've got a bet. Most likely you will lose. You could have increased your chances somewhat by "hooking up" #6 with two horses in the second race; there's no law against playing more than one combination. In fact the management will be more than happy to sell you all the tickets you want. Therefore, if you weren't too sure of #10 in the second race and kind of thought #1 might beat you out, you could play 6 and 10 and 6 and 1. Now your chances are better—but not much. Ol' #12 has a good Past Performances record, too. Course he's been away a long time and may not do anything; nevertheless, just to be on the safe side, you'd better include him too. Now you've got 6 and 10, 6 and 1, and 6 and 12. And then there's #7. And #2, #3, #4, etc. In fact, just to be absolutely certain—maybe you had better play #6 in the first race with *everything* in the second race. There will be no mistakes today. Such a bet is called Wheeling the field, and there are separate Daily Double windows for such bets called Wheel windows. You have now wheeled the field with ol' #6 at a cost of $24, 12 tickets times $2. Of course at about this time you may begin to have a suspicion lurking in the back of your mind that there is a possibility of a very horrendous thing happening; good ol' #6 could conceivably lose—at which time you could stick all 12 tickets up your sleeve. Maybe you had better turn the damn thing around and play all the horses in the first race, with #10 in the second race. It's permissible to wheel the field in either direction. Or something else maybe. No, sir. By God, you are a man of deep convictions, and it's going to be wheel the field with #6. First race winner? #6. See there—see how easy. Now all you have to do is let them run the second race and see just how much money is going to roll in. Second race winner? The odds-on favorite. Daily Double pays $23.60. Damnation. Lost 40c. You throw away the eleven losing tickets and go collect $23.60.

All right, you goofed once; now you're a little wiser. Tomorrow instead of wheeling the field and having to throw away eleven losing tickets you will simply buy 12 tickets on #6 in the first race coupled with the favorite in the second race. First race winner? #6. Second race winner? An eight-year-old Maiden who had never finished closer than 6th in his whole life. The Daily Double pays $1,320.40. Damnation.

Tomorrow it will all be different. Tomorrow you can wheel the field with #6 *and* buy 12 tickets with the favorite. Or something. Now you have $48 invested, and #6 with the second choice in the second race, where you will have only one ticket, may not pay $48. And then there is still the slight possibility that good ol' #6 might dog it and short-circuit the whole scheme. Maybe you had better try something else. Or something. No matter how you work it, you will do it wrong. Even if you play only one combination and it comes in to the tidy little sum of $77, we'll say, you will still feel bad. Why? Because you bought only one ticket. Why didn't you get 3 or 4 tickets on it? Or even a $10 ticket. Yes, Daily Double tickets of the $10 variety are available. And, man, that's my definition of an optimist—a guy who buys $10 Daily Double tickets.

The Daily Double is under criticism frequently; even horse players get disgusted with it. And no wonder—it's a pistol. Some punters will tell you it is better to parlay the first two races than to fool around with the Double. A parlay means that you bet a horse and when he wins, assuming he does, you then bet back all the money he paid on a second horse. Example: First race #6. Wins and pays $10. You go collect the $10 and then bet it all back on your choice in the second race. In other words—you are still kind of playing the Double, but you are doing it all by yourself. I still string along with the Double, and for two reasons. First, as a rule, the Daily Double pays more than a parlay of the two winning horses would have. And secondly, once you have bet a Double, there is no chickening out. You've got a bet. For instance, let's say the parlay player has a 39-1 shot in the first race and it wins. He now has $80 in his hands and is supposed to go bet it all back on a 10-1 shot in the second race. I'm sore afraid that about halfway down to the betting area all of his sporting blood is going to turn to horse piss and he'll wind up betting only a part of the $80, or maybe none of it at all. At times a parlay may pay more than a Double—on paper. That's on paper. As an actual accomplishment, it may be something else again.

And the zombies periodically attack the Daily Double. A few years ago the zombies of New York decided Daily Double wagering was not bona fide pari-mutuel betting at all. They saw it as a legalized numbers game. People were betting 1 and 2, 7 and 3, 5 and 8, etc., and what kind of horse racing was that? And thus they abolished Daily Double wagering forthwith. Such a legislative stroke brought about a mass migration of horse players across the river over into Jersey where there was and is a Daily Double. So the Empire State zombies, noting the dwindling handle, a mortal blow, held a caucus and reconsidered. They then said Daily Double wagering was forsooth horse race gambling, after all. And so, after a short hiatus, it looks like the Daily Double is here to stay.

However, lately there has been a new method of wagering

introduced. This one is called a Pic 6 or a Big Bonanza, or any other of a variety of names. This is the sucker bet to end all sucker bets. Here you are asked not to pick two consecutive winners, but *six*—the last six races. Of course the odds are very high and if you should ever hit one, the payoff will be away up there—$1,000 on up (for $2). You may not even have to pick 6. If no one does, the pool is divided amongst all those who selected 5 winners, then 4, etc. And as the number of selected winners decreases, so does the payoff—it has to be divided among more people. Some few other tracks have modified or "simplified" this many-winners game by introducing the "Twin Double." Here you do not have to pick 6 winners; it's a Twin Daily Double—"only" four winners are required. Practically a cinch. (This Twin Double on the later races is in addition to the regular Daily Double on the first two races, of course.)

This is a hell of a thing to say, but on these multiple-choice forms of wagering I'm going to have to agree with the zombies. When things have wandered off into a Never-Never Land of picking 4-6 straight winners, it has turned into a numbers game. At least the odds are right; however, even a bet with good odds can be a bad bet. Here is an anecdote from *This Was Racing* to illustrate the point:

But the story I was getting to started with a poker game in Havana, in which our hero (W. T. [Fatty] Anderson), because of the mistaken assumption that three queens was the high hand, came out into the gray light of morning with several hundred miles of water and a $5 bill between him and his homeland.

On the way to his hotel he met a man carrying a large fish. "What kind of a fish is that?" he asked.

"Red snapper," said the fisherman.

"For five dollars it's not," said Anderson.

It developed that the fish was on the way to be sold, and it was agreed that the decision of the fishmonger would be final.

"What kind of a fish is this?" said the fisherman, tossing it on the block.

"No jokes in the morning," said the buyer. "You've been fishing these waters for years and you ought to know. Get on with you."

"Never mind that," said the fisherman. "To decide a bet, what kind of a fish is it?"

"It's a red snapper," said the merchant. "You know cursed well it is."

Anderson handed over the $5 bill.

"You win," he said, "but it was still a good bet. I had every other kind of fish in the ocean running for me."

So there is the moral. Anybody can make a losing bet; just be sure you get the right odds.

On the 5th of May, 1962, the Twin Double at Suffolk Downs paid $56,677.40 for each $2 ticket sold . . . of which there was one (1).

## 10th. SUMMARY

WE have tried here to introduce the sport of horse racing to all those who know nothing about it, since I am convinced that when most people say, "I don't like horse racing," what they really mean is, "I don't know anything about horse racing." One of the easiest things in the world to do is to condemn something you know nothing about. Like opera, for instance. Mention the opera and most people groan. They don't like it. That's OK. That's their choice. But, when you think about it—the very fact that opera has been around for so long always leaves that outside chance that there just *might* be something to it. And racing, too. Racing in some form or another has been going on for thousands of years. And the fact that it involves an expenditure of over 2½ billion dollars a year causes you to have that lingering doubt that there just *might* be something to it. This figure of over 2½ billion dollars represents only the total amount of money *bet*; it does not take into consideration the total cost of the racing plants, the cost of the horses, the employees' salaries, etc. So you can readily see that horse racing is a pretty big business.

Racing is a sport and a diversion. Ben Hogan has said that one of the appealing aspects of golf is that it gives you artificial problems to substitute for the real problems of everyday living. Well, if it's problems you're looking for, just meander out to your local oval and try to latch on to a Daily Double. You'll find more problems out there than you ever knew existed.

One of the great appealing factors of racing is that it is unique in that it is a turnstile sport which allows audience participation. Allows it? Man, it depends upon it. Everything you do out there is strictly up to you. You can bet the Daily Double or pass it. You can bet win, place, show, or combined. You can bet $2 or $200. You can skip the 3rd race and bet the 4th. (At least I hope you can.) Any which way you want to run things—it's all up to you. At a baseball game you may hope the batter bunts, but you certainly can't order such a maneuver. You paid to watch, and you're going to watch. Not so with racing. You paid to watch, but you have a few things of your own to attend to.

Racing requires no partner; it requires no team. It will not be postponed due to rain. Rain only adds a few more factors. You won't go all the way out there only to be told the card has been canceled. It's a poor sport that's called off on account of a little sprinkling.

We started with the horse and explained the sexes and the age groupings as they are used to card races. We discussed the jockeys and why some of them receive an apprentice allowance. We "graded" all the various race tracks in the East to let it be known that different race tracks offer varying calibers of horse racing. We must know this to be aware of the fact that a consistent winner at one level of racing may not be able to get in the money when elevated in the racing scale of values, and, conversely, a chronic loser at an important track may pull off quite a "form reversal" if entered in a cheaper form of racing.

Next we discussed the different types of races. This was to show you that an habitual loser in the Allowance ranks must be given new consideration when dropped into a Claiming Race, that a winner for Maidens Claiming $5,000 has almost no chance in a Claiming Race for $5,000—and to clarify all the other shifting around done by both the winning and the losing horses.

Then we went into some detail about how to cope with the problem of Major League racing and Minor League racing—how the two more or less mesh together by accident, rather than by design. The winners in the lesser races move on to bigger and better things. Some of the small-time winners keep right on winning and others, after eating the dust of superior horses for a few trips, call a strategic retreat. Losers from the Big Apple drop down the scale in a search for a bunch of horses they can beat. Some immediately take on a new stature and a new aura of respectability. Others keep right on losing.

And with all of our discussions concerning Major and Minor League racing you may have gotten the impression that the more modest forms of racing are at best only inferior imitations of the "Big Time" and should be avoided.

Such was never the intent of this piece. I grew up within walking distance of a ½ mile track. All the racing I knew during that period was a bunch of nobodies racing for peanuts. Man, when a $3,000 Claimer stepped out on the track, it was time to sit up and pay attention. But the Daily Double was still there, the win, place, and show pools were still there, and the fast horses won and the slow horses lost. Let me say this: If you go out to Belmont Park and bet $2 to win on a 5-2 favorite and he wins, you will collect $7. And if you go out to the Great Barrington Fair and bet $2 to win on a 5-2 favorite and he wins, you will still collect $7. There is neither a surcharge on the bet nor a deduction on the payoff because it was a lesser horse at a lesser track. The "little" horses pay the same kind of money as do the "big" ones.

And the cheaper horses can be figured just as well as the "milers." The fact that the horses are cheap is just another excuse offered by Alibi Ike as to why he lost. No horse player has ever been known to bet on the wrong horse. When he lost, it was because the stretch was too long, or the stretch was too short, or the horse made his move too soon, or too late, the jockey was dumb as hell, the horse got a poor start, got knocked off stride, the sun was in his eyes— anything but the fact that he bet on the wrong horse. And so the fact that he is handicapping $1,250 and $1,750 Platers gives him a perfect out. The horses are no damn good. He's OK, but the horses are no good.

And so racing on the Gyp circuit is all right. They just don't have the best horses in the world, that's all. Still, each race will have a winner; all you have to do is pick it—and no excuses.

Next we became acquainted with the racing papers and how to read them. Of the *Form* and the *Telegraph* it may be said that one of them is as good as the other. And that's as it should be, since they both come from the same place. We used a series of horses to learn how to read a racing paper, discovering which segment of the presented material is important and what part of it is not. I do hope you can now read a racing paper and understand all of its markings. The problem here was to present neither too little material nor too much, lest you founder and sink somewhere between the pre-stretch call and the track variant.

Then we came to the task of actually handicapping a horse race. And here I am almost sure most of you were disappointed with the way the material was presented. Instead of a 1-2-3 procedure of just how the winner can be made to miraculously rise to the surface, you were shown instead a one-horse, one-race example of just how to go about evaluating a horse's chances.

You were not even shown any examples of any of the hundreds (?) of winners I've picked. And that little seemingly insignificant detail right there is my proudest accomplishment in this whole book. I could have shown some races with the Past Performances of each horse and then proceeded to tell you all the reasons why Fleet-Footed was the one superior horse. Next would follow a chart of the race, and, sure enough, there would be Fleet-Footed right on top. Paid $16.60. Very good.

Well, friends, it took some self-restraint, but I did manage to refrain from exhibiting any such examples of my uncanny handicapping prowess—and for a very good reason.

One time I attended a Medical seminar on oncology of

the head and neck. The doctor conducting the seminar was showing the results of his X-ray therapy via the medium of color slides. The first slide would show a fungating mess, or nearly so. Then subsequent slides taken after exposure of the growth to X-rays would be shown. And finally, on the last slide, aside from a little redness, the face of the patient would look almost as good as new.

And these slides went on and on, patient after patient. It got to the point where most of the members of the audience began to get the opinion that Big Casino had been licked. A little X-ray therapy was all that was needed. Finally one member of our group asked why research was still being carried on if X-rays could effect such dramatic cures. The doctor looked a little shamefaced and confessed, "Men, I'm not showing you any of the failures."

And so with me. If I presented a few winners, I could do it only by "not showing you any of the failures." So there'll be no heartaches tonight.

And let me say again that the title of this book is still *A Primer for Eastern Racing* and not "How I Made $1,000,-000 at the Races," or, "Beating the Horses Made Easy," or any other such get-rich-quick blueprint. To refresh your memory by repeating a thought from Chapter 1: ". . . the novice and/or the uninitiated racing fan should glean a sufficient amount of racing information to enable him to attend a race meeting and to participate in its excitement with more than an aimless, thoughtless series of blind stabs. He will recognize and understand the problems that beset him when he undertakes to select a winner. How well he succeeds will depend upon him." It's all up to you. If you do not want to think, if you do not choose to apply yourself to the problems at hand, and if you are better suited to sitting and watching and doing nothing which requires an expenditure of effort, then you had better quit horse racing right here and now before you even get started. You belong in a baseball park or a football stadium or some similar spectator sport where the only intellectual acuity necessary is the ability to find your seat. And if your day at the races proves to be a complete bust, you have no one to blame but yourself. Mighty Casey didn't strike out; you did.

If you bog down somewhere along the way in this book, then you will still have learned something in spite of yourself—namely, why winners are so damned hard to come by. It isn't easy, friends.

If the problem at hand is a Claiming Race for $7,000, then seek out the contenders by finding all the horses which have demonstrated they can win for $7,000. Their winning efforts will show in the Past Performances; it's no secret. And a horse who has won for $7,000 and then run a few clinkers is still a contender. He's done it before and he can do it again. Now note all the horses which won their last race, if there are any. *All* of these horses coming off winning efforts figure in today's race; can't improve on finishing first. That takes care of all the winners and all the horses moving up the scale; now, are there any class horses dropping down? Any $10,000 or $12,000 Claimers looking for cheaper opposition? Have they shown anything at all? We know before we even look that the Past Performances of any such horses will be bad; that's why they are dropping down. Any apparently hopeless also-rans which are coming down out of the Allowance ranks? They may not be as bad as they look. The Past Performances of any such horses will undoubtedly be terrible, but don't be afraid to bet such a horse if you think he can beat a bunch of Platers. He certainly won't have finished second his last time out, or within 3 lengths of the winner, or anything else as good as all that. If he had been doing that well in the Allowance ranks, he'd still be up there. His odds will probably be very good, because most people won't bet a horse who has been finishing way back. And don't be duped by a "speedy cheapie." If the "Allowance" horse under consideration has a very *good* record—then check *where* this good "Allowance" record was established. You will see it was at a lesser track, and hence this horse isn't dropping down at all; most likely he is actually overmatched.

How about the consistency of the various entrants? Which ones usually finish well up? Many times you can come up with the winner by simply noting which horse is the most consistent. (Ignore the empty consistency of CCL's, of course.) Blending the in-the-money consistency figure with the class figure is where the trouble comes in. The cheap horses will excel in consistency but are moving up and may be overmatched. The losing horses dropping down will be awfully short on the consistency aspect but will have been racing against better horses. But at times it will be possible to find a horse which stands out in both respects. And he won't necessarily be 6-5, either.

*Read the conditions of the race in question and then compare each horse's capabilities with what the winning horse must be able to do.* Sift out all those which meet the specifications, and then determine which one is in the best form today, which is going the proper distance, which has the weight advantage, and then—and only then—if the track is off, check your selection's mud-running ability. And if all of this handicapping work is too trying, you can help matters a lot by utilizing *Turf and Sport Digest* ratings. These ratings will quickly give you an indication of the contenders, but they will not enable you to effortlessly and thoughtlessly grind out endless stacks of winners and concomitant windfalls of cash. Any set of numbers which could do that would not be published. Nevertheless, they are a big help, especially for the beginner.

And, finally, we discussed betting. If you don't know how to bet intelligently, then all the handicapping knowhow in the world isn't going to help you. I once read an article which stated that if 100 people were given 1 horse a day to play for 30 days, at the end of the 30-day period, even though a $2 flat win bet on the 30 horses would show a profit, 95% of the bettors would be in the red. Now why? How can a group of people be given profit-producing racing selections and still lose? Oh, you'd be surprised. There are a few hundred ways. After the first two horses ran 3rd instead of 1st, many players would drop back to the show hole. And then when the third horse won and paid $25.60, they wouldn't collect exactly that much—more like $3.60, the show price. Then after a $25.60 winner, they would double their bet on the next horse—only that one lost altogether. So the only sensible thing to do then was to pass up the next one too—which won and paid $12.80. And then when the series of designated horses went into a tailspin and clunked out 12 straight losers, they abandoned the whole thing and went back to the more scientific method of betting the horse with the skinniest legs. Of course then the next horse roared in to the tune of $37.60, only they didn't have that one either. From then on until the end of the month it was strictly panic-button time and the losses continued to mount. Like the Music Man said, "It takes a cool head and a keen eye."

I will confess that the odds I set for place and show betting were very high. And this was done purposely to put the point across that before you bet any money in the place or show pools, you must be certain the return on such a ticket is going to be worthwhile. And even then, *all* place and show bets are made only *in addition* to the win bet. Always bet the horse to win. There is nothing worse than picking a $44 winner and then collecting $7.60. You see to it that you collect the $7.60 *and* the $44. Minimum-place odds of 40-1 are very high, and ditto for a show minimum of 80-1. The point is that you don't bet 4-1, 6-1, 9-2, 8-1, etc., horses to run second or third. Keep your money up front.

There are just three more things I want to say about betting. And the first one is this: The Feds have just come up with a new tax source. Some sniffling ass, pasty-faced, dole-seeking bureaucrat, or some group of same (zombies, Federal grade—the winners and still champs), decided that when a horse player's winnings reached $600, the sum was taxable and must be included on one's income tax return. How they arrived at the figure of $600, I don't know. I think $400 is a fair figure myself, or $200, or $100. And then there's $50 or $20, or even $5.40 or $2.80. In other words, the public charges who must forever seek new sources of revenue to perpetuate their existence are going to see to it that you learn to love Big Brother even if it takes all of your goddamned money.

If winnings are taxable, then how about deducting the *taxes* which were paid on the losers (@8%)? Heresy! Heresy! Oh, hell, no. That's no good. This parasitic blood-sucking works in only one direction—toward bigger government and more usurpation by the ever-increasing complexities of the political subdivisions. How in the hell are the zombies ever going to get all the citizens lined up like so many rows of rabbits if there are always going to be a few individualists who do not want to live on a handout?

The second thing is something I've said a time or two before, but I'm going to say it again. Your trips to the track are supposed to be fun. The primary prerequisite to having fun is that the player must be free from any undue pressures or strains. Therefore, all betting should be done with some few *extra* dollars you have. Don't go out to the track with the grocery money and try to run it up into the rent money; you may instead deficit finance yourself right into beans for the next week.

And lastly, with regard to betting, I want to offer some solace in advance for the bad days which are bound to come. When you are plagued with a seemingly unending string of losers, when you too are suffering from the "slows," and when the horses, to your way of thinking, are forsooth running backwards, rationalize away your melancholy by recalling to mind the definition of the word "year" as found in the *Devil's Dictionary*:

year, noun. A period of three hundred and sixty-five disappointments.

And now, since we do not want to end our discussion of Eastern Racing on such a sad note, we will close instead with an explanation of a racing will-o'-the-wisp called "holt." "Holt" is what makes the racing world go 'round What is it?

We'll begin to answer that by first making the observation that horse owners are a very determined lot. Some of them will throw their charges into races for Maidens Special Weights for two or three years without giving up. Week after week they watch their horse struggle in a distant 10th or 12th, and week after week they reassure themselves that *next* week will be different. Both these horse owners and their horses develop a very stiff upper lip.

And not only the non-winners continually race too high. Moderately successful Allowance horses compete in Handicap-Stakes races and instead of bringing home sizable portions of Allowance purses, they bring home dust and despair. Fairly high-priced Claimers habitually race in the Allowance ranks and habitually come back badly beaten horses. Moderately priced Claimers race with the elite of the Claiming division and just can't keep up. And then there are horses at the Major League tracks which suffer from a bad case of the "slows"; they can't make a decent showing no matter what the claiming price is. And yet they'll stay there and continue to chase their tormentors week after week, meeting after meeting.

Why? Now why? Because all of these horse owners are waiting for the day their horses get what trainer "Jimmy"

Jones calls his "holt." And that means the day when the horse is no longer a distant trailer or a bedraggled also-ran, but a galloping winner. And in whatever classification he cracked down, next week will bring more of the same. He'll go on winning and improving until he can beat any horse on the grounds—just you wait and see.

And all of this whistling in the dark and all of this wishful thinking is not based entirely upon whimsey. At virtually every meeting at race courses of all calibers, there will almost always be that one "sleeping beauty," that one potential demon of the turf—if he could only just get started. The $1,500 Plater at River Downs finally wins one. And then it's two. And then he's entered for $2,000 and does it again. And the next thing you know, he's being unsaddled in the winner's circle after soundly thrashing some of the best $3,000 Claimers on the grounds. He's done it, by God; he's got his "holt." Just wait till next Saturday—you ain't seen nothing yet!

In higher circles a $10,000 Claimer finally hits it. For $12,500 he's still an eased-up winner. Bring on the Allowance horses and we shall see just who can run how far and how fast. Just a breeze. Handicap-Stakes. Now we're up here where the money is. Can he do it? Well, El Mono did it, from the $10,000 Claiming ranks to a smashing victory in Hialeah's Widener Handicap—$50,000 added—now there's a pretty good-sized "holt." And if you should ever happen to examine the chart of Hialeah's 1948 Widener Handicap, you may be surprised to find a couple of pretty fast-stepping campaigners listed among the "also-rans"— Armed and Assault. It just goes to show you that when a horse gets his "holt," it doesn't matter who in the hell he's running against.

And then of course there's Stymie. Stymie and his image probably give more hope and more encouragement to down-at-the-heels horse owners than does any other single factor. Who was Stymie? Stymie, friends, was a horse—a Cinderella horse—in fact, *the* Cinderella horse to end all Cinderella horses, the lowly $1,500 Claimer who rose up out of his valley of sin and smote the whole damn racing outfit. He won and moved up, and continued to move up, right to the top—Handicap-Stakes—not any form of Chinese stakes races either, nothing but the best for Stymie. He beat 'em all. For a while it looked like he was going to become our first equine millionaire, but the rigors and the stresses of racing's wars and a few too many trips around the track carrying a few too many pounds of the racing secretary's lead forced him to pull up short. He didn't get his million, but he did bring home $918,485. And there, friends, is one hell of a lot of "holt." Not bad for a $1,500 Claimer.

Well, let's see now. 1st Race Rockingham Park. Six furlongs for 4-year-olds and up. Claiming. Claiming Price: $2,500. Horse #1 Cheap Sort. Win his last race. That's good. In-the-money consistency rating, 72%. That's very good. Been racing at Scarborough Downs. That's not so good. Let's see . . .

Well—you'll have to excuse me now; 'tis time to compute. I want to thank you for your time and trouble. Goodby, good luck—and most of all—good racing!

# INDEX